George Henry Calvert

Travels in Europe

Its people and scenery, embracing graphic descriptions of the principal cities,

buildings, scenery, and most notable people in England and the continent

George Henry Calvert

Travels in Europe
Its people and scenery, embracing graphic descriptions of the principal cities, buildings, scenery, and most notable people in England and the continent

ISBN/EAN: 9783337292294

Printed in Europe, USA, Canada, Australia, Japan

Cover: Foto ©Andreas Hilbeck / pixelio.de

More available books at **www.hansebooks.com**

TRAVELS IN EUROPE:

ITS PEOPLE AND SCENERY,

EMBRACING

GRAPHIC DESCRIPTIONS

OF THE

PRINCIPAL CITIES, BUILDINGS, SCENERY, AND MOST NOTABLE
PEOPLE IN ENGLAND AND THE CONTINENT.

BY

GEORGE H. CALVERT, ESQ.

TWO VOLS. IN ONE.

BOSTON:
PUBLISHED BY G. W. COTTRELL, 36 CORNHILL.
1860.

ENTERED according to Act of Congress, in the year 1852, by
GEORGE H. CALVERT,
In the Clerk's Office of the District Court for the Southern District of New York.

PREFACE.

CERTAIN classes of books are such favorites, that nearly the whole responsibility of publishing them should be borne by the public. The eagerness with which they are read is a premium on their production. The traveller in foreign lands finds the privacy of his letters and journal encroached upon while writing them, by the thought that they may be turned into "copy" for the printer. To so many others has this happened, that the possibility of its happening to himself cannot be kept out of his mind, spotting, it may be, the candor of his statements. Afterwards, when he has been at home long enough for the incidents of his journey to grow by distance of time into reminiscences, what he wrote on the spot comes upon him with unexpected freshness and distinctness. Himself gets information and entertainment from the perusal of his notes, letters and diary. In this state of semi-self-complacency, the public urgently invites him to its broad tables—invites him through the kindness wherewith it has loaded so many of his book-blazoned fellow-travellers. He begins to criticise his manuscript; to shape it by excisions, by additions; to calculate quantity; to confer with a popular publisher,—who is of course in close league with the public,—until at last, he finds that his manuscript has been made away with and in its stead he has proof sheets. His private doings and seeings, and thinkings, and feelings, are about to cease to be private and to become public, and himself is to be thrust in every page personally before the world by the printers, notwithstanding his constant endeavor to merge his individuality, and, like modest editors, to multiply and disperse himself by means of the indefinite *we*. He is in the case to claim the favor that is shown at a feast to a guest especially summoned for the entertainment of the company. The host is the public, whose part it is to bear with his waywardness, to be indulgent towards his shortcomings, to overlook his deficiencies. The author of the following little volume scarcely need add, that this claim of the author-guest is strong in proportion as he possesses the one virtue, the rare virtue, of brevity.

March, 1846.

CONTENTS.

CHAPTER I.

PAGE
THE RHINE—BINGEN—WIESBADEN 7

CHAPTER II.

HEIDELBERG—SUNSET—PRUSSIAN SOLDIERY 11

CHAPTER III.

THE NECKAR—STUTTGARDT—ULM—NAPOLEON 14

CHAPTER IV.

LAKE OF CONSTANCE—SWITZERLAND—LAKE OF THUN—THE YUNGFRAU—LAUTERBRUNNEN—THE WENGERN ALP 19

CHAPTER V.

MOUNTAINEERS—ISOLATION—PRACTICAL ART—MAN'S AGENTS—PRINCES AND PRIESTS—SACERDOTAL DESPOTISM—CATHOLICISM—JESUITISM—CONCLUSIONS 23

CHAPTER VI.

SWISS REPUBLIC—BADEN-BADEN—THE NUN—PEACE-CONGRESS IN FRANKFORT 31

CHAPTER VII.

STAGE-COACH AND CAR—CONSERVATISM—GERMAN BURGHER AND POSTILION—PRIMARY EDUCATION IN GERMANY 37

CHAPTER VIII.

MARBURGH—MONUMENT—RAILROAD TO CASSEL—CASSEL TO DRESDEN . 42

CHAPTER IX.

A DAY IN DRESDEN 47

CHAPTER X.

WEIMAR—CEMETERY—SCHILLER'S STUDY—GALL AND GOETHE—CRANIUM OF SCHILLER—WEIMAR'S HIGH INHABITANTS 55

CHAPTER XI.

EISENACH—THE WARTBURG—LUTHER 64

CHAPTER XII.

WHO FOLLOWED LUTHER—RACES—COLOR—CHRISTIANITY—PROTESTANTS AND CATHOLICS—ENGLISH AND SPANISH AMERICA—CONVERSIONS TO ROMANISM—RELIGION 72

CHAPTER XIII.

SUPPER-TABLE AT THE "HALF-MOON" IN EISENACH—ANNADALE—GRIMM'S TALES—MIGRATION WESTWARD 88

CHAPTER XIV.

GIESSEN—LIEBIG—MARIENBERG—PRIESNITZ—THE RHINE . . . 95

CHAPTER XV.
LOGNE—DUSSELDORF—ARTISTS—LEUTZE'S WASHINGTON—FREILIGRATH 99

CHAPTER XVI.
ANLINESS—BELGIAN PROSPERITY—STATISTICS 104

CHAPTER XVII.
ANCE—DEMOCRACY—BONAPARTE—LOUIS PHILLIPE—LOUIS BONAPARTE . 110

CHAPTER XVIII.
DAY IN PARIS 119

CHAPTER XIX.
WALK IN THE LOUVRE 151

CHAPTER XX.
AGMENTS 164

SCENES AND THOUGHTS IN EUROPE.

CHAPTER I.

THE RHINE—BINGEN—WIESBADEN.

To be taken up by a steamboat on the Rhine is always a lively incident. Out from her level path to the pier the strenuous gay boat glides with a grace that captivates the traveller, like the smiling welcome of a beautiful hostess. On the morning of Monday the 22d of July, 1850, there was a fog on the river, so that the *Goethe*, due at Boppart at half-past one, did not arrive from Coblenz till past two. Seated on the quay with cheerful company, we escaped the vacuum which, to the idle as well as to the busy, ever comes with waiting.

To be ushered of a sudden, hungry, upon the scene of a repast that has been, with the fragments of good cheer strewn around, is not a happy beginning. When we got on board dinner was over. Under the awning, at the long, narrow tables, with tall, empty Rhenish bottles in the midst, a medley of nations were chatting German, French, English, with the volubility and complacency of satisfied appetites.

Man is the creature of food. To be well fed is the first condition of thriving manhood. Let the others take rank as they may, this is the basis. The British tar was right, who, on seeing the beef destined for an American man-of-war, exclaimed, "D—— 'em, no wonder they fight so." Let Europe look to it. The twenty-five millions of the United States take in daily as much nutriment as almost double the number of any other Christian feeders. Not that the Americans are overfed: the Europeans are fearfully underfed. John Bull is getting puzzled and alarmed at the pace at which Jonathan is " going ahead." Let him bethink him, that while to his millions roast beef is a tradition or a festival, to ours it or its equivalent is a daily smoking reality. Democracy and " a good bellyful" go together. The which takes precedence as cause, we will not now stop to determine. Our well-being depends primarily upon what we eat. Nature ordains that man should feed well, plenteously, variously. To mortify the flesh, except to counterbalance a surfeit, is a sacrilege and an impertinence.

Reflections like these come up, without forcing, from an empty stomach into the brain of a man waiting for his dinner.

I had not talked three minutes with my neighbor at the table before he brought in California. Neither the resumption of payment by defaulting States, nor the feats of the Mexican war, have raised us in European esteem so much as the possession of California. Virtue with the Romans meant courage, it now means cash. If men were not hypocrites they would call the Rothschilds the most virtuous family in Europe. California is in everybody's thought and mouth. Gold! gold! Protean potentate, flexible omnipotence, gentle conqueror—what can it, what can it not? By giving it, we get peace within and good-will without; by lending it, gratitude and six per cent.; by promising it, the service of the strong; by spending it, profit or pleasure; by hoarding it, we have the more of it, and by having it we are masters of most that the world prizes. He who speaks contemptuously of gold is a dissembler or a simpleton.

—— The Rhine, fatted by the maternal glaciers of Switzerland, rushes down resistless, like a headlong herd of buffaloes on a prairie. But we drive steadily up, and heed not his torrent, taming his counter-flood to our will with the wizard hand of

Genius. How divine, to wrest from the great heart of Nature a pregnant secret, and endow the world with a new force, immeasurable, infinite. The boats on the Rhine have good fitting names, but not one of them the best and fittest, the name of Fulton.—I look up, and above the modern landscape, still cresting his vine-mantled hill, a stern old ruin paints his jagged outline on the sunny sky, and brags of the past, like some weather-beaten grandpapa. At the water's edge the blackened broken wall fences in part the compact little town, from whose midst rises the bulky church, triste, heavy, unsightly from without; triste, chill, prosaic within; where mechanical priests still drive their huckstering trade, selling what they have not earned, and cannot possess without earning, fuddling the green imaginations with doctrinal strong-waters, compressing the expansive intellect, paralyzing the vivid soul, frightening to subject, enlarging themselves to belittle the multitude, whom they darken where they should enlighten; thus blaspheming while they affect to pray. The churches that arose under the inspiration of Beauty, the which it is a joy and an exaltation to behold, are as rare as are the spiritually-entitled priests, whom it is a privilege to hear.

—— As you stand on the heights in its rear, Bingen smiles up to you, enwreathed with vineyards,—Bacchanal Bingen. The precious, petted vines,—just now in their pride of leaf and fresh luxuriance of new juicy shoots,—press up to the walls, and over them into the town itself. Opposite, Rudesheim piles its fruitful terraces, and a little further is Geisenheim, and beyond Johanisberg,—inspiring names, that stand high and highest on the scroll that the traveller pores over with daily renewed zest. All around is one green wine-promising abundance.

The happiest eyes that from the deck of the boat gazed upon the warm, expanded landscape between Bingen and Biberich, were those of a German, naturalized in the United States, and revisiting, after ten years' absence, his native Germany. The man seemed to feel for the first time, in all its fulness, the sweet strength of his new ties. The joy of rebeholding the land of his birth disclosed to him the intensity of his love for the land of his adoption. Of what "we" had and did in America he spoke with the glow of one who had been raised to a new dignity. As watching the mellow shifting landscape, we talked of America, his countenance beamed with a compound delight. Through the present enjoyment shone the deeper satisfaction of thoughts that were busied with his new home. There, in democratic America, he had been reborn and rebaptized. He was conscious that he had become a larger, abler man than he could have been in Germany. He could not conceal his happiness, that he had exchanged a home that was so dear to him for one that was still dearer.

—— Wiesbaden owes its summer life to two poisons,—its boiling mineral spring, and its ravenous roulette-tables. Early in the morning, round the "Koch-Brunnen" (boiling spring) a motley crowd of pallid dupes cool their smoking glasses to below the scalding point, credulously abiding the sulphurous self-infliction of repeated seething draughts. In the evening, a denser throng encircle in eager morbid silence the gaming-tables, where rich and poor, men and women, sick and well, fascinated by the gloating eye of Mammon, throw their tens and thousands into the monster's maw. On one of the few days that we stopped at Wiesbaben, a rich banker lost in a single evening four thousand pounds sterling. I was told of another player whose eyebrows turned white in a few days after continued heavy losses.

These crowded summer resorts represent the pursuit of pleasure under difficulties.

CHAPTER II.

HEIDELBERG—SUNSET—PRUSSIAN SOLDIERY.

Could a man be said to have travelled from Dan to Beersheba, who had compassed the space between the two by steam? Travelling implies effort, a concurrent locomotive activity, and a self-guidance on the part of the traveller. Once in a railroad car, he is passive, subordinated, without will or authority, with but even a tatter of personality left to him, in the shape of his ticket. He doesn't travel, he is transported, and is hurriedly thrust out on the platform of a station, just as though, instead of being a bag of electrified capillaries, he were but a bag of oats. In this way we came in a few hours from Wiesbaden to Heidelberg.

The beautiful structures of man's making rise from the earth like a favored growth out of it. They are adopted by Nature. The sun rejoices to shine on them. The Castle of Heidelberg we reached in time to behold it by a sunset of American gorgeousness. The rosy atmosphere deepened the expression of the beautiful inward façade which stood again before us, ever young and fresh. Perennial youth is not a fable, or a futile longing: it is the gift of Genius to its handiwork, and is the touchstone of Art. But a work of genuine art is not only young itself,—it makes you young. To revisit it, annihilates time. The intervening years are bridged over by a rainbow.

Through time-rents and vacant casements the rich horizontal beams fell with a glow of celestial gladness. From the terrace, the town beneath, with the valley and plain that stretched far away towards the burning west, lay in a blissful tranquillity. Alas! only to the outward eye, bribed by the purple opulence of light. In this seeming Paradise the ubiquitous Serpent is at work, and here is neither bliss nor peace, but in their stead, unrest, misery. This magnificent leave-taking between Sun and Earth, this illuminated farewell, this broad parting look of love, which lights up the countenance of the responsive Earth with an intense flush of beauty,—how many see it or share it, of the tens of thousands there below, on whom it falls? In torpid imbecility, in exasperated conflict, they lie and writhe there, with senses closed to the eloquent heavenly message. This beauty, which is for them, they cannot claim; this magnificence of nature, they are too poor to accept. The few who, by fortune or spiritual effort, possess freedom enough to enjoy, revel on such spectacles, and in them escape from the omnivorous evil around, their imaginations purged by this transfiguring light. Only for a moment they escape, for the ghastly realities can be but momentarily laid. Not as the evanescent demons of a dream do these come, but as the abiding terrors that leap upon the awakening criminal. So begirt are we by implacable hostilities; self-doomed to have every joy shadowed by a sorrow, every love dogged by a hate, every possession haunted by a fear.

Descending into the town, we came upon squads of Prussian soldiery. Whenever I meet these mechanized men, these soul-informed machines, these man-shaped irresponsibilities, I feel saddened, humiliated, insulted. Plainer than words they say to me,—speak not, think not, act not. In their presence I am utterly quenched. I feel myself supplanted, and in my place a musket. In their speechless tramp there is something terrific. This steeled silence controls my speech: this noiseless movement paralyzes my will.

The European armies hang on the nations, a monstrous idleness, a universal polluting scab. In them are condensed into one vast blight the seven plagues of Egypt. Like the "frogs," they "come upon the people, into their houses, their bed-chambers, their ovens, their kneading-troughs." How this picture fits them in all its traits. Look at those knots of lounging dirty soldiers: they swarm and buzz over the whole land, like the "lice and flies," only more befouling than these. Are they not "sores and blains" on the people, a moral and physical corruption, and a drain upon their strength? "The fire that ran along on the ground"—what could realize it more vividly than the march of armies, smiting like the "hail" as they pass, both man and beast, and herb and tree, and eating like the "locusts" the fruits of the earth and every green thing. In the crowning "Plague of Darkness," the likeness is the most palpable. Standing armies are the very fomenters of darkness. Their office is to propagate night and make men sleep on. They are coarse, brutalizing Force, in contrast and conflict with the subtle, humanizing, liberating power of the intellect and heart of man. They are a million-mouthed extinguisher plied ceaselessly by the hand of Despotism, to crush out the light so fast as it jets up. They exist to enforce man's law against God's law, to be the jailers of thought, the executioners of freedom.

CHAPTER III.

THE NECKAR—STUTTGARDT—ULM—NAPOLEON.

Going up the valley of the Neckar, one runs over with impracticable desires, and their tantalizing importunity is an index of the overflowing abundance of its beauties. How many sites that one longs to halt at for a day; how many hills that one would climb, to compass a wider enjoyment. But we must be at Heilbron in time to dine, before taking the railroad to Stüttgardt. To no one is dinner a more important item in the day's account than to your traveller.

Stüttgardt is a "Residenz." A "Residenz" is a German town, lifted into consequence from its being chosen by the sovereign of a petty dominion for the residence of his petty self and his petty court. In the body-politic of Germany, these reiterated capitals assume to be ganglia, or nervous centres, whence political vitality (so much as there may be) is diffused through the little circle upon each dependant. They are absorbents rather, and of a wen-like turgescence, seeing that they suck in, as well of spiritual force as of material substance, more than they impart. Here, in a small theatre, is performed, without interlude, the serio-comedy of Kingship, wherein Usurpation brazens it out by a prescription of impudence, and Servility is so low that it knows not its own lowness; where the emptiest actors play often the highest parts; and where the audience is terribly out at elbows, being forced to forego, most of them, even some of the necessaries of a meagre household, to furnish the gilded trappings of the performers. To an American, there is no more astonishing feature in European existence, than the patience of the people. Their forbearance is to me a daily marvel.

—— Railroads lay open the landscapes of a country; they take to the valleys. At Geislingen, between Stüttgardt and Ulm, there is one of rare beauty, which, before you issue out of its upper end, narrows to a gorge, where the ascent achieved being of several hundred feet, the delight of the traveller is redoubled by admiration of man's mechanical art. With noiseless ease the heavy train rolls up the valley. True power is so unostentatious. I know not a clearer image, at once of might and beneficence than a silent shower, that slakes the thirst of half a continent. Witnessing it, one wonders at the large facility of Nature. A great idea or discovery, offspring of the prolific brain of man, works and fertilizes with a like breadth and bounty.

—— Ulm is historical. It is one of the many Continental towns branded with notoriety by the fatal hand of Napoleon. It was here, in 1805, while Europe awaited with breathless intentness his descent upon England, that Napoleon, sped by his demoniacal instincts, having rapidly traversed France from Boulogne to Strasburg, suddenly faced the astounded Austrians, cut in two their force, and by the capture of sixty thousand men at Ulm, opened the campaign, which in a few weeks was to end with the victory of Austerlitz.

What grasping thoughts now swelled that vivid brain, making even the new diadem too small for it. As on the daily outspread chart the sure eye of the General tracked the marches of the enemy, the Imperial glance ranged far beyond the lines of a campaign, and kindling with dark power, devoured land after land on the broad map of Europe. Between him and his hope, no majestic figure of Justice, no tearful countenance of Humanity uprose to rebuke his desires. The higher his eminence, the less he felt the wants of his fellows. As he ascended, he put away from him more and more the nobler attributes of man's nature; until, at the culmination of his path, he had become an icy ambition-mastered inhumanity, illuminated by intellect.

He was now rapidly mounting. From the height gained by the victory at Ulm, his horizon widened of a sudden. Into the future he glared with exultation. The foes before him he felt were his prey. He strode on to clutch them. Munich he entered as a deliverer. Elated with conquest, exalted by Bavarian homage, flushed with ambitious visions, the new Emperor seized in his audacious thought a boundless sovereignty.—A courier arrives from the west. What brings he? A tremor seizes Napoleon's frame. His face is livid. His lurid eye rolls, as though tortured by the brain behind it. Fled are those gigantic visions. Far away from the Austrian are his thoughts. He writhes with anger and hate. In his hand is the report of the battle of Trafalgar.

Napoleon has himself said, that but for the obstinate resistance of Sir Sidney Smith at Acre, the course of history had been changed. From the beginning to the end of his career he was baffled by the sturdy Islanders. This was part of his "Destiny." At Acre; at the Nile; at Trafalgar; at Copenhagen, where their seizure of the Danish fleet, disconcerted again his plans, and poured gall into the brimming cup of his German triumphs; in Spain, where he boasted that he would drive that Sepoy (Wellington) into the Atlantic. At the high tides of his affairs came ever this adverse potency to make an ebb in his fortunes. When his fortunes had waned, it was England that gave, at Waterloo, the finishing blow, and then bound the Imperial Upstart to a far rock in the tropical ocean, there to be slowly devoured by the vulture of his own sensations.

This strength to master the giant, England drew from her freedom. The Continental States were all Despotisms. One after the other they fell before democratized France. Napoleon, a child of the Revolution, wielded its fiery vigor to crush the old tyrannies. His own new one he set up in their stead. He cheated France of her revolutionary earnings. In exchange for the gold of political rights, he gave her the gilt copper of military glory. Her people were again effaced before his will. She became a new despotism amid old despotisms. She was shorn of half her new strength. England was the only great nation where the People were for something in the State. Like Austria and Russia, she had made war against Napoleon for self-preservation; but unlike them she never succumbed to the despot. But for her, they would have been his subordinate fellow-despots. In her the feeling of national independence was kept erect by the breath of freedom. Napoleon, who would that no one had a will but himself, who hated any and every man's liberty, who strove to centre in himself all political vitality, who sucked the French nation dry of its liberal juices, felt that England, the only home for freedom in Europe, was his most dread foe. He struck at her with his whole might; but her might, nurtured by liberty, was stronger than his, poisoned by slavery. Thus, his very power became his weakness. In his prosperity, he had absorbed into himself the life-blood of France: in his adversity, he found himself the head of a corpse.

The Emperor of Russia takes the place of Bonaparte in hatred of England. Russia would rule Europe through despotism. National rivalries are not barriers enough to check her. Austria as a State, has the most to dread from Russia; and yet they are, through the paramount necessities of despotism, fast allies.

In the struggle between regal governments, backed by autocratic Russia, and the governed, or more properly the misgoverned, led by France, aristocratic England must back the Peoples. And this, not alone ambitiously to thwart Russian ambition, but from the deep instincts of her national being, whose health and strength spring from the democratic element in her

Constitution. This makes her the political enemy of Russia and Austria, and at the same time gives her the force to withstand them. The intensity of life and the resources of a nation, are in proportion to the political participation of the people.* Therefore it is, that in Europe, England ranks first in wealth and power. Therefore, the United States,—who left behind them in their nest the impure political principles, the monarchical and the aristocratic, and carried with them only the pure principle, the democratic—have grown with such astounding rapidity, that already, within three generations, in intrinsic resources they take the lead of England, their European mother, and who alone could have been their mother. In this conflict between Peoples and Princes, between Right and Wrong, between Light and Darkness, shall it become necessary for Democratic America to intervene, otherwise than with the daily influence of her principles and her example, let the strongest beware.

By the having achieved a larger liberty than has yet been enjoyed, we march in the van of all the nations of the Earth. With us, humanity unfolds itself in broader, deeper strata. Liberty cannot but purify, enlarge, invigorate. It harbors an inevitable, an involuntary virtue. Even martial conquests it transmutes into beneficences. Thus, where we conquer, we emancipate. Our taking possession is not an enthralment, but a deliverance. We cannot subjugate, we must elevate.

* So morbid is their condition, that in European States there are two divided constituents,—the governing and the governed, the privileged and the despoiled. Only to the latter, that is, the laborers, the *vile multitude*, as M. Thiers calls them, is now applied the generic term, the People. With us there is but one constituent: we are all People.

CHAPTER IV.

LAKE OF CONSTANCE—SWITZERLAND—LAKE OF THUN—THE YUNGFRAU—LAUTERBRUNNEN—THE WENGERN ALP.

From Ulm the railroad carries you in a few hours to Friedrichshafen, on the Lake of Constance. This is one of the best routes for entering Switzerland. You come upon it suddenly. The transition from plain to mountain is across the Lake, whose level expanse magnifies the contrast. You get out of the cars and find yourself in the sublime presence. Just over the clear water, quite near, is the strange land, that leaves the earth and goes up into the air, a land built into the heavens. It looked like a discovery.

When the sun shines, travelling in Switzerland is a perpetual festival. Mother Earth holds here a jubilee. She welcomes her children with the laughter of water-falls, the thunder of avalanches, the smiles of green valleys, the salutations of towering granite, the gaze of snow-glistened peaks. You share the sublime joy that beams from her countenance. Your soul and senses expand to be in accord with her grandeurs. You are magnified by the magnificence around you. Nature here pours out her generic power in floods. She is in a mood of Titanic revelry. She leaps and shouts. The Earth is heaved up and down in exuberance of beauty, so inundated is matter by creative spirit.

—— On the 18th of August, 1850, the clouds, that for days had darkened the Lake of Thun, and hidden all save the bases of the nearest mountains, lifted their compact curtain of sombre vapor, let in light upon the Lake, turned up their broken masses to be dried and whitened by the sun, and re-opened to the grateful eye the far-shining snow-peaks of the Yungfrau. A good day, like a good deed, makes you forget a score of bad ones.

At two the little steamboat, with its freight of cheerful tourists, issued from the port of Thun for its afternoon voyage to the eastern end of the Lake. The deep water, like a deep heart, took in and gave back from its tranquil surface the grandeurs and beauties about it. The mountains and the vapory mimicries of them built in the air, painted themselves with the warm light into the depths of the Lake, breaking and beautifying with their images its liquid level. Before us, to the right, the far Blumlis peaks of eternal snow shone whitely among the clouds that they had gathered about them as a foil to their own whiteness. Looking back when half-way up the Lake, the Niessen, that rises from the water's edge a regular pyramid a mile high with a base equal to its height, presented a magnificent spectacle. To one side and round the head of the mountain, an isolated, dark mass of cloud clung with a mysterious, threatening look, as though, blackened by anger, it would wrestle with it as with a foe. The sunbeams behind, that seemed to issue up from the Earth, illuminating one edge of the black cloud, added to the splendor of the effect. A little later the cloud had risen, and shrouding just the peak of the mountain, gave it the aspect of a volcano in travail.

The Lake being ten miles long, we landed in an hour, and soon had our faces turned southward towards the Valley of Lauterbrunnen. From the hot plain of Interlachen, beyond and above the high angle formed by the interlapping green mountains of the narrow valley, the Yungfrau shone a dazzling front of white, clear and palpable, yet dreamy and unreal, from its unearthlike beauty. Of the snowy surface, the eye, from this point, takes in probably a mile square, a wall of solid white two miles up in the air, bounded below by the outline of mountains, in the inverted angle of which it seems to rest. It was like an abstraction, a sublimated essence of the Earth; so calm, so pure, out of common reach, up-piercing, predominating. Like a high abstraction too, infolding the condensed substance of truth—which it cherishes and widely imparts, to the enrichment of many and distant minds—those pre-eminent white peaks are inexhaustible fertilizers, sending down from their heavenly elevation food for great rivers. In Nature there is no waste, nothing useless or idle. Everything works. Everything has its life, its purpose, its dependence interlocked with its power. The distant flats of Holland feel the power of this cold pinnacle of the Yungfrau, which helps to keep full the freighted channel of the Rhine; while on the rivers that she feeds she is herself dependent, the impalpable exhalations from them, condensed in the upper air, furnishing the snow, which in her sublime strength she sends back in avalanches, that give to the torrents, born in her bosom, the volume and speed to hurry to the plain. On her summit the Creative Spirit is enthroned in unspeakable grandeur, and works thence with a ceaseless bounty.

We were soon inclosed in the wonderful valley, whose sides are steep fir-clad mountains, or perpendicular planes of bare rock a quarter of a mile high. Down its stony path, the Lutchine, whose source is in the near glaciers, comes shouting fiercely, as it were the bearer of an angry message from the mountains.

At the village of Lauterbrunnen, our resting-place for the night, is the brook which falls into the valley over a precipice nine hundred feet high, and thence, from being shivered into spray by the wind and the height of its fall, gets the name of Dustbrook (Staubach). Itself a wonder, it is a type of this valley of wonders. From the twilight below, we beheld, over the green mountains, the rosy sunset that bloomed for several minutes on one of the snowy peaks. It was like a glimpse into a brighter world.

The next morning at half-past five, my young companion and myself, well mounted, were on our way up the Wengern Alp. The cool clear air gave us a good appetite for a bad breakfast at the inn near the top, which we reached at eight.

Now we are face to face with the white giantess, between us a deep, black chasm. We stand a mile above the sea level, and even with us is the snow-line of the *Yungfrau*. The summit is more than two miles above the sea; so that we have, right in front and above us, distant from one to two thousand yards, and seeming but a few hundred, a mass of vertical snow more than a mile high, and several in breadth. The eye strives to grow familiar with these sublimities. Far below are all sounds of the common Earth. About us is a sublime silence, so wide and deep, that nothing small can break it; common noises only scratch its surface; it is broken by the avalanche. This solid, up-stretching, white immensity! This mountain-measured distance! This unearthly silence! This thunder-voice of the avalanche! Nothing is ordinary and every-day-like but the sunshine. We heard and saw several avalanches. They look like a fall of water, and sound like a roar of thunder. Over the chasm an eagle is circling.

Before noon we were again on the road to Gründelwald. As we advanced we had in view successively, and at times several or all together, the *Yungfrau*, the *Monck*, the *Eiger*, the *Wetterhorn*, the *Schreckhorn*, and the *Finster-Aarhorn* the least of them more than 13,000 feet above the sea-level, and the *Aarhorn*, the highest of the sublime group, over 14,000. What company for a morning ride! We passed the relics of a forest blasted by avalanches, and far down the descent a patch of snow. At Gründelwald we visited one of the glaciers—a huge, creeping, Saurian monster, with its tail high up among the eternal snows, its body prostrate in a rocky gorge, and its head flattened upon the green valley, into which it was spouting turbid water.

CHAPTER V.

MOUNTAINEERS—ISOLATION—PRACTICAL ART—MAN'S AGENTS—PRINCES AND PRIESTS—SACERDOTAL DESPOTISM—CATHOLICISM—JESUITISM—CONCLUSIONS.

MOUNTAINEERS cannot but be hardy. They have a constant fight with Nature to win a livelihood. The stern, fixed features of their abode limit their being, and give to it a one-sided intensity. From these causes they are courageous, independent, with a strong, fond clinging to their home. Witness the Swiss, the Caucasians, the Highlanders of Scotland. At the same time, from being isolated and confined, they are inflexible and stationary. Dogged, persevering, tough, they are not expansive, not progressive.

Isolation withers whether man or community. The first need for human growth is contact. The closer, wider, more varied the contact, the stronger, fuller, straighter will be the growth. Heeren says justly, that a great source of Phenician, Grecian, Roman development was the Mediterranean. Besides its practical facilities, a sea acts healthfully on the mind by motion and fluidity, inviting its capabilities, giving it a broad impulse. Here is an immensity, and yet to be compassed,—a boundlessness, and yet to be explored. The Swiss want this ever-urgent opportunity of expansion. Their geographical completes their political isolation, their country being withal circumscribed. The very sublimities of their land are practically a hindrance, rather than a furtherance. These awful heights do not lift up, they press down the people. These grand glaciers feed the Rhine and the Rhone and the Tessino, for the use of others. The centres of Swiss culture are away from proximity with avalanches and precipices, in the midst of warm arable fields, at Zürich and Geneva, near the frontiers of Germany and France.

A rugged, ungenerous soil, inland, cannot rear a strong people. Scotland and New England could not have nurtured so thorough a breed, but for having at their door the land-embracing ocean. Through it, the whole world, open to their enterprise, is made tributary to their invention. For development, nations need the sea. The ancients had the Mediterranean. Since that the earth has grown larger, and nations with it. The Atlantic is now the Mediterranean. Soon all the oceans will form but one Mediterranean for all the continents—a universal path for intercommunication among all the peoples.

——With an ever deeper embrace Art encircles her elder sister, Nature; the two co-working with man for his deliverance. The highest service of practical Art is, to bring men together. For this, greater instruments are needed in the modern enlarged field, than in the ancient confined one. Types, steam, electricity, these are the mighty modern instruments. They are at once the signs and means of elevation. They are cause after having been effect.* They denote moral as well as intellectual activity; for in productive action there is always virtue. The most selfish workers carry forward undesignedly the common cause.

* These great tools are but growths, elongations of the intellect,—helps, which in its fulness it contrives for itself. All machines are but man-made fingers, legs, eyes, ears. Thence, the mind that has not swelled to the want of them, cannot use them. What are types or the telescope in the hands of the savage? And thence, the degree of activity wherewith those tools are plied, marks the rank of nations in the scale of humanity. Pass from the heart of Russia to the heart of England, from the sterile animalism of Africa to the affluent humanity of America. In Africa, types and steam are unknown; in Russia they are still in embryo; in England and America, to arrest them for a day, were to arrest and confuse the great currents of life.

Life is movement. On the earth man is the centre of life. For invigorating, multiplying, beautifying life, all Nature is at his service. At first he uses partially, grossly, passively, only her palpable simple qualities. Compare the tools, and the work done with them, of the savage, with the tools and work of the civilized.

The subtler his agents, the larger is man's gain of power. Who can compute what he has gained by steam? Enter a crowded capital by night, to learn what a centupled flood of light comes from an imponderable substance. What are battering-rams to gunpowder, whose terrible force is in the sudden liberation of a gas. Subtler than either, electricity,—now our postman,—has a speed which cannot be calculated. Subtlest of all, master of them all, clutching their combined force in its grasp, out-shining the sun, out-running the electric flash, in resources infinite, in power immeasurable, is the mind of man! the centre, summit and consummation of earthly being, the quintessence of things, the jewel of the world, the citadel of humanity, the final superlative in Nature,—the boundless receptacle, the exhaustless source, whither and whence, backward and forward, flow the streams of the multiplex movement which we call the world,—the mystic womb of thought, in whose vast depths lie the Past, the Present, the Future,—the mighty generator, who on earth generates all the deeds of men, and with man-like shapes peoples the infinite beyond,—the dauntless seeker, who on the dread confines of being confronts the Creative Spirit of the Universe, and wrestles with him for his secrets.

This divine fire, who dare wish to quench or control it? The sacrilegious, who would handle this sublime essence as they do gas and steam, who are they? They are Princes and Priests.

In the beginning, natural superiorities are readily acknowledged. By their sympathies not less than by their weaknesses, men yield to guidance. So long as it is guidance and not direction, so long as real superiority is the condition of leadership, the relation between guides and guided is healthy. But in the imperfect social organizations, for the elastic play of natural tendencies, is soon substituted the rigid pressure of artificial arrangements. Men invent laws, instead of discovering them. Then humanity is turned awry. Then in place of impartiality and freedom and natural growth, there is—in proportion to the rigidity of the conventional ordinances—one-sidedness, compression, tyranny. The human-arbitrary takes place of the divine-free. Willingly or not, men have abdicated their native sovereignty; there is enforced submission; they are governed, ruled, commanded. Their strength has passed away from them, to be centered in a caste, a class, a family. Above them, in permanent possession, absorbing their wills, controlling their thoughts, ordering their acts, are irresponsible masters, greedy monopolists of power. Scorning men, defying God, jealous, self-seeking, unsympathizing, the first objects of the suspicion, envy, wrath, of these self-constituted, unhallowed leaders, are the men commissioned by Nature to be the guides of humanity. The mission of these is to enlighten, to exalt; the aim of the former is to domineer over, to possess men. The inspired benefactors, the parents of new thoughts, the revealers and champions of great truths—they who are endowed with genius to vivify and enlarge the minds of their fellows, when they have not ended a life of persecution by the cross or the fagot, have mostly lived unacknowledged to die unregretted.

Two hundred years ago, a tribunal of Theologians sitting in Rome, pronounced the assertion, that *the earth moves*, to be not only heretical in religion, but absurd in philosophy; and to the assertor applied the rack to extort a retraction of this truth, which his genius had revealed in its high communings with God. More presumptuous, more blasphemous than the angry denial of the movement of the earth, is the denial of the movement of the human mind. The same tribunal still sits in Rome, and to its officials in all quarters of the globe proclaims, that in matters the most vital,—his duty to God, his duty to his fellows,—judgment shall not unfold itself in the brain of man, but be passively accepted from this tribunal, the privileged fabricator of religious and moral laws. This inhuman, this godless proclamation, it endeavors to enact by means adapted to the condition of each land; by the gaol and gibbet in priest-rotten Italy,—by gilded sophistries, by feigned pliancy, by Judas-kisses in Protestant America.

Of all despotism, the sacerdotal is the most desolating, both its end and means being the direct subjection of the mind. Irresponsible priests are worse enemies of mankind than princes. Hating each other as rival usurpers, with an unchristian hate, they have from necessity mostly leagued together to bemaster the intellect and soul; believing, that he who could possess himself of the minds of men, would own the treasure of treasures. But the selfish are ever short-sighted. It is seldom given to thieves to enjoy their thefts. When priests have robbed their brother of that which makes him poor indeed, the wealth that he has lost enricheth not the robber; for, by a deep law of Nature, which decrees the inviolability of the human soul, the moment the mind is invaded it ceases to be a treasure. The contiguous breath of the possessor bedims the splendor of the jewel. Freedom gives the only light by which it sparkles. In subjection, the mind pines and perishes. On itself must it be poised, out of itself draw its life, within itself must be its supreme tribunal. Else it has no spring for elevation, no self-renewing vitality, no self-rectifying force. It languishes, it sickens, it dwindles. But not alone. They who on the holy of holies lay impious hands, the Cains who kill their brothers' souls, they dwindle with it; they become little with the littleness they have caused. Look at Spain, at Portugal, at Italy, the People and their Priests. What an intellectual wilderness! What children are the People, what wet and dry nurses their pastors!

Rome being the centre of Catholicism, in the upper ranks of the Hierarchy there, an intellectual activity is maintained by the conflict thence directed against Protestantism in the freer countries of Christendom. No correspondent moral activity is visible. On the contrary, being predominant, absolute, irresponsible, living in isolated grandeur high above the people, the upper clergy in Rome is further than almost any class of men in the world out of the circle of the conditions needed for the growth and nourishment of Christian morality, of self-sacrifice and brotherly love. Hence the Prelates in Rome have ever been noted for rapacity, arrogance, ambition, sensuality; alternating these indulgences, on occasion, as at the present moment, with vindictiveness and cruelty.

Follow the Catholic priests to England, or, better still, to the United States. Here, without losing the vices inherent in such a theocracy, they become morally as well as intellectually invigorated in the light kindled by Protestantism, to the which they are so unwillingly exposed. They do their best to put out this hated light, feeling that they can never be at home in it, that in the end it must be fatal to them. In Protestant countries priests of Rome always cut somewhat the figure of owls by day.

What intellectual force it has, Catholicism owes to Protestantism. By Protestantism I do not here mean merely Calvinism, or Anglicanism, or Lutheranism, or any other sectarian *ism*, but the imperishable spirit of mental freedom which has in all ages burst up through the crust of ecclesiastical usurpation—the perennial protest of the soul against spiritual authority—the continuous assertion of the rights of conscience. This spirit is the moral life of humanity. The Romish Church, striving ever to crush it, has found in this strife a permanent stimulant to intellectual exertion. In the midst of Protestant churches themselves, this same spirit, struggling ever for absolute liberty, rises up from a deeper deep, protesting against priestly dominion, however tempered. Its sublimest manifestation was against Catholicism through the great Luther, under whose mighty blows the Papacy staggered. In the throes of its despair it gave birth to Jesuitism, which is the offspring of the collision between light and darkness, and which gives evidence in its nature of its monstrous parentage, exhibiting the cold glitter which intellectual light makes on a ground of moral gloom. Jesuitism is henceforth the indispensable armor of Popery.

With the advancement of culture the clerical is overtopped by the literary and scientific classes. A vivifying book rarely comes now-a-days from the clergy, Protestant or Catholic. Creeds are not the nurseries of originality. Original minds on their side are prone to interrogate creeds with very little reverence; and a heart of deep sympathies solves all theological questions in the flame of its love and justice.

On the other hand, priests, while arrogating to themselves a spiritual superiority, reflect the moral condition of the population around them. Like man, like master. Thus the priest of Mexico fights cocks, and the Cardinal in Rome, and the Anglican Bishop in London play whist. The successors of St. John and St. Peter fighting cocks and playing whist, while Christendom is agasp for want of a vivifying faith! In all things how effects and causes interplay one upon the other.

Some conclusions :

That a man should never give permanent or irresponsible power over himself to any other man.

That as men are wisely wary of trusting their purses or their persons to others' keeping, much more should they refuse to trust their souls.

That to do so, is to abdicate one's manhood.

That Nature designs the mind to be developed, not moulded.

That irresponsible rulers, priestly or princely, must in the main be knaves; for irresponsibility indurates the conscience.

That force is the law of evil, that is, no law, but like all evil, a breach of law.

Let us return for a moment to Switzerland, whence we have been floated away on this current of thoughts, which are, however, pertinent to her condition; for, republic as she is these five hundred years, she too has had her princes and her priests.

CHAPTER VI.

SWISS REPUBLIC—BADEN-BADEN—THE NUN—PEACE-CONGRESS IN FRANKFORT.

For the most part in Switzerland, political power was from the first absorbed and retained by a few families. In the greater number of Cantons a majority of the inhabitants had no voice in public affairs. Those in which the whole people participated did not contain one tenth of the entire population. Switzerland, strange as this may sound, has learned democracy from France. Until the French revolutions, especially those of –30 and –48, what between the predominance of aristocratic families or of Roman priests, Switzerland was as little progressive as any of her neighbors. She was a Republic with aristocratic institutions—a Republic of the bastard Venetian species. But the democratic element was there and recognized, only not developed. Thence, the popular impulse, communicated by France to Europe, if not caught up with more alacrity by the Swiss than by the Germans, found in them a mould fitted to give it at once practical shape. In the coming conflict between Democracy and Despotism, Switzerland is destined probably to play a part worthy of her origin.

After having been a short time in Switzerland, to be out of it is like resting after work. For the mind that has been weeks on the stretch, heaved up into mountains and furrowed with gorges, the subsiding back to its normal level is a repose. Joy as it was to get into Switzerland, to get out again brought its pleasure. So it ever is with healthy enjoyments; they end naturally, leaving the spirit refreshed for the soberer tenor of its way.

—— From Basle steam hurried us in a few hours to Baden-Baden, whose crowd of motley visitors was waging, as at most "fashionable watering-places," an hourly battle with ennui. By successive assaults of dressing, driving, dining, dancing, gossipping, gambling, strolling, they manage to keep Time under; so that even the professional idler, whose sprightliest companion is his cigar, finds that he can beat "the enemy" day after day, without the trouble of a thought to help him. Then, a Congress of plotters against freedom would hardly have assembled more Kings, and Queens, and princes, the very presence of whom, in such abundance, so magnetized to most of the company the common air, that simple breathing was a continuous intoxication, enough of itself to make life delicious. It would be unjúst not to particularize, as the chief attraction of Baden-Baden, its green, varied valleys, and the wooded hills that make them. By help of these, a few choice friends and books, with the privilege—which need not be despised—of cutting at will into the above mentioned artificial stores, a summer might be spent in Baden-Baden in a way that would make one desire to repeat it.

—— From midst the town flights of steps led me, on a Sunday morning, up a steep height, about two hundred feet, to the palace of the Grand Duke. Begilded and bedamasked rooms, empty of paintings or sculpture, were all that there was to see, so I soon passed from the palace to the terrace in front of it.

A landscape looks best on Sunday. With the repose of man Nature sympathizes, and in the inward stillness, imparted unconsciously to every spirit by the general calm, outward beauty is more faithfully imaged.

From the landscape my mind was soon withdrawn, to an object beneath me. Glancing over the terrace-railing almost into the chimneys of the houses below, my eye fell on a female figure in black, pacing round a small garden enclosed by high walls. From the privileged spot where I stood, the walls were no defence, at least against masculine vision. The garden was that of a convent, and the figure walking in it was a nun, upon whose privacy I was thus involuntarily intruding. Never once raising her eyes from her book, she walked round and round the enclosure in the Sabbath stillness. But what to her was this weekly rest? She is herself an incessant sabbath, her existence is a continuous stillness. She has set herself apart from her fellows; she would no more know their work-day doings; she is a voluntary somnambulist, sleeping while awake; she walks on the earth a flesh-and-blood phantom. What a fountain of life and love is there dried up! To cease to be a woman! The warm currents that gush from a woman's heart, all turned back upon their source! What an agony!—And yet, could my eyes, that follow the quiet nun in her circumscribed walk, see through her prison into the street behind it, there they might, perchance at this very moment, fall on a sister going freely whither she listeth, and yet, enclosed within a circle more circumscribed a thousand fold than any that stones can build,—the circle built by public reprobation. Not with downcast lids doth she walk, but with a bold stare that would out-look the scorn she awaits. No Sabbath stillness is for her,—her life is a continuous orgie. No cold phantom is she,—she has smothered her soul in its flesh. Not arrested and stagnant are the currents of her woman's heart,—infected at their spring, they flow foul and fast. Not apart has she set herself from her fellows,—she is thrust out from among them. Her mother knows her no more, nor her father, nor her brother, nor her sister. In exchange for the joys of daughter, wife, mother, woman, she has shame and lust. Great God! What a tragedy she is. To her agony all that the poor nun has suffered is beatitude.—Follow now, in your thought, the two back to their childhood, their sweet chirping innocence. Two dewy buds are they, exhaling from their folded hearts a richer perfume with each maturing month,—two beaming cherubs, that have left their wings behind them, eager to bless and to be blest, and with power to replume themselves from the joys and bounties of an earthly life. In a few short years what a distortion! The one is a withered, fruitless, branchless stem; the other, an unsexed monster, whose touch is poisonous. Can such things be, and men still smile and make merry? To many of its members, society is a Saturn that eats his children—a fiend, that scourges men out of their humanity, and then mocks at their fall.

A nun, like a suicide, is a reproach to Christianity: a harlot is a judgment on civilization.

—In the last days of August, we found ourselves again in Frankfort, at the heels of the Peace-Congress.

Arms can't free a people; ideas only can do that. But at certain stages of the liberating work of ideas, arms have to clear the track for their further march. Otherwise they would be first stopt, and then stifled by gross obstructions. Arms may thus be the instruments of ideas,—impure instruments, but the best, on occasions, that an impure world affords. Threatened with drowning, would you be nice in the means of extrication? Freedom has always used arms; without them she would have been crushed. If honest men should all turn members of the non-resistance society, the rogues would soon have the upper hand.

What can a Peace-Congress do against wolves? Put your preachings into practice in face of a bear. Without compunction or a moment's theoretical cogitation, the meekest zealot of you all, would meet Bruin's hug with the thrust of a bowie-knife. There may be a time when even a bowie-knife can do good service. But a bear is a beast forever inaccessible to thought, which is the parent of freedom and peace. What if you were set upon by a foot-pad, who first wounds you with a pistol-shot, and then rushes forward to rob you, or to finish you with a poignard?

Could you keep your finger off a trigger, or, if you had none, help cursing your stars that you were unarmed. There is but one way of dealing with a murderous assailant. "He who slays with the sword, he shall perish by the sword." The text clearly applies to him, and not to you. Upon him you have fulfilled it, and there an end.

The two millions of soldiers that garrison the continent of Europe, are but legalized foot-pads. They hold bayonets to the throats of the nations, while kings and popes, and their minions, rob their souls and their pockets, and their lives. It is brute force, compelling the mind in its lowest as well as its highest needs, crippling it in all its means. Freedom of speaking, of printing, of meeting, of going and coming, of buying, of selling, of associating,—all are curtailed, hampered, or suppressed. Every right of manhood is maimed or crushed. Against such violence what defence is there? Incalculably more effective arms than pistols, even against pistols themselves, are thoughts—when you can use them. And at this moment, in the face of artillery and the haugman, they are used with an efficiency that startles the gods of gunpowder.

Were the conflict confined to civilized Europe, it might be brought to an end without bloodshed. Vienna and Berlin, and even bemitred Rome would soon capitulate to the fiery assaults of all-conquering thought. But semi-barbarous Russia, who fears freedom and proscribes ideas, puts herself at the head of the brute cause, and gives it her million of muskets. Here is a bear that, under pretence of love for order, would hug freedom to death. And shall Freedom, in this strait, not thrust the sword, not pull the trigger?

Let the Peace-Congress address itself to the Emperor of Russia. He is the chief, nay, the only obstacle to peace in Europe. With an unchristian infidelity the Emperor of Russia puts his trust in the despotism of muskets. With his brute force he upholds the regal governments of the Continent, the which, being dead, can only be upheld by brute force. At Paris and Rome, as well as at Vienna and Berlin, Russian policy rules. But for her, Freedom, the nursery of peace, would be already founded on the ruins of Austrian despotism, and her cause be triumphant in Germany. The logical place for the next Peace-Congress is Warsaw.

The Despots have divined, that peace can only be the fruit of freedom. Thence they regard the Peace-Congress as a Freedom-Congress. It is a Freedom-Congress. But can it devise how, in the actual array of hostilities, freedom can triumph without a temporary alliance with gunpowder? Most of its members are, I suspect, of one mind with three American delegates whom I had the pleasure of meeting in Switzerland on their way to Frankfort, whose tongues warmed at the talk of a universal armed uprising of the Peoples against the tyrants that degrade and despoil them.

CHAPTER VII.

STAGE-COACH AND CAR—CONSERVATISM—GERMAN BURGHER AND POSTILION—PRIMARY EDUCATION IN GERMANY.

AMONG agreeable contrasts cannot be classed that between a steam-driven car and a German stage-coach. On the railroad from Frankfort to Cassel, there was, in 1850, between Friedberg and Giessen, a chasm which we were three hours in getting over by coach. What a good thing is a McAdam road! It deserves the point of admiration. Wherewith then shall we point the sentence that tells of the railroad? To pass from the one to the other is like poverty after affluence, like a good whistler after Jenny Lind, like beer after Burgundy. How we grapple to us what we once get possession of. Who would give up the railroad or the newspaper? Ask the freshman to go back to the schoolroom. A progress takes hold of us like the growing fibre of our frame : it enfolds our life. To go back, is against nature. Our lot is, to go forward.

Let Conservatives bethink them. Our moral life is as sluggish as the "Royal Mail." Only twenty years ago the mail' ten miles an hour was very fast. 'Twas the most that turnpike and coach could do. Who then talked of twenty miles the hour, not to speak of fifty, was a dangerous innovator or an impractical Utopian. The ten miles is the most can be got out of the old Church and the old State. We want a new Church, as different from the old one as iron and steam are from horse-flesh and granite. Who dare say "Halt," to the moral man? Why should I doubt that we may have a belief so inspiring, that our social condition shall, like locomotive speed, rise from ten to fifty. Are we only mechanical? Can we reform roads and not institutions? Are no more discoveries to be made in the upper sphere? Have we read to the end of the book of life, that we turn back the leaves to the first chapters again? In the presence of miraculous man, and the mighty Providence above him, who dare define his possibilities? Ye think yourselves believers, and ye believe only in the dead and the dying. The Barbarian believes naught but tradition and what he sees. Ye bandage your vision with his limitations : ye forego the right of reason, which bids ye look before as well as after. Talk to the Barbarian of the railroad and the electric telegraph ; he will laugh at you, if he does not frown. Talk we to you of methods whereby evil shall be exorcised and good made to prevail like sunshine, of harmonies that shall convert human labor into a life-long joy, of conditions that shall fulfil your daily prayer, " thy kingdom come, thy will be done on earth as it is in heaven,"—ye laugh or frown. Ye civilized barbarians, ye believing skeptics, upon ye be this triple malediction ; ye shall sail without the compass, travel without steam, and read never a printed page.

—By my side on the top of the coach, was an average sample of a German Burgher,—stout and kindly, intelligent and accessible. It did me good to hear him curse all kings, particularly his own of Prussia. Not that as a democrat I need to be fortified in my political creed by this verbal pulling down of monarchies ; or, that as a man I take delight in hearing a fellow-man, even a king, abused. It was as evidence,—such as I have had much of in the past few weeks,—of the emancipation of German feeling from the thraldom of regal prestige, that I listened with pleasure to my neighbor's king-cursing fluency. No "divinity doth hedge a king" any more in Germany. In the Frankfo*t*

Assembly, two years ago, an orator said bitingly of his countrymen, "A German without a prince, is like a dog without a master." He could not and would not have said it, if it had not already begun to cease to be true. In these two years the Germans have not made progress simply, they have made a leap. They have, in opinions and convictions, leapt clean out of princedom. One is astonished to hear of and to witness the so rapid and general conversion to democracy. Principles of political liberty and resolves to put them into act, are widely spread and deeply rooted. Among this thoughtful, reading people, the ground was well prepared, and the princes by their perfidy are doing almost better for the growing crop, than could have done those who are to reap. There will be a plentiful harvest; if it be gathered in blood, the blood be on the heads of the traitors who, having been again trusted, would again rule with the old tyrannies. In two years what a revulsion! After the popular victory in 1848, how forgiving, hopeful, magnanimous, trustful, was the whole German race: in 1850, how full of wrath, bitterness, menace. There will be no forgiveness of the past the next time.

In the postilion, who from the back of the near wheel-horse conducted our cumbrous vehicle, I had a sample of a German proletarian. Proletarian means a producer of men. The day-laborers of Europe are esteemed, first as workers, who can be bought at about twenty-five cents a day, to do all agricultural and manufacturing work; and secondly, as breeders, whose function is to keep full the supply of workers. Hence this appellation, which denotes that the masses here are valued as muscle-endowed animals, not as soul-endowed men. Our postilion had been twenty-six years on the road, passing over these same few leagues almost daily; and yet, of the small neighboring towns or villages, so near that the spires and highest buildings were visible, he knew the name of scarcely one. His countryman by my side, poured upon him from our elevation, volleys of bitter ridicule.

The postilion was annoyed, not at being found ignorant, but that he was expected to know such things. In his *naïveté* there was wisdom, as there so often is. His feeling was an unconscious protestation, that personally he was blameless for his ignorance. They are the blamable, who, under pretext of governing, convert a man into a carriage-conducting machine.

Much praise has been bestowed on the schools, and on the universality of primary instruction in Germany. For the comparative excellence of methods and the breadth of their application, let the praise stand. Good schooling is never a bad thing. Nevertheless, when for twelve hours out of the twenty-four, men are turned into beasts of burden, and can then barely earn the coarsest food and raiment, how much does schooling profit them? Many of the German peasants are found in mature life, to have forgotten how to read and write. What time or occasion have they to use these high instruments? To men so belabored, so disfranchised, schooling is almost a mockery. This postilion can read and write. Had he been never taught a letter, but been allowed a voice in naming the mayor of his village, and the parson of his church, I warrant he would have known the names of every hamlet we passed; and this in itself, barren knowledge, would have been the attendant and sign of a productive knowledge of men and things, denoting that his understanding had been cultivated by animating contacts, and his heart enlarged by sympathies beyond the petty routine of the postilion's duties. Let him vote for his burgomaster, his pastor, and his tax-imposer, and no fear but he will take care that his children be provided with the humanizing media of intercourse, reading, writing, and arithmetic; and no fear either that they will forget them from want of practice. The mere introduction of the penny-post in England, led tens of thousands of poor people to learn to read and write, just to avail themselves of the facility thus opened of communicating with their distant relatives. Open to the laborer the facility and necessity of communicating with his neighbors and fellow-men,—his political relatives,—on their common interests and rights; give him as man the practical education acquired by a manly share in public affairs, and he will be sure to provide,—whether by public or private means,—for the school-instruction of the boy. But this elevation of the proletarian is the reverse of what European governments desire.

CHAPTER VIII.

MARBURG—MONUMENT—RAILROAD TO CASSEL—CASSEL TO DRESDEN.

To the traveller on this route, who travels to see, I recommend half a day at Marburg. A prettier site for a small inland town, he will seldom meet with. It stands on the sides of a hill that projects like a sudden promontory into the valley of the Lahn, and whose summit is crowned with the old castle of the Landgraves of Hesse, round which the town gradually built itself in the middle ages. At the outer base of the promontory is the church, pure and simple Gothic, six hundred years old, with double towers, remarkable for its symmetry. The station is a quarter of a mile distant from the town. As you sweep up to it on the curve of the railroad, the castle on the top of the hill, the old town on its sides, the graceful church at its foot, with a valley running back from its northern slope, make a picture so captivating, that you rejoice to learn that this is Marburg, where you are to stop.

On our way up to the castle, we passed the houses wherein had lodged Luther and Zwingli, when they met here to discuss transubstantiation. They of course parted without agreeing. To settle a theological question is as easy as to pin a ghost to the wall: they are both so purely within the province of the imagination. In the castle is a chapel, in which Luther preached. I mounted into the plain oaken pulpit, whence the thunderer had launched his church-rending 'ightnings.

The town, partly in shadow, clustered round the protecting castle, the twin, tapering spires, and the soft valley of the Lahn, seen up and down, combine to give a view from the terrace which, in the afternoon especially, is enchanting. As we gazed, a train from Cassel came down the valley. After rushing noisily past in front of us, it shot away in silence to the south, under its white canopy of mist, like a cloud before a hurricane.

—— To "take mine ease in mine inn," the inn must be good. The inn is the traveller's home, and he can't feel at home in it unless it be cleanly and kindly. Mine host and hostess are the wayfarer's father and mother. When he alights they receive him with welcome, good cheer, and a clean bed. These he will find at the "Golden Knight" (zum Goldnen Ritter), in Marburg. Mine host was a good specimen of the German Boniface of a small town—portly, thriving, communicative, familiar but respectful, a good judge of meat and drink, and sharing fairly with his guests the fruits of his judgment. Twice a year he goes to the Rhine to replenish his cellar. While there he keeps his palate susceptible by abstinence, and surrenders himself to the gustative joy which the Rhine offers to the discriminating connoisseur, not until after he has made his purchases. He warmed towards me as he perceived that I drank in with relish his discourse about the localities where *Liebfrauenmilch*, *Oppenheimer*, *Niersteiner* ripen. As compliment to his publican qualities, and as index of his thrift, he owns a garden on the skirt of the town. His landlordship were incomplete without these few acres within an easy walk of his door, where he rears fruit and esculents, and has a daily pastime for his latter years. I am bound to mention, for the truthfulness of my sketch, that at parting the next afternoon, he played me a very unfatherly trick, having—after we had paid his bill and set out on foot to the station—manifested a hard-hearted indifference whether our luggage arrived in time or not. Had I met him within the ten minutes of excruciating suspense caused by his coldness, I should have had difficulty in refraining from paying his unparental insensibility with very unfilial phrases.

After exploring the pretty valley that runs back and brings a tributary brook of most limpid water to the Lahn, we ascended a hill across it directly opposite to the town, wishing to get a view from this point, and attracted too by a monument on the summit of the hill. The view is a reward for the ascent to any one who does not find in the walk itself its own reward; and the monument I would not have missed seeing had the road to it been rugged and steep.

I defy all the millions of guessers in the United States to divine why this monument was erected. No American imagination could in such a search come near enough to have even " warm" cried to it, as in the game of Hunt the Slipper. After looking round at the panoramic landscape, I turned towards the monument, an obelisk twelve or fourteen feet high, built of freestone. When I had read the inscription, I read it over again. Yes, there could be no mis-reading; the words were plain, well-cut German. I am counting perhaps much too largely upon my character for veracity, in hoping that it will be able to withstand the shock of the reader's incredulity, when I tell him that their purport was as follows. A princess of Hesse-Cassel had one fine day walked up to this spot, and enjoyed the views thence. To commemorate this fact this monument of stone was built by some grateful inhabitants of Marburg. And these good Germans would at times take airs over us on account of African slavery! I must in justice add that it is a monument of the past, having been raised about thirty years ago.

—— At every station of the road to Cassel on Sunday afternoon, crowds of peasants were assembled to see the steam-wonder. At the snorting monster, fire-souled, and wheel-pawed, they stared as the aboriginal Americans did at the vessels of Columbus. But not like them with wild wonderment and a dim presentient fear. The white civilizee is within reach of the beneficence of machinery; for the yellow savage it is an unsparing destroyer, which mows him down the faster in proportion as itself is the stronger. At the flying "locomotive," whose wings, laden with a hundred men, outfly the eagle, the sun-browned sons and daughters of 'abor gazed with an intelligent admiration, as half conscious that t is a harbinger of better days.—For the emancipation of man all oowers must co-work; the intellect with its logic and its invenions, the soul with its expansive wants, nature with the revela.ions which she so gladly makes to penetrative genius. Industry must join hands with Christianity, Science with Sentiment, Intelligence with Faith. The momentum of humanity must have been already incalculably accelerated by the unfolding of its capacities, ere it can swing itself into a wider orbit. This momentum it now has; and as the train, burthened with its scores of tons, swept with fabulous speed past turretted burgs and stately castles in ruin, it was a symbol of the present eager movement among the foremost nations of Christendom, striding forward with new energy and new hope, leaving behind the old walls and towers of defence, and careering into a sphere of untrammelled freedom and unvexed enjoyment.

―――― At Cassel, the population was all out of doors, in the great streets and in the public walks, as is the continental custom of a Sunday afternoon, the peasantry from the neighborhood flocking in to diversify and thicken the crowd. Puppets, mountebanks, and monkeys were entertaining full-grown men and women. The pleasure of the lower classes in these childish spectacles, is reflected in the upper, who delight to see them enjoy such coarse emptinesses, it being a sign that they are themselves empty and childish, and therefore governable. To be easily governed is, in the eyes of governors, the highest virtue of a people. I am happy to bear witness that this virtue is here growing weaker and weaker. A manly consciousness is awakened in the laborious masses. Thence the multiplication of soldiers, who are the constables of tyrants. On these musket-shouldering drones, the people now scowl with feelings anything but childlike.

Between Cassel and Dresden lie five or six degrees of longitude, and the territories of half a dozen sovereign states. This space, dotted with towns of historic name, has on the map a formidable look, Cassel lying in the west, and Dresden in the east of Germany. But the wishing-cap of Gothic mythology finds its realization in a railroad ticket. Wish yourself three hundred miles off, and by having in your pocket a printed slip of paper, your wish is in a twinkling fulfilled, even in Germany, where the fiery "Locomotive" has to curb his impatience, and adapt his flight somewhat to the proverbial Teutonic slowness.

CHAPTER IX.

A DAY IN DRESDEN.

DRESDEN, the capital of Saxony, contains 90,000 inhabitants; its collections of works of art have gained for it the title of "the German Florence;" its two unequal parts are united by a broad substantial stone bridge over the Elbe, "built with money raised by the sale of dispensations from the Pope for eating butter and eggs during Lent," &c. &c. The &cs. covering twenty closely printed pages, the reader, curious in such details, will find in "Murray's Hand-Book for Northern Germany." Here he will have only the sketch of a day in Dresden, from notes, taken down on the spot, of such "Scenes and Thoughts" as presented themselves successively to the writer, from early morning till bedtime, on Monday, the 9th of September, 1850.

Through a window of No. 16, a spacious chamber on the second floor of the Hotel, *Stadt Rom*, I look, while dressing, into the square of the *Neu-Markt*, yet in shadow, for it is half-past six o'clock. Carts, and women bearing on their backs heavily laden baskets, are coming slowly in from the country. Opposite, across the square, is the great Picture-Gallery; at the right, the "Church of our Lady," with its stone dome, large and lofty, illuminated by the rising sun.

—— Before seven, out in the cool morning. Fires are already lighted, in people's mouths. We have just past a cart drawn by a woman and dog, pulling sociably in harness together, and at every few steps, we come upon women stooping as they walk, under burthens on their backs. Striking into a street raked by the sun,—for the air is chilly,—we soon issue upon the *Wills-druffer* Place, set off by a fountain in form of an elaborate, feathery, Gothic pinnacle; and thence onward to the *Zwinger*, an extensive showy edifice, where are the Historical and other Museums, partly destroyed during the late civil conflicts. The sides of the building enclose a square, laid out in walks and shrubbery. Before entering, let us read the printed notice at the gate-way:— " These grounds are recommended to the protection of the public." A greeting like this, wins at a stroke the affection of the stranger. Such gentle fraternal words, tell of refinement and mutual trust. They made sacred to us every blade and leaf within the enclosure. We walked back to the inn with the sensation that one has, after receiving welcome unexpected news.

The carts in the New Market-place have emptied their loads, which are now piled up breast high on one side of the square, pile next to pile of huge loaves of rye bread, baked in the neighboring villages.

Waiting for breakfast in the public room of the *Stadt Rom*, from a seat by the corner window, I have a level view of the whole square, and a close one of the current of passers in and out of it, through a street that runs by one side of the hotel. People have not a brisk auroral air; they look relaxed instead of braced. They don't go at the day vigorously. This early aspect of awakened Dresden, is of a town that takes its leisure. After breakfast, I sauntered across to the sunny corner of the square, towards the church, where the market-women with their baskets of vegetables are chatting and chaffering. Their heads are without covering. If upon the living brain the sun could breed thought, as upon the dead he breeds maggots, what vaulted brows would crown the faces of European peasants, what Moses-like coruscations would shoot from their parturient foreheads. But then they would cease to be peasants, to be the drudge-horses and patient oxen that they are. The sun breeds only brownness and dryness, which embellish not the feminine physiognomy. The market-women, however, look ruddy and cheerful, and show well, as country people always do, by the side of the townfolk.

—— At nine, by appointment, with other sight-seers, to the Green Vault (*das Grüne Gewölbe*),—a regal curiosity-shop, stocked with Mosaics, jewels, trinkets, miniature-carvings in wood, ivory, and precious metals, and other costly rarities. Here and there is a bit having the unworn stamp of beauty; but the most of them are not works of Art; that is, works embodying thought, sentiment, or vivid corporeal reality in beautiful forms. They are skilful handiwork, with little head or heart-work; the toilsome shapings of uninspired fancy; the lifeless leavings of Art, elaborate nothings; fruits of the patronizings of tasteless Princes. The most precious jewels were absent, having been removed for safe-keeping to the Fortress of Königstein. They showed us one unique natural product,—a crystal globe twenty-two inches in circumference, a solid transparence, a flawless mineral purity, purged by subterranean fires.

The Historical Museum is an abstract, written in daggers and breastplates, of the history of war during the latter half of what are called the middle ages. These coats of mail are contemplated with a certain favor if one will regard them as life-preservers during the stormy period of chivalry. After all, these old-time brawlers and spoilers took devilish good care of their skins. Just before quitting the Museum we came unexpectedly upon arms of a totally different and immensely more effective kind, the pen of Goethe and the modelling-stick of Thorwaldsen. These modest, tiny weapons, what conquests have they not made! They lay in their little case a mordant irony on the performances of the Duke Georges and Prince Henrys, whose effigies on horseback, armed cap-à-pié, we had just seen, and whose exploits, only heard of through the mouth of the droning cicerone, we had already forgotten. It is a humane surprise prepared for the visitor, thus to quicken his spirit with these modern holy relics, after it has been wearied with such a flat reiteration of profane antiquities.

—— We have time before dinner to look upon some of the splendors in the Collection of Pictures, one of the richest in Europe. Passing with hasty glances through the broad galleries, hung by the procreant hand of genius, we soon found ourselves at their centre, before the masterpiece of masterpieces, the *Madonna di Sto. Sisto* of Raphael. When, after gazing at it often, you happen to be in the congenial receptive mood, which a work of art demands, in order to be appreciated, the wonderful perfections of this picture reveal themselves. Those two heads, the Mother and Child! In the Madonna is the plenitude of womanly life and beauty; grace united with power, strength with sweetness. What a grand contour of head, yet soft and feminine; calm, earnest, with a deep look of unspeakable beatitude. The whole and the individual features, regular as Greeks could have made them, and yet without coldness or limitation, but warm as happiest maternity and of infinite suggestiveness.—The Child has a wise, almost wizard look. But for the earnestness and mystic depth in the eyes, one might think it the head of an urchin who would prove hard to manage,—and in truth the man Jesus was unmanageable, a protestor and reformer, a rebel against the priestcraft of his time. The big eyes look like loop-holes through which the Past is peering thoughtfully and sadly into the Future. The hair is wild and unkempt. The head and face are not regular, but running over with beauty; infantile and beyond childhood; shining with an inward light, that ennobles the features with the glow of human intellect and sympathy. With the instinct of genius, Raphael has made the head large, but the size is absorbed by the light of the expression.—The two up-gazing Cherubs at the base,—the types of love and joy, the focusses of

infinite rapture, marvellous little winged heads,—are in power
and beauty entirely subordinated to the unwinged Jesus.—This
is a picture that Fame has never caught up with.

Ere we quit the Gallery let us pause for a moment before
another of its chief treasures,—Neptune stilling the Tempest, by
Rubens. At the command of Neptune, standing in a shell borne
on the waves by sea-horses with heads and necks above water, and
followed by sea-nymphs, the angry winds with black wings are
reluctantly retiring. What breadth and power of conception, expression and coloring. One is nerved by looking at this picture.
Those three prancing heads are a great creation. Rubens has
here brought to view the original types of the horse species, the
progenitors of the whole equine race, such fire is there and inexhaustible strength, such a nervous dilation in those heads, darting
lightnings from eye and nostril.

—— At one,—a wholesome hour,—we sat down with a score of
fellow-diners to the public dinner in the hotel. The dishes, served
successively, were soup, fish, mutton-chops with red cabbage,
roast veal, rice pudding—a modest repast which cost forty cents
in money and one hour and a quarter in time.

—— The human capacity of adaptation is nowhere more forcibly exhibited than in the acquired callousness to the suffering
which, in Europe especially, assaults the compassion at every
turn, and which, but for this pliancy to circumstances, would keep
the spirits forever low and banish smiles from the countenance of
man. But there are spectacles to which no use of custom can so
harden us but that the heart will always sadden in their presence.
In going up to our chamber after dinner we had one of these,—a
woman bearing on her back such a load of wood, that as she
slowly set foot before foot in the ascent, so bent was she under the
weight that her face and hands almost touched the step above, her
burthen thus converting her corporeally, as it tends to do spiritually, into a down-looking quadruped. One hurries by such

sights, that the pang they give may be quickly quenched in the sea of busy movement about us; but against them, and even against those to which we are outwardly hardened, men enter more and more frequently and more and more deeply an inward protest as they pass. A fact full of hope is the accumulating protestation against cruelty and wrong. This ceaseless heart-cry is a prophecy. Feeling precedes conviction, conviction precedes action. The one predicts the other. A present ideal of healthy minds is the promise of a future reality. They whose convictions outrun their practice, whose aspirations are purer than their deeds, who know the littlenesses of our dislocated existence for what they are, let them cherish uplifting thoughts; these are not barren dreams, they are the roots of a more generous life.

Who is this that greets us at the landing with an humble smile from her arch face? Her face is more than arch, it is pretty besides, and would be more than pretty, were the soul that lights it itself fully lighted. Her brown hair is carried back in that easiest simple manner called Grecian. Her head turns gracefully on a fair round neck; and her shoulders, bust, waist, and whole figure are in harmony with her head. Her arm, bare and white, would fix the eye of Greenough or of Powers in admiration, while on his organ of form he took its impress for ideal uses. Were you to meet her in a cottage, you would think the cottage blest by her sweetness,—in a drawing-room of jewelled beauties, she would seem to be born for this elegant rivalry,—in a Palace, you might forget the Princess in the woman. Poor Saxon Girl, whose mien doth beget for thee such divers perfections upon the imagination of a passing stranger, lower than the most modest of these conditions is thy lot. Not for thee is even the cottage, with the breadth of earth and sky to compensate for its cabined uncultured existence. Perhaps from its rustic hearth thou wast lured by the glare of the city, towards which,—impelled by the deep need of human communion,—so many of thy sisters rush to burn their ignorant wings in its fire, and to drag ever after their blackened bodies towards an obscure grave. Thee Nature destined for a higher sphere. Where the texture is, the sculptor's creative hand fashions the Goddess from the raw block: thou hast the texture wherewith the plastic power of favoring circumstances could have fashioned a household Goddess, an honored accomplished woman. But Fortune, to whose caprices so many are committed in this blind-folded world, not joining hands with Nature, thou wast disorbed, and now dost perform,—and that with the cheerfulness of a happy temperament,—the low daily routine allotted to the chambermaid of an inn.

How few people are in their right places. And worse still; were there to be a thorough shuffling, a general change and interchange of conditions and positions, forward and backward and sideways and upward and downward, still we should not get into them. The right places are not there.

—— Dresden has attractive environs. But the weather is just now so unseasonably cold, that an open carriage is rather a penance than a pleasure. We shall content ourselves this afternoon with an intramural stroll. The town has an air of old-fashioned elegance. There is a courtly quiet in the streets. Business and traffic are secondary. Many of the people that you meet seem to have nothing to do, and those who bear on them some badge of business are going about it so leisurely, that most of them, one would think, will be overtaken by to-morrow ere they get through. The absence of commercial bustle is an agreeable characteristic of Dresden.

At six we walked to the large, commodious theatre lately erected near the river. The piece was an opera, a good one, *The Water-carrier*. About the time that the curtain of the opera in London and Paris rises, that of Dresden falls. At half-past eight we were back to the hotel, taking a late tea, while our neighbors, male and female, at the public table were busy with the early German supper of meat, bread, cheese, and salad, of which last, especially, the Germans, who have an enviable gift of copious feeding, consume a huge quantity.

—— It is past nine. Although the opera is over, the Dresden day is not yet closed. If the reader will go along with me, I will bring him where he will witness what, if he has not been in Germany, he never has witnessed. In a few minutes we are on the *Brühl* Terrace, which forms a delightful walk within the town, along the river and high above it. Here is a *café :* we pay a few coppers at the door, and enter a hall capable of holding three hundred people : it is now quite full. At the opposite end, a large band of good performers is executing excellent music. The company, half females, are seated at numerous tables of different sizes, supplied with coffee, tea, beer, wine, and some with eatables. This kind of cheap, good, sociable, conversational concert, is characteristic of Germany. One feature caps its Germanism : nearly all the men are smoking. One hundred of them simultaneously puffing out smoke generated in their mouths by their lungs, which act as bellows on ignited tobacco, in a closed hall neither large nor lofty, where, intermingled with the smoke-producers, are one hundred and fifty of the softer (I cannot here say sweeter) sex, witnesses of the production, and absorbents of the product. The throng of people sit for hours in the compound rankness of this unventilated hall, with an insensibility to bad air that verified with clenching emphasis, how custom may usurp upon nature. If the lungs and olfactory nerves of delicate women will not protest, their shawls and silks should, against this foul violation of the rights of women. For ourselves, as dutiful sight-seers, we bore the pressure upon the arterial circulation of this deoxygenated nicotenized atmosphere for twenty minutes, and then fled to the terrace. The Germans do not smoke, they are smoked. Tobacco has got the upper hand of them.

By ten we were back to the hotel and No. 16.

CHAPTER X.

WEIMAR—CEMETERY—SCHILLER'S STUDY—GALL AND GOETHE—CRANIUM OF SCHILLER—WEIMAR'S HIGH INHABITANTS.

The next day towards noon we were suddenly beset by a desire to be in Weimar. I like in travelling to give way to an impulse of this kind. In the wilful breaking up of the set sequence of things, there is a remunerative assurance of freedom. You start without the ceremony of giving yourself notice. You go solely because you want to go. In this there is an enlivening breach of routine, a luxury of liberty. You snatch a sunny holiday from amidst the sombre slaveries of this conventional, whip-driven world. After a hurried packing, we provided ourselves with the modern wishing-cap, and alighted by early bed-time at the "Hereditary Prince," in Weimar, having rushed through book-selling Leipzig and book-fed Halle, just as though, instead of being populous, notable towns, they had been only relay houses by the wayside.

—— I walked again in my old paths through the tranquil town of Weimar. 'Tis like arresting, and fixing in hard corporeality, the airy images of a dream, thus to re-behold after twenty-five years, the scenes of careless, laughing youth. The solid recognized forms are as cold and sad-speaking as the sarcophagi of departed friends. One hovers about them with a melancholy self-abandonment. I think I know how a ghost feels who revisits the haunts of his sublunary sojourn. I peered as I went into faces, with a hope of recognition or reciprocated interest; but all were cold, exclusive, introverted, just like the faces of other streets. I passed before Goethe's house. At that door I had once knocked, —with timidity, as having no claim to admittance but that which his fame gave me,—and within I had met, shining with kindliness, that great glittering eye. For what is left of his mortal part I must now seek in the vault.

And thither I bent my steps. He who after the lapse of a quarter of a century revisits the resorts of his youth, must betake him to the graveyard to find the vestiges of his former acquaintance. The cemetery of Weimar, lying just outside the town, has an untrimmed look which suits a cemetery. Flowers and shrubbery and grass are not much curtailed of their natural freedom. This wildness and unclipt exuberance is in harmony with the spot, and gives to it a softer and a quieter aspect. In the centre is a small chapel for funeral services. Through the middle of the floor a large round opening, guarded by a balustrade, communicates with the Grand-ducal vault below, wherein, with those of the sovereign family, lie the bodies of Goethe and Schiller. We descended by the stairway into the vault. It was neither dark nor damp, and was mildly perfumed by burnt incense. Here was naught of the gloom of a charnel-house. 'Twas as though the immortal spirits of the great inmates had purified it of all stains of death. Beside their holy remains we lingered with feelings of cheerful elevation. It was not a place for sadness. The coffins are raised three or four feet from the ground. Those containing the bodies of Goethe and Schiller are side by side, apart from the others. I stood between them, with my hands resting one on either coffin.

The late Grand-Duke of Weimar, Charles Augustus, the friend of Goethe and Schiller, and who is illustrious by that friendship, requested that his body should be placed between the bodies of the two Poets. He had a right to make the request: he was worthy of that exalted place. He was not merely their friend and generous protector; he had a soul that sympathized with theirs. Whether it be, that his successors, animated by a low jealousy, are unwilling to recognize his right to this great privilege, or that they are influenced by a still more ignoble motive, his request has not yet been complied with. The coffin containing his body lies by itself.

———— In the study of Schiller I sat down one morning at his desk, and with ink dipped from an inkstand of Goethe, I took phrenological notes on a cast of Schiller's head. There was a seat and an occupation! But nothing is complete in this loose, fragmentary world. Why was there no mould from the cranium of Schiller's renowned friend? Because men are such laggards behind truth. The momentous, brilliant discovery of the physiology of the brain was promulgated in the beginning of this century, and first in Germany by its great discoverer, Gall. And still, though so easily verified, it remains unacknowledged by scientific men on the continent of Europe. In freer England, and freest America, its truth has been forced upon the scientific in a great measure by the enlightened perseverance of the laity. Goethe, whose sympathy with the spirit and processes of Nature was the source of his wisdom, meeting with Gall, who, in a tour through Germany, was expounding his newly-made discovery, received it at once into his mind, with that large hospitality which he always extended to new-comers from the realms of Nature. Pity that he had not cultivated acquaintanceship into intimacy. His name would have been a passport to this fruitful truth, and thus have hastened by half a century its acceptance among his countrymen. In that case, moreover, his friends and executors, knowing the scientific value of a fac-simile of his noble head, we should have had his by the side of Schiller's, to compare together and contrast the two.

The brain of Schiller, from its large size and general conformation, denotes uncommon energy, great force and warmth of character, and irresistible mental momentum. In his organization there was a rich mingling of powers. What he undertook he went at with a zeal that rallied his whole nature to the service, with a volume of impetus that bore him on with burning velocity, and with a resolution that no obstacle could stay. His undertakings were high, his aspirations noble. Onward, onward, upward, upward! might have been his device. With all this fiery enthusiasm, this impatient activity, he undertook naught rashly. He was at once impetuous and prudent. He was self-confident, but with consciousness of his gifts he united an insatiable thirst for better than he could furnish. His ideal was so exalted it kept him ever learning and expanding. Goethe was often astonished, when they would meet after a not very long separation, to find what progress he had made in the interval. His intellect was under the spur of his poetic expansions fed by his hearty impulses. His mind was kept at red heat. His nature was earnest, and even stern. If there was in him no sportiveness or humor, neither was there any littleness. His love of fame was strong, but he sought to gratify it by lofty labors.

Schiller's intellect was broad and massive, not subtle nor penetrative. Hence, with all his material of sympathy and inborn passion, wherewith he energized and diversified his characters, they lack individuality and compactness. In the most finished there is a certain hollowness. It is not so much, that they are not distinctly enough differenced one from the other, as that each is not tightly knit up into itself, as in Shakspeare and Goethe. Schiller was not the closest, most scrupulous thinker, and thence in creating characters he could not thoroughly interpenetrate the animal and sentimental vitality with the intellectual, which interpenetration must be in order that each personage have his definite, rounded, vivacious existence. Nor is the action in his dramatic structures always bound up in the severest logical chain. Schiller was not a Poet of the highest order; he was not prophetic, not a *vates*. He did not deliver truths, or embody beauty in creations, so much above the standard of his age that they have to wait for a higher culture to be fully valued. His generalizations have not the unfading brilliancy which those truths have that are wrought in the mine of emotion by the intensest action of reason. Between his intellect and his sensibility there was not that perfect accord which makes the offspring of their union at once veracious and ideal, and elastic from the compactness of their constituents. His grasp of intellect was not so strong as was his imaginative swing. When the cast was put into my hands what first struck me was the want of prominence in the upper part of the forehead.

Speaking of his early flight from Wurtemberg, Schiller describes the joy he felt in having thenceforward no other master than the Public. To an ardent young Poet it could not but be a joy, akin to that of moral renovation, to escape from the suffocation of tyranny, to find himself rid of a narrow King and face to face with the broad multitude. But there is a still higher Tribunal,—through which too the Public is in the end more surely and permanently won than by direct appeal to itself,—the tribunal of Truth. To this and this alone the true Artist feels himself amenable. For, the Artist's function is, to purify the sensibility of his fellow-men, to instruct them by awakening a poetic admiration, to chasten their taste. By creations in harmony with the absolute true and beautiful, he develops, and cultivates the latent æsthetic capability of the mass. His part is to be a teacher, not a flatterer or prosaic purveyor. Great Artists are always above their Public. Did Shakspeare suit himself to the common judgment of his day? So little so, that even the shrewdest of his contemporaries discerned not half the meaning and merit of his wonderful creations. He himself,—sublime isolation,—was the only one of his time who knew their transcendent worth. To think, that for more than a century there was in the whole world but one man who entirely enjoyed the Tempest and Lear, who was capable of fully loving Imogen and Juliet, and that man was Shakspeare. What kind of appeal to the general judgment of Charles the Second's generation was Paradise Lost? Wordsworth scorned the Public, who laughed at him, and having survived a half-century his earlier Poems, had the personal enjoyment of a tardy justice, his genius being acknowledged by a more "enlightened Public" than that which first so coldly greeted him, his later contemporaries paying him reverence as a true Priest in the service of Beauty and Truth. He had to make the taste by which he was appreciated. Goethe, mentioning in a letter to Schiller, the limited sale of one of his best Poems, *Hermann and Dorothea*, comforts himself by adding ironically,—" we make money by our bad books." And Schiller himself, who always wrote in pursuit of a refined ideal, says somewhere, that the Artist's mission is to scourge rather than to truckle to the spirit of his age.

It is much for a man to possess several eminent qualities that keep him on a high level. Schiller was upborne by his poetic nature and his love of humanity. He had not the deepest sensibility for truth. Thus, although, under his poetic and generous inspirations, he appreciated and practically fulfilled the Artist's function, his impulse when first freed was towards fame. From the same source,—that is, the absence of arched rotundity in the region of conscientiousness,—I would infer a want of punctuality in engagements, literary and other, and venture to conjecture, that by this failing his friend Goethe was occasionally somewhat put out.

Among the precious relics was the bedstead whereon Schiller slept, and whereon he died at the early age of forty-six. Often at night, he put his feet into a tub of cold water, placed under his writing-table, in order thereby to keep himself awake. He worked his brain to the uttermost, and wore himself out with the noblest labor. It were easy to figure him seated at his desk, with " visionary eye" and furrowed brow, intently elaborating thoughts which his pen hurriedly seized, when a knock, drawing from him an unwilling "Herein," he would lift his eyes with a look of almost sternness, for the unwelcome interrupter; and then suddenly his countenance would relax and beam, as the tall figure of Goethe advanced through the opening door, and rising with an eager motion, he would greet his friend with cordial words and hand-grasp. And the fever of his mind would subside. The calm power of the self-possessing Goethe would soothe him without lowering his tone; and when, after Goethe's departure, he set himself again to his work, it would be with the refreshed feeling of one who, towards the close of a midsummer's day, has just bathed in the shady nook of a deep, tranquil stream.

On one side of the desk is a sliding chess-board, to be drawn out when wanted. Here, the guardian of the house declared, Goethe and Schiller sometimes played. This I refused to credit, and put it down as a false tradition. Games,—even those involving bodily exercise,—are the resource of the vacant; and I would not believe that two such full-brained men, whose interviews were to them both enlivening thought-breeders, would ever dedicate their tête-à-tête meetings to this solemn frivolity, this ingenious emptiness, this silent, sapless pastime. Still, against the circumstantial conclusions of reason, there was the sliding chess-board.

——Owing to some misunderstanding between Goethe's heirs and executors, his house is only opened one day in the week, and even then his study is not shown. On entering the drawing-room, I perceived that there had been crowded into it sets of porcelain, piles of prints, vases, and other articles such as a man of Goethe's celebrity and tastes would, in a long life, collect by purchase or gift. The room looked like a crammed curiosity-shop. Without exchanging a word with a person who was there to serve as expounder, I turned back, and with feelings of disgust instead of satisfaction, left the house.

I contented myself with the outside of the abodes of Herder and Wieland.

―――After I had studied the cast from Schiller's cranium, and had thoughtfully wrought out a correspondence between it and his mental endowments as exhibited in his life and writings, fitting the cast to the character, and the character to the cast, as is the pleasant way with phrenologists, I learnt from a gifted physician in Weimar, that there was a slight—a very slight—doubt as to whether the cranium from which the cast had been taken, was that of Schiller. When, many years after his death, the bones of Schiller were dug up, to be removed to the Grand-ducal vault, it was found, that his body had been buried so near to two others, that the sexton was not absolutely certain which of the three skeletons was his. Goethe confirmed the sexton's decision, from the arm-bones of that one which the sexton believed to be Schiller's, declaring, that no other man in Weimar had arms of such length. The testimony of the sexton's memory and Goethe's inference, I make bold to corroborate with the cranium, whose size and shape are in harmony with the man and poet Schiller, such as we know him from his life and writings.

―――Goethe, Schiller, Wieland, Herder. They still inhabit Weimar. Once they trod its streets as flesh-and-blood men, whose daily living was a benefaction and an adornment. Now they abide in it as genii, and make the little town large by their large spiritual presence. They attend you wherever you go, sanctifying and beautifying your path by their magical potency. They beckoned me into the palace, where four rooms have been dedicated to them, one to each, whose walls are ennobled by painted scenes from their works. Walking in the park, the Grand Duke passed me with his simple equipage; but I had just come from the "Garden-House" of Goethe, and the presence of the great poet and sage was so vivid, that to me he was the living reality, and the reigning Duke went by like a phantom. I might say with the concluding lines of the beautiful, touching dedication to Faust,—

> Was ich besitze seh' ich wie im weiten,
> Und was verschwand wird mir zu wirklichkeiten.*

The great dead are the most living inhabitants of Weimar. The town was to me a cemetery, and each house in it a sepulchre, which sent forth by day instead of by night, its coated or gowned ghost. The time best to enjoy the company of Weimar's high inmates, were midnight, when the present generation being in their tombs, one would be free from their petty intrusion. But at that solemn hour the wearied traveller sleeps, and if perchance he dreams, his visions are apt to be more dyspeptic than poetic.

> * What I possess I see as in the distance,
> And what is gone comes back in firm consistence.

CHAPTER XI.

EISENACH—THE WARTBURG—LUTHER.

On our way back from Weimar to Frankfort, we stopped at Eisenach, that we might go up to the Wartburg, and look out over the wooded hills and valleys of Thuringia, from the same window through which Martin Luther daily looked for ten months. In this little room, himself a prisoner, he kept on at his sublime work, the liberation of Christendom from papal imprisonment. Here, plying his sinewy pen, he wrote those words which Richter calls half battles; and taking off from the Bible the Latin cloak wherewith priestcraft had hitherto concealed it, he clothed it in warm, homely German, which the newly invented types snatched up, and poured by tens of thousands upon his awakening, spirit-hungered countrymen.

Pause we a few moments on the Wartburg, while we recall the early life of this wonderful man. The best monuments of men are their lives, and those of our benefactors we never tire of contemplating. In their self-written inscriptions there is an enduring significance. We are fortified by coming near to their greatness. It is a profitable curiosity that pries into the modest beginnings of men whose matured lives have swollen to so broad a current, that they inundate the history of their kind. Only the greatest rivers are eagerly traced to their source.

The boy out of whom grew the gigantic man, Martin Luther, once begged in the streets of the town there beneath us, singing before houses to earn bread, as was the custom then in Germany for poor school-boys. Dame Ursula, widow of John Schweichard, taking pity on the child, gave him a home in her house, and kept him at school in Eisenach for four years, after which he entered the University at Erfurth, where his father was then able to support him. " Luther," says Michelet, " writes of his benefactress with words of emotion, and on her account showed gratitude towards women all his life."

Luther's father was a worker in mines. Like other peasants of that day, some of whom, in imitation of their seignorial masters, adopted armorial bearings, John Luther took for his arms a hammer. This symbol of his humble trade was prophetic of the vocation of his son, for Martin proved to be a hammerer whose blows, struck with the boldness of a martyr and the force of a Titan, reshaped Christendom. He hammered Catholicism out of its catholicity; he broke its universality. With the mighty sledge-hammer of reason, he knocked half the limbs off of the Pope, who since that hops on one leg.

Luther was destined for the law; but like all men in whom are conjoined a large soul with a large intellect, the study of what has been falsely termed the " reason of humanity," had for him no attraction. Literature and music were his delight. " Music," he says, " is the art of prophets; it is the only one which, like theology, can calm the troubles of the soul, and put the devil to flight." He seems to have had feeling for Art; he was the friend of the famous German painter, Lucas Cranach. The early spontaneous tendencies always denote important elements in the nature of a man. The geniality which in Luther underlay the dogmatic theologian and brawny combatant, was an ingredient of his greatness.

The more powerful the nature, the less is it liable to be directed by circumstances. A warm, vigorous mind makes new circumstances as a medium for itself, and resists the old ones. This initiative potency is the source of progress in the world. But the strongest cannot wholly withdraw himself from the action of outward pressure, nor even from the controlling effect of single events. Luther had just entered manhood, when the current of his life received a new direction from a startling incident. One of his companions was struck dead at his side by a flash of lightning. In his terror he made a vow to St. Anne to become a monk if he escaped. Fourteen days later, after having spent the evening gaily with friends in making music, he entered at midnight the monastery of the Augustines in Erfurth, carrying with him nothing but Plautus and Virgil. It was two years before his father would be resigned to this his son's self-immolation. At the end of that time he consented to be present at Martin's ordination. A day was chosen when the poor miner could leave his work, and he brought with him and gave to his lost child all the money he had laid by, twenty florins.

There is beauty in this early passage in the life of Luther. That he should have kept a vow taken at such a moment, is proof of his truthfulness and his resolution. In the act there was fidelity and strength. Then, the grief of the father, ending in the bestowal on the son of all his savings. One rejoices to meet with touching facts like this in the early life of a great man. Such are always to be found where men are manly and truehearted, and it is by the substance out of which they spring that greatness is nourished.

To turn monk is for a man to abdicate his humanity. He truncates himself of his upper endowments. He extinguishes the higher lights of life, those that are fed by the sympathies of labor and of love. He cuts the myriad threads that, binding him to his fellows, are the sole means of unfolding and fortifying his manhood. Thus isolated, the mind,—which can not be totally stifled,—preys upon itself. The monk is abandoned to a moral self-defilement. He dwindles to be the shadow of a man, or he bloats out to be a beast with feeding for his chief work. Luther could not stay monk, but his initiation into a monastery was for himself and for Christendom an immense event : it was decisive of his career. Monk-like, he preyed upon himself, but thereby a stirring was given to his deep nature. In the terrible tussles of the spirit, light went up in him that otherwise had probably smouldered forever. He stumbled upon a neglected Bible. Conceive of Luther, with a conscience as inexorable as Radamanthus, an intellect like St. Paul's, unaided by other human insight or sympathy, imprisoned with unthinking, unbelieving monks, unlocking the Book. There was food and an appetite ! Job and Isaiah, and David and St. Paul first made known to Luther. We are now familiar with the Bible. On entering manhood we find ourselves possessed of its substance without knowing how we have come by it. The Bible is a universal heir-loom in protestant families. But in 1505 it was a sealed book. If a few learned recluses had read it, they had merely read it ; it fructified not in them for their or others' profit. Were a cohort of Angels to come singing from the Heavens visibly and audibly celestial symphonies in our ears, we should hardly be more amazed than was Luther, as his deep eager spirit suddenly found itself in full communion with the inspired singers and sages of the Old and New Testaments, their large solemn souls receiving his as the ocean receives a turbid great river, which there finds calm and transparency.

In the monastery Luther had his first great lesson. He learnt there faith, not from his brother monks, who had none, but from his own thirsting spirit that had found its mate in the grand, fiery soul of St. Paul.

Without faith a man is not a full man. By self-reliance a strong man can do much, but to do the most, to self-reliance he must add reliance on the HIGH. " Things hoped for" must become " substance" to his eyes by the intensity of his belief in

Good. Into such strength are his powers knit up by this spiritual attraction, that he is then, and only then, ready and fit for greatest undertakings.

In the providential schooling that Luther went through to train him for his destined task, the second lesson was his journey to Italy. Had his heart not been opened in the monastery, his eyes would not have been opened to see what was to be seen in Italy. The poor Augustin Monk set out on foot, full of joy and hope and spiritual life. On the way he was harbored at the monasteries of his order. Coming down from the mountains upon Milan, he was there received into a monastery of marble and seated at a sumptuous table. He passed from monastery to monastery, that is, from palace to palace. Venturing once to tell some Italian monks that they would do better not to eat meat on Friday, this freedom nearly cost him his life. Astounded, saddened, the single-minded German pursued his foot-journey through the burning plains of Lombardy. He arrived ill at Padua; still he would not halt, but pushed on and reached Bologna almost dying. Restored to health, he hurried forward, traversed Florence without stopping, and at last entered Rome. He fell on his knees, raised his hands to Heaven, and cried out, "Hail, holy Rome, sanctified by the holy martyrs, and by their blood which has been shed in thee." In his fervor he ran from one holy spot to another, saw everything, believed everything. He soon discovered that he believed alone. He was in Rome, but Christian Rome no more.

The fallen Marius, seated on the ruins of Carthage, was a less sublime spectacle than the erect Luther in Rome, amidst the ruins of the Christian faith. One spiritually-minded priest, amid that sensual throng; one living soul, amid all those deadened souls; one believer, amid Rome's mitred scoffers; one humble, God-trusting man, amid haughty atheists. What a sublime thing is the mind of a true strong man! In that festering darkness shone,—invisible then and there,—a spark of living fire, from the which was to be kindled a light that would illuminate and rewarm Christendom.

At the end of fourteen days Luther quitted Rome. He fled as from a town smitten by the plague. He says: " I would not for a hundred thousand florins not have seen Rome. I should have been troubled for fear that I did the Pope injustice."

When Tetzel, the papal vendor of Indulgences in Germany, having to the long list of orthodox sins added crimes and infamies of his own imagining, perceived his auditory struck with horror, he declared with *sang froid*, " Well, all this is expiated the moment the sound of hard cash rings in the strong-box of the Pope." In this announcement the Dominican church-broker embodied in the most transparent formula what gets to be the aim of all Hierarchies. They traffic in souls for gold and dominion. Through hopes and fears, stimulated by their fictions, they draw from men's pockets the money wherewith to consolidate their power, and then use their power to get more money.

After the Roman the richest church in Christendom, is the Anglican ; and it is so because it is, after Rome, the best organized. The recent schism sprang from an effort at a still tighter organization, and this unavoidably brought the Pusey party nearer to Rome. Organization as applied to a Church involves independence of the People. By organization the Priesthood gets a permanent existence above, aside of, more or less independent of, the masses, according to the completeness of the organization. This independence, isolation and organic self-subsistence feeds ambition and encourages the impudent blasphemous assumption of especial God-derived sanctity.

The moral duties of priests are well or ill performed, according to the moral atmosphere of each country. *But the good that priests do, they do as men not as priests.* And the richer they are as priests the less good will they do as men.

The acme of priestly greed, impudence, and imposture, is the selling of Indulgences,—a practice by no means yet disused.

At the time that Tetzel commenced the sale of indulgences in Germany Luther was Doctor in Theology, Professor in the University of Wittemberg, provincial vicar of the Augustines, and charged with the functions of the Vicar General in the pastoral visits to Misnia and Thuringia. He was high in place, of great consideration and influence. But he was one of those true men upon whom high trusts impose high duties. Indignant at this vile traffic, he applied to his Bishop, praying him to silence Tetzel. The Bishop answered him, that he had better keep silent himself. He then wrote to the Primate, the Archbishop of Mayence, but distrusting him, on the same day that he despatched his letter he affixed to the Castle-Church of Wittemberg his celebrated propositions.

A great truth or idea is something so deep and subtle, even when most simple, that the great man who announces it conceives not its full import. He is the depositary of a germ from the Universal, the which he is commissioned to plant and to till, but it is a new seed, and to what it will grow he cannot foresee. But ideas once planted by man are watered and nourished by Providence, for Providence doth ever countenance genius. A far bolder and broader act than Luther himself knew was the publication of those propositions. Striking at the most accursed of tyrannies, that over the mind, he opened a breach through which by gradual enlargements man was to come out from all prisons, civil as well as ecclesiastical, out of royal bondage into republican liberty, out of Lutheranism itself as well as out of Romanism, —such progressive life is there in truth. Not only were the immense historical after-consequences of his first act necessarily invisible to Luther, but so vigorous and rapid was its fecundation that its effects upon his contemporaries astounded him. Upon no one did it work more potently than upon himself. Of the emancipation of his own mind, not only from papal but from regal au thority, brought about, unconsciously to himself, by the working of his first great anti-papal act, there is lively evidence in the new treasonable freedom wherewith he soon after wrote of Princes. He says of them ;—" You ought to know that from the beginning of the world a prudent Prince is a very rare thing, rarer still an upright Prince. They are generally great fools or great reprobates."*

It was on the 31st of October, 1517, that Luther affixed to the Castle-Church of Wittemberg his propositions.

Since the first day of the Christian era there had been in human annals no day so pregnant, so solemn as this. To Americans especially this day ought to be holy. Without it there had not been that other memorable epoch-marking day, the 4th of July, 1776. On the 31st of October, 1517, was made to the world the Declaration of Mental Independence. Upon Germany, upon Europe, it fell like a trumpet-tongued summons from a better world. Luther found himself hostilely arrayed against the Pope. That was a fearful position. Even the great Luther shrank back ; and had he not had above his strong intellect a conscience that would know no compromise of principle, and behind it a courage that could brave all the Powers of Earth and Hell, he would have succumbed. In the middle of the 19th century we can scarcely conceive what strength, what moral grandeur that man must have had, who, in the beginning of the 16th defied the authority of the Pope. Luther did defy it steadfastly. He asserted the spiritual self-sufficiency, the moral dignity of man. By all freemen he should be revered as one of their mightiest deliverers. Noble, stout-hearted Brother ; we thank thee for thy great courage, we thank thee for thy great intellect, and above all we thank thee for thy great conscience.

* The truthfulness of Luther's picture of Princes has lately been acknowledged in Prussia, where a volume selected from his writings, containing his opinions of them, was burnt by order of government. Luther burnt in protestant Germany! What a close hug Kingcraft and Priestcraft are giving each other to strengthen themselves against Democracy.

CHAPTER XII.

WHO FOLLOWED LUTHER—RACES—COLOR—CHRISTIANITY—PROTESTANTS AND CATHOLICS—ENGLISH AND SPANISH AMERICA—CONVERSIONS TO ROMANISM—RELIGION.

It is of deep historic interest to note, who followed Luther in this vast stride; who in that age was capable of being freed from the yoke of sacerdotal usurpation.

"O! the difference of man and man,"

cries Goneril. So different are men, that there never were two just alike; and at the same time all are so alike, that we must acknowledge the cannibal for our brother. Nations,—organic multitudes geographically defined,—like the individuals whereof they are composed, likewise differ one from the other. Races, too,—numbered by naturalists at from three to six, each embracing many nations,—differ broadly in aptitudes, habits, manners, physiognomy, color. This last quality, color, be it observed, is not a mere superficial mark, but denotes deep differences, being an index of mental capacity. At one end of the human scale is the black man, at the other the white, between them the brown and yellow. The white man never comes into contact and conflict with the others that he does not conquer them. The brown and yellow he subjugates or exterminates, the black he holds in bondage. The two extremes meet in this close union.* In color

* They who, assuming for themselves a pre-eminence in philanthropy, run into such extremes of opinion and indignation, because their white

there is great significance. Nature is never arbitrary, nor shallow, nor illogical. She would not stamp one man white, another brown, another black, and mean nothing thereby, or no more than surface-diversity as among cattle or flowers. White and black—light and darkness—these are deep words. Whence is it that the white is always at the top of the scale of humanity, the yellow in the middle, and the black at the bottom? Not of choice, not of outward influences are these pervading, enduring facts the result, but of law and inward motions.

None but nations of the white race, and only a few of these, have a civil, a political history; that is, a development and the record thereof. History implies growth; that is, childhood, youth, maturity. National growth implies depth and a fund of resources. In the current of centuries, a people of high organization unfolds itself from within, until it reaches a refined multiplex life. Slowly it traverses degrees, planting itself on its advancements still to ascend. Its annals are written in comprehensive institutions that fortify its progress, and in monuments, not merely solid and enduring, like the Pyramids of Egypt,—for that were not enough,—but deriving their durability from their instructiveness, like the statuary and architecture of Greece, and the books of the Hebrews, Greeks, and Romans,—statues and books that still live, not because they reflect the thoughts and deeds of those nations, but because in their thoughts and deeds was the vitality that springs from the beauty there is in truth, and the truth there is in beauty. These three are the only nations of Antiquity that were nervous enough to create history, and therefore the only ones from whom the moderns have learnt.

In each of them, be it noted, the democratic spirit was strong, but only partially developed; for its full unfolding, Christianity

brothers hold by inheritance their black brothers in bondage, let them look discerningly into Natural History. The search may have the effect of enlarging the range of their fraternal solicitude.

was needed,—Christianity, which is the highest moral generalization; which would substitute charity for force, broad faith for petty hopes, justice for expediency.

The other races, ancient or modern, the colored, have not in them the spring for indefinite progressiveness, for God-clasping development, no upward yearning for moral or intellectual generalization. Feeble on their path are the traces of beauty or wisdom; shrivelled or immature their intellectual fruit. They have no ripe art, no great books, no history. They are not expansive, not creative. They cannot clear the circle of animal littleness. They lie bound in the sterility of savageism, or the immobility of barbarism: their life is an intellectual and moral pauperism. They are unfinished, and according to both history and philosophy,—whose testimony when concurrent is clenching,—destined not to be finished.

When we use the phrase, "the great cause of humanity;" when we speak of man as capable of being indefinitely enlarged by thought and invention, and exalted by poetry and sentiment; when we triumph in the growth of science and culture, our words, whether or not we will it or know it, apply only to the white race. History declares that the only æsthetic, the only scientific man, is the white man.

Christianity is confined to the white race, and does not embrace all that. This is an enormous fact in the natural history of man. Christianity involves a struggle of man to put himself under the rule of his highest sentiments. Only the white race has had the inward impetus, the conscious need, the swelling vitality to make this struggle, to escape from the tyranny of sensualism into the upper region of possible liberty where predominates the spiritual.

Christianity, promising the reign of justice, leads to liberty, for men can only get to freedom through the dominion of their noblest faculties. It has been a path for going forward and upward. Upon this path mankind could only enter after it had reached a certain growth. Far ahead of all others on the earth are those nations that entered it. They and only they have gone continuously forward. Where they have not, is owing partly to this—that the spirit of Christianity—the aspiration for a higher life—has been smothered by ecclesiastical usurpation. In the 14th and 15th centuries, after ages of priestly tyranny and sophistication, it had got to be so smothered. Wickliffe, Huss, Jerome of Prague, Savonarola re-uttered this spirit to priest-ridden Christendom, and prepared its soul to hearken to Luther.

To some nations are allotted high functions in the life of Humanity. In ancient times the Hebrews, the Greeks, the Romans, predominated in turn over the race. In modern history, Italy emerged first out of the mediæval darkness. Among the Italians there was, in the 13th and three following centuries, a revival of the Greek and Roman genius. In the struggle for emancipation from ecclesiastical dominion, commenced by Wickliffe, and triumphantly conducted by Luther, the German breed led the way. The Reformation embraced northern and central Germany, Sweden, Denmark, Holland, and Great Britain, all belonging to the German family. In mixed France it took deep root, but did not gain over openly more than one eighth of the whole population. In Spain and Italy the priesthood was too strong, and manhood then too weak for it even to take root. In Poland it scarcely got a footing. In the Austrian dominions, out of a population of thirty-five millions, but three millions two hundred thousand are protestants. In Switzerland, more than half the inhabitants are protestant.

The place held among nations, at the time that Luther put forth his propositions, by Spain, who rejected them, is now held by England, who accepted them. It is no longer the petty Queen of Spain, it is the mighty Queen of England, that can say, " The sun sets not in my dominions." Like the Ariel of her Shakspeare, England has put a girdle round the globe. The influence upon the thought of Christendom exercised by Italy through her Dantes, her Machiavellis, her Galileos, in the 15th and 16th centuries, has been, in the 18th and 19th, transferred to the Goethes, the Niebuhrs, the Hegels of Germany. Protestant Holland shook off the dominion of Spain, and erected herself into an independent Republic, that for a time disputed the sovereignty of the seas with growing England, and was strong enough to resist the power of Louis XIV. Catholic Belgium remained subject to Spain. Where are the colonies founded in America by Spain and Portugal and by Englishmen? The Protestant United States, in power and influence, take rank beside the first nations of Europe. If a people, like a man, is prosperous and strong in proportion to the number, variety, elevation and vigor of its thoughts and sensations, which are the parents of deeds, the life of the United States for fifty years exhibits such an unprecedented growth and success in all departments of human activity, as to entitle them to claim a place, not beside, but in front of all the nations of the earth. To the spirit which made Protestantism, that is, the spirit of individual liberty, of manly independence, we owe this progress and unexampled welfare. What is Mexico, or Brazil, or Bolivia? What part do they play in the stirring, striving, Christian community? What conquests are they making in the domains of Nature—what fruitful secrets do they wrest from her deep heart? What discourse is heard among them of great human interests? New ideas, winged thoughts, what acceptance do they find among the nations of South America? Ask their oracles, their priests.

In France the massacre of St. Bartholomew and the revocation of the edict of Nantes tell the strength of Protestantism, and with what dread it filled tyrants. At this moment hardly the half of Frenchmen can be claimed by Rome. With the mass, Catholic observances are a habit rather than a faith. Among the educated there is an almost universal religious disbelief in the Church, coupled with a political belief in it as an engine for keeping the people ignorant and dependent; and for this end it is the most efficient apparatus that human ingenuity stimulated by human egotism could devise. The French Revolutions that have pulled down the throne and set up man, have shaken the altar and put God in the place of the Pope.

In Italy the open profession of dissent from the Romish Church is not tolerated. But those who, despising its mummeries and hating its extortionate tyranny, reject in their hearts as well its spiritual as its temporal assumptions, are to be numbered by millions. Let Italy become independent, and there will be revealed a sum of Protestantism, of protesters against Priestcraft, a tithe of which will counterbalance the trumpeted conversions to Romanism from among the idle, ennuied "Nobility and Gentry" of England.

Conversions* to Catholicism in Protestant countries should in most cases be looked upon as a throwing out of morbid particles, a salutary moral crisis. People who, brought up in the light of Protestantism, feel too weak to bear that light, why let them in God's name retreat and shield themselves in darkness. Liberally speaking, these losses are a gain. We want to go forward, and these good souls have not even the self-supporting life to stand upright; they must go back for support out of themselves. Peace go with them.

In this survey of Protestant and Catholic nations, what presents itself as the most striking contrast between them? It is this, that not one of the purely Catholic is independent. Popery, which, as an Italian writer says, "is a Theocracy founded on the absolutely moral slavery of man," destroying individual independence, undermines national. Italy, the fountain-head of

---

* These conversions, be it noted, are chiefly from the Church of England, which has features of likeness to that of Rome. To weak minds, or to those that to a sensuous quality of intellect unite a peculiar sentimental organization, the transition from Anglicanism to Romanism is logical.

Catholicism, where Protestantism is proscribed under penalty of imprisonment or death, has been for centuries a prey to the foreigner. Portugal, as Catholic as Italy, the favorite torture-house of the Inquisition, is a dependence of Protestant England. Spain, where by a late concordat the ban against Protestantism has been renewed, is so helpless, that she had within thirty years to call in a French army under the Duc d'Angoulême to uphold the tottering Bourbon throne, and having lost nearly all her immense colonies, is now obliged to appeal to England and France to prevent the last remaining one from falling into our hands. Poland,—blotted from the list of nations. Austria,—saved lately from destruction by the sword of Russia. Ireland,—compare Ireland with Scotland. France, vigorous, independent France, has not only four or five millions of Protestants, but how many millions besides of Voltairiens, until lately, when Skepticism, which is by the nature of man short-lived, having passed away, Socialism, or a belief in man involving a deeper belief in God, is begetting a higher Christianity than has yet animated Christendom, —a Christianity destined to be far more fruitful than ever was the theological, the which however is now everywhere almost as good as dead.

But deeper and stronger than either, than Catholicism, than Protestantism, both perishable, is the imperishable Christian principle of liberty, the quenchless longing for absolute mental freedom. Protestantism was the assertion of this principle against the usurpation of Rome. It was a conflict for truth, but not itself the broadest truth, that it could not be; a struggle for emancipation, but not itself the largest liberty, that it could not be. It quickly put bounds to its own essence, the right of private judgment, of free inquiry; it narrowed itself to *isms*. It is not universal in its embrace; it is partial, and thus runs into Sectarianism. It has no Pope, but it has creeds; it has no monasteries, but it has theological seminaries; it has no independent hierarchy (except in England), but it has dogmatic priesthoods. In its churches ecclesiastical abuses are vastly mitigated, by no means fully abated. Protestantism has its army of priests, who are, too many of them, Jewish in their narrowness and their hates, and in their assumptions papal; and who, if they could, would, like their Romish colleagues, persuade us that priests are essential to salvation, the very depositaries and dispensers of spiritual life, the indispensable bond to unite men to God. In this they serve themselves more than God and men. When a man places himself between God and another man, he intercepts the light and casts a shadow upon his brother. He is a false priest who would make himself indispensable to men as a medium of union with God. The true priest aims to unfold the soul, and thus disclose to it its own innate powers and grandeur.

A primary and pre-eminent element of our mental being is religion. To say of a man, he is without religion, is as much nonsense as to say he is without lungs. Breathing is not more essential to the physical life than is to the moral a recognition of the Infinite, a reverential consciousness of the Absolute and Unspeakable. So sophisticated are men's minds by one-sided teachings, that they come to regard religion as a something they get from the priest, a spiritual treasure guarded and dispensed by the priesthood. At stated periods they go to Church to receive their share of it, like stockholders to the Bank to draw their dividends. They have made an investment in the Church and leave the management thereof to the priests, who pay them in prayers, sermons and liturgies. In this way forms usurp the place of substance, dead material husk of spiritual kernel.

As are the temperament and the moral and intellectual wants of a people so are its divinities, who are modified, aye moulded, by the mental characteristics of each. Hence the difference between the Gods of the Greeks and the God of the Hebrews, between the worship of the Hindoo and that of the African. Men can only conceive God according to their own capacities. To the low man ever a low God. As individual men in their narrowness would have other men like themselves, so aggregate men, men in tribes and nations make God like man. Anthropomorphism is the egotism of unemancipated humanity. Through culture and moral enlargement we attain to the conception of he vitalizing omnipresent Deity as incorporeal essence. As man rises, the Deity shines the more purely upon his heart, God and man exalting one another. To the upstriving man the Deity holds out a helping hand, ascending ever higher and higher, the more and more effulgent with intellect and love as man mounts after him towards the centre of Liberty and Truth, the eternal home of the infinite Good.

Jesus, an inmate of this heavenly home, from the depths of his large soul proclaimed the law of love, justice, unity. This solemn, momentous proclamation has remained a prolific abstraction, kept present to the human soul by the inborn need of its fulfilment. Only in Jesus himself burnt purely the light of his revelation. The Apostles his agents were tainted with Judaism. And soon the spirit of priestcraft, which had crucified Jesus, took possession of his doctrine and soiled it. It is not yet purged of the soiling. The God of priestcraft is a God of wrath, inspiring fear more than love, a priest-made God to serve priestly ends of dominion; gloomy, revengeful, the oppressor not the liberator of humanity, whose messengers are oftener devils than angels. Do you purify man by defiling God with cruelty ? By abasing man do you exalt God ? Do you strengthen the heart by compressing it into intolerant creeds, do you shelter it under mystic imaginations ? Out of trite fancies and sour sensibilities you would build up Deity, and present as the Infinite the image they make on your finite brains. In flimsy phrases you would word the Unspeakable, in fleeting vesture clothe the Eternal, and then you solemnly declare the outcome of these your theological inventions to be God, and summon us to worship as the Creator this your dwarfish misshapen creature.

What profit hath the soul from these degradations of Deity? Is it not akin to image-worship, this petrifaction of fallible interpretations into staunch creeds? Beams from the central Light deflected through Judaic imaginations, can they retain any warmth for the 19th century? What knowledge or nourishment is there now in these ancient aspirations? Is spiritual life replenished by feeding more on the man-made than the God-made? This temple built with hands, what is it to the sanctuary within the heart? This formal conned ritual, what is it to the spontaneous aspiration of the soul? What are your loud prayers and hymns to the voiceless communion with the Infinite? The silence of a Church is voiceful to the solemnity of a man's conscience! Your altars, your surplices, your mitres, your cathedrals, your consecrations, all are but verbiage and stitchwork and brickwork, ostentatious, transitory, in face of the eternal self-renewing life, the deep sacredness of the soul of man. Protestantism, one-sided and short-coming as it is, was the rehallowing of this desecrated sanctuary, the reassertion of this unacknowledged sacredness. The Reformation of the 16th century rescued men from much of their captivity to priesthood. It shattered many of the bars that made churches prisons. It is an illuminated phasis in the history of liberty, of Christian deliverance.

* The light then kindled in a few souls now shines over Christendom. From the door of the humble church in Wittemberg, where it was first set up, that light spread from land to land, from generation to generation, vivifying and fortifying wherever it fell, so that at the present day those nations that opened their hearts the widest to its rays are the foremost on the earth. But from it,

---

* Chapters xi. and xii. were delivered as a "Lecture on Protestantism" in Newport, R. I., in January last. On that occasion this concluding paragraphs was added.

all the peoples of Christendom, those who are struggling to achieve, as well as those who possess liberty, be they Catholic or Protestant, chiefly draw their animation. Whether in America, where to the disenthralling, life-cherishing principles of the Reformation* we owe the best of what we have done, of what we are, of what we have, including the privilege so happily habitual among us that we forget its value, the privilege I at this moment use of publicly speaking on things of universal interest my honest thought, without fear of gaol or gibbet;—whether in steadfast England, the mighty mother of nations, who owes so much of her might to her protestantism, and to her truth-loving heart that made her accept it, where together with an obsolete aristocracy and an unspiritualized church, a load of dull Dukes and carnal Bishops, there is a fund of large manhood and freedom;—whether in France, where by means of tyrannical centralization and military organization, both inherited from monarchy, a pigmy miscreant has just been enabled to enact a gigantic crime against a long-suffering but never disheartened nation;—whether in Germany, where protestant princes, faithless alike to God and man, are foully leagued with Jesuits and Cossacks to cheat and berob an enlightened, temperate, and too trustful people of what is dearest in life, a patient people, too, but who now knowing and valuing their rights, give their robbers their hate, biding the time, which must soon come, when they can give them their vengeance;—whether in Italy, bleeding, beautiful Italy, where in the north the brutal Austrian vainly strives to trample out manhood with the soldier's heel, where in the south the Bourbon, fanatic in ferocity, slaughters men like cattle, where in the centre, in majestic Rome, the Arch-despot of the world blasphemously calls himself the vicar of Christ, while, seated on a throne built of foreign bayonets fleshed in the breasts of his subjects, he gives one hand of fellowship to the man-shaped tiger of Naples, and the

* See note at the end of the Chapter.

other to the perjured traitor of France, and, encircled by greedy, lowering Cardinals, whose red robes are dyed redder in their brothers' blood, he hearkens for the secret curses of his awakened people, who ceaselessly lust for the blood of their oppressors, and ceaselessly sigh for freedom, having learnt their cruelty from their priests, and their aspirations from their own hearts.—Wherever the breath of freedom swells healthfully in man's breast, or gasps painfully in sobs and sighs; wherever men possess, or are striving for the blessings of freedom, not one in any land of Christendom, whether Catholic or Protestant, not one of these many, many millions but owes much of what he has, or of the will and courage to desire and to dare, much of his richest inheritance or his noblest resolution, to the poor German miner's son, to the moral boldness, the intellectual might of Martin Luther.

NOTE.

In a Lecture entitled "The Catholic Chapter in the History of the United States," delivered in New York in March 1852, Archbishop Hughes says,—" It is altogether untrue to assert that this is a Catholic country, or a Protestant country. It is neither. It is a land of religious freedom and equality." General usage justifies the calling of a people Catholic or Protestant, according as a large majority of its inhabitants belong to the one or the other of these religious divisions. Thus, southern Germany is called Catholic, northern Germany Protestant; Ireland Catholic, England Protestant. The United States, where only a fraction, about one tenth, of the population, is Catholic, are called, therefore, Protestant. But, apart from common parlance, what strictly authorizes a designation is, the principle which rules a country in religious matters. By this logical test, the United States are thoroughly Protestant, and the Pope's dominions in Italy thoroughly Catholic. In the United States, there are absolute religious tolerance and liberty; in papal Italy, constraint and absolute religious intolerance. Absolute intolerance is a fundamental Catholic doctrine, which is not merely preached but severely practised, as the world knows; and practised not only against Italians, but also against strangers, so that American Protestants, while in Rome, are not permitted to meet together for public worship; such outlaws and damnable heretics are they regarded by Pope and Cardinals. In this country, on the contrary, not only is there absolute religious tolerance, but so productive is this high Christian principle, that even Romish prelates here are obliged to avow it, in the teeth of the theory and practice at headquarters. Thus Archbishop Hughes, in this Lecture, "hopes that it will remain a land of religious freedom and equality to the latest posterity." On other occasions he has made like declarations. These avowals have no significance as signs of the wishes and purposes of an Archbishop; for Catholic prelates exercise—especially, we presume, when dealing with heretics—a right of mental reservation, which paralyzes any positive interpretation that the ingenuous might put on their words, and is probably large in proportion to the hierarchical elevation of the dignitary. But they have significance, as showing what is the power of Protestantism here, and what a very Protestant country Archbishop Hughes thinks it, that he, a nominee of the Pope, drawing from Rome his archiepiscopal breath, should feel obliged to reiterate so unpapal, so uncatholic a sentiment, the which he would no more utter in Rome than he would there laud Luther or deny purgatory.

"If," says the lecturer, "there had been only one form of Protestantism professed in all the colonies, I fear much that even with Washington at their head, the Constitution would not have been what it is in regard to religious liberty." But it is the very nature of Protestantism, when it has free play, to break a people up into many sects. The essence of Protestantism is the right of private judgment in religious belief, which right leads unavoidably and healthfully to multiplication of creeds. Protestantism is a protest against sacerdotal dominion, and the assertion of individual religious independence. It frees men from the yoke of priesthood; it empowers every man to define his own creed, to choose, or to be, his own priest. This, the fundamental principle of Protestantism, involves absolute religious liberty. That Protestant sects and men have violated this principle, proves only the fallibility of men, but shakes not the foundations of the principle itself. However uncharitable some sects in this country may have been, or may be, in their feelings towards each other, a higher law controls them—the law of Protestant freedom, which, if not complete, goes yet to the extent of guaranteeing to each man immunity from interference of State or Church, against his will, in his religious profession. Granting that the multiplicity of sects led to this general tolerance; the multiplicity of sects is the robust offspring of Protestantism, and by its excess here proves, that this country is ultra-protestant.

In a "Catholic Chapter in the History of the United States," Maryland would of course not be omitted. What right has Archbishop Hughes to say "Catholic Maryland," he who a few pages before asserts that this country is neither Protestant nor Catholic? If this country was not at first and is not now Protestant, how can Maryland be called Catholic? Among the first colonists of Maryland there were Protestants, as there were Catholics among the first colonists of the other provinces. The proportion of Protestants in the Maryland colony was at any time as large as that of Catholics in all the other colonies, or in the United States, after their independence. With his own words we contradict Archbishop Hughes' designation, and say, that Maryland "was neither Catholic nor Protestant. It was a land of religious freedom and equality."—And as such it was in its birth eminently uncatholic.

To learn what the Catholic view of a subject is, we must go to Rome, to the Pope who appoints the Archbishops Hughes, to the Cardinals who appoint the Pope. Rome is the fountain of all Catholic doctrine. Now we find that in Rome, at present, and at the time that Maryland was founded, and at all times, nothing is more abominated than this very religious liberty. "I will not, by myself or any other, directly or indirectly, molest any person professing to believe in Jesus Christ, for or in respect of religion." Such was the oath prescribed by Lord Baltimore for the Governor of his Maryland. Did he get that from Rome? Does the Pope prescribe such an oath for the Governor of his Rome? Papist or the dungeon of the Inquisition, that is the alternative of the native Roman. Torture or death awaits him who there presumes to exercise what Lord Baltimore fully and formally granted,—freedom of conscience. Not even can strangers there worship after their choice. Let a score of Maryland Protestants try it within the walls of Rome; they will find that they dare not even meet together to say their prayers. They will not be indirectly, but most "directly molested," lest by their Protestant communion the capital of Catholicism be desecrated, and Pope and Cardinals insulted and scandalized. And yet Rome's bemitred minions here, claim the founding of Maryland as Roman Catholic work!—If a Quaker were to forget the precepts of his religion, and take to swearing and fisticuffs, would the odium of his aberration fall on the whole "Society of Friends," or only on the exceptional member? If a lawgiver inserts in his code a clause in flat conflict with a fundamental dogma, an inflexible maxim, of the church to which he belongs, a clause the directly opposite of which finds place in the code of that church itself; in after-years, when this clause turns out to have been wise and creditable, is the church to claim the merit thereof, and that too when her own practice is still as hostile as ever to the very principle embodied in that clause? As the Quaker, for his unquakerly conduct is read out of meeting, so Lord Baltimore, for his official unpapal religious tolerance, would doubtless,—but for worldly considerations,—have been sentenced to do penance or to pay a round sum for absolution, if even he had not been excommunicated. For the sin of liberality (although only verbal and calculated) in this lecture and other similar occasions, Archbishop Hughes has, I dare say, penitently to mortify the flesh, or else be absolved (beforehand probably) by the Italian Prince, his master.

The original Constitution of Maryland, drafted by the Proprietor, was the work of a clear-headed, large-hearted man,—a man so strong, that, in founding a state so early as the beginning of the seventeenth century, he put at its basis the broad human rights of civil and religious liberty,—a man so Christian, that the unchristian intolerance of even the Church he had chosen, did not taint his heart. If the King who endowed him with this domain on the Chesapeake did, as has been surmised, as a Protestant, exact religious tolerance in the organization of the new government, Lord Baltimore, if this tolerance had been unpalatable to him, would have applied for lands to the King of Spain or of Portugal; and these "most Catholic" sovereigns would eagerly have granted to one so honored in England as he was, a choice tract in their rich American possessions; and there he could have established himself, like his neighbors, to his Catholic heart's content, in severest Catholic exclusiveness. But the papist was not uppermost in Lord Baltimore's nature, and therefore he had not recourse to Spain or to Portugal, and he sought not help of the Pope. The liberal clauses of his charter, so hostile to the spirit of Romanism, and so deservedly celebrated in history, were dictated by his own high human feelings; and no heretic-cursing Pope, no ambitious sophistical Archbishop, has claim to a tittle of his noble deed. The illustrious founder of Maryland belongs not to their side, but to the opposite one of humanity and freedom; and to him their eulogy is no honor.

CHAPTER XIII.

SUPPER-TABLE AT THE "HALF-MOON" IN EISENACH—ANNADALE—GRIMM'S TALES
—MIGRATION WESTWARD.

In the evening the company at the supper-table of the "Half-Moon," in Eisenach, was enlivened by the news, just arrived from Cassel, of the flight of the Duke. It was the opening act of the Hesse-Cassel political melodrama, which afterwards ended unmelodramatically with the triumph of the guilty and the fall of the innocent. Except that the end is not yet, and will only be after that the whirlwind,—which ere long will envelop all Germany in gloom and terror,—shall have passed over, and from the bosom of the enfranchised people shall have arisen a higher justice than has ever yet presided over German affairs.

As I have generally found this summer at German Inns,—except those of fashionable watering-places,—the majority of the little circle at the "Half-Moon" was democratic. The discussion of the doings in Cassel was conducted with vivacity, but with good temper. One of the speakers was the head-waiter, who, without either forwardness or timidity, took part in the conversation, and expressed moderate opinions in good language, performing at the same time his duties round the table with watchfulness and alacrity. The spirit of the great Wartburg prisoner, that animates so many millions all over the globe, had made a man of this humble servant.

The traveller through Eisenach should take two or three hours,

—whether he has them to spare or not,—to visit Annadale. After a drive of two miles through a beautiful valley, you enter on foot a narrow winding gorge, whose rocky sides are embowered by overhanging trees, under which you walk on a gravel path not wide enough for two abreast. But what constitutes the peculiar beauty of the place, and marks it as a unique natural curiosity, is the fine moss on the rocks, covering them as completely and as smoothly as if silk velvet had been carefully fitted on them by feminine fingers, and kept of the most vivid green by the shade of the forest and the moisture from springs.

It is a place to tell fairy tales in. With such poetry before the senses, the mind grows fantastic. So much beauty should not be wasted on solitude; it solicits you to people it. One can readily conceive how an imaginative race like the Germans should, in their robust youth, have populated the dells of their virgin forests with fays and fairies. These attended the Saxons to England, where Shakspeare by adopting, after educating them, has given them an everlasting home.

Of the safety wherewith traditions travel down through many generations, with no other vehicle than the tongues of nurses and grandmothers, I had, while a student at Göttingen, a remarkable exemplification. One of the Grimms had just published a collection of children's stories all gathered by himself from the mouths of aged women,—chiefly in the Hartz Mountains. In looking through them I came upon one that was in its minute and absurd particulars precisely the same tale that I had heard as a child in America. A thousand years ago it had gone over to England, had there lived from mouth to mouth through thirty generations, had then traversed the Atlantic and dwelt for two hundred years near the shores of the Chesapeake, and now, brought thence packed away in the memory of an American, back to its starting-place, was found, after having changed its vesture from Gothic to Anglo-Saxon, and from Anglo-Saxon to English, to match as accurately a tale now for the first time printed, as one proof-sheet does another taken from the same form of types. In rude Gothic the two had parted more than ten centuries ago, and now met, the one in German, the other in English, and in the many vicissitudes of that long separation, neither had changed a feature.

It were curious to seek the origin of these tales in the East. The affinities of language and similarities in many words point to the neighborhood of the Caspian Sea as the cradle of the German tribes. To some of the many inquisitive travellers, who are eager for new fields of exploration, here is a captivating enterprise, to penetrate to that region and bring away the popular and nursery tales as philological and ethnographical treasures.

Tradition and researches do not entirely concur with the Mosaic record in placing the origin of man in the East. Yet it were not unreasonable to suppose that man first appeared in the highlands of Asia because there the Earth was first humanly habitable. From what is now observed and known, we are authorized to infer, that the whole surface of the Earth was not at once put in condition to be the abode of man. Asia may have been first ready, and America or Australia last, perhaps thousands of years later.

Facts justify the line of Bishop Berkeley that

Westward the march of Empire takes its course,

shifting its seat as the streams of population,—of white population,—pouring down from the centre of Asia towards its western confines and Europe, grew stronger and clearer the further they advanced. From Asia the march of Empire was to Greece, and thence to Italy, and from Italy still further westward to Spain, France, England. Driving ever westward, population followed Columbus across the stormy Atlantic, and founded on its American shore an Empire that will as much exceed England in power as England does Rome in Rome's proudest day, and as Rome herself did the Assyrian monarchy in its broadest magnificence. But America had already been peopled. This population, coming out of Asia eastward, was met and driven back again towards Asia by that which came out of Asia through Europe westward, and is destined to be extinguished by the latter.

That it is a law of Nature that migration should "go with the sun," we have startling proof in this fact, that the aboriginal inhabitants of America, who in peopling that Continent had violated this law, are thus thrust back by those who obeyed it. This, it may be said, is only the superior white subjecting the inferior brown race. In India too the white man has subjected the brown, but he has not overflowed his territory and displaced him. The British and Dutch Indies are held by a handful of whites through military possession. So the English, who have set an armed foot in China, may subdue it as they have subdued Hindostan. But the peopling of the eastern shore of Asia with swarms from the great white hive, is to take place by migration westward, that is, from Oregon and California.

The strong, the white race, streamed westward; the western Asiatics are to this day white. Those who from the region which according to Oriental tradition is given as the starting-place of mankind went eastward, the Chinese, the Siamese, the Japanese, belong to the inferior brown and yellow races. It may be objected that all having originated from one stock, the difference of color was caused by climate, food, water and other external influences. The force of these influences is undeniable; but admitting, what is by no means demonstrated, that the parents of the whole human family were a single couple, their color must remain a mystery; and therefore we cannot know whether climate re-changed brown to white in Western Asia and Europe, or white to brown and black in Eastern Asia and Africa.*

* A recent French writer, M. Henri Lecouturier, in a remarkable work,

Color, in races, is not a mere outward cutaneous painting by the sun, but comes from within, from the blood. That long action of the sun with other outward agencies will change the quality of the blood, may be believed. But a strong race may carry within itself the vigor to resist and even to reverse the effect of these agencies. In figure the Anglo-Saxons in America have as-

entitled *Cosmosophie ou le Socialism Universel,* endeavors by an ingenious exposition to prove, that the birth-place of man was in the Polar region. According to his deduction the first man was black and covered with hair, and like certain tribes still found in Africa, was nearer to the Ourang Outang than to the white man. Towards the Poles, it was that the Earth first became cool enough to be habitable; and when man first appeared, the climate there was as warm as it now is under the Equator, while that of the temperate and torrid zones was so hot as to be uninhabitable. With the receding of the Ecliptic,—which at first extended over the whole ninety degrees,—and the corresponding receding of the focal fires within the Earth, the cooling of the surface, which began at the Poles, extended gradually to the temperate zone. At the same time the polar region grew cooler and cooler, and the first men, adapted to the greater warmth, followed it and gradually approached the equator, in the heats of which their descendants are now found in Africa.

His hypothesis is, that the first man was preceded by the monkey, who went before him also in migrating towards the equatorial region, where he is still found. As the monkey left man behind him, so the first race of black hairy men left superior men their descendants behind themselves, the race improving in color and quality with the cooling of the Earth and the purification of its zones, until, after many ages of successive migrations, the inferior breeds following the heat and the superior taking their place, the whole Earth was peopled, and the highest types were found in the temperate zone and the lowest in the torrid.

The genealogy of man, says M. Lecouturier, may be learnt by beginning with the present occupants at the tropical regions and going northward. The most advanced will be found in the temperate zone, and the most backward, that is, the primitive and oldest races, in the torrid. For a general classification he divides the human family into three races, the lowest, the middle, and the highest; the Ethiopian, the Mongolian and the Caucasian; each embracing several varieties.

The Finns, Laplanders and Esquimaux, a stunted and misshapen race living on the borders of the Arctic circle, are remains of the primitive races, who refused to follow the current that drew them towards the warm latitudes. Philological researches have shown such an affinity between the Finns and the Hungarians, that Berghaus puts them down on his Ethno-

similated somewhat to the North American Indians; but who would thence conclude, that they are to grow downward to them? On two races so wide apart as these, the one having an organization so superior to that of the other, is it not reasonable to presume, that external influences, telluric and solar, magnetic and material, might act with opposite effects, weakening the weaker race and strengthening the stronger; and that thus, while the Europeans in North America, under the above influences, should come to resemble in some minor characteristics the natives, the gulf between them would in the main be widened, and the original organic superiority of the white race be not only maintained but augmented?

This proclivity of man, or rather of the white race, westward,—exhibited in subordinate movements as well as in the great cardinal migrations,—would seem to proceed from an instinct that harmonizes men unconsciously with the order of Nature. Westward is the path forward, the path of progress. Conservatism looks backward, that is, eastward. Thus at this moment, princes in Germany look with hope to Russia, in Spain to Rome; the People, with a deeper intuition, to America, and themselves. On the other hand, Russia dreams of another Scythian invasion, and Rome is straining to get command of the advanced guard of humanity in America,—which she will do when printing shall be there prohibited as the abettor of crime, and steam suppressed as a disturber of the public peace, and the reasoning faculty proscribed as an obstacle to virtue,—a prohibition, suppression, and proscription practised in the papal dominions, and which the paternal chiefs of the Roman Church are making a last agonizing

graphical maps as belonging to the same tribe, thus confirming the opinion of M. Lecouturier, who says, the handsome valorous Maygars are directly descended from the poor emaciated dwarfs of the polar regions.

This curious theory of the peopling of the Earth is not in contradiction with the westward migrations, which only commenced with the white race, that is, after that all the zones of the earth were peopled.

effort to perpetuate by means of the dungeon, the hangman, and Louis Bonaparte. In the great capitals, London, Paris, Berlin, New York, the west is the chosen quarter. Is this accidental, or is it not an undesigned, instinctive conformity to the saying, "The devil take the hindmost?" a saying, the significance and sad truth of which, few people suspect.

But it is time for us to obey the westward law, and move towards the Rhine.

CHAPTER XIV.

GIESSEN—LIEBIG—MARIENBERG—PRIESNITZ—THE RHINE.

On the way back to Frankfort, we stopped for the night at Giessen. It would have been a satisfaction to have availed myself of the genial accessibility of German professors, to visit Liebig, one of the stoutest living scientific pioneers,—one of the precocious band that with the sharp edge of thought are hewing for their fellow-men paths into untrodden domains,—one of that bold brotherhood of discoverers who, in the holy privacy of the laboratory and the closet, reveal new truths by light struck from the contact of genius with Nature. But we arrived late and tired. I did not see a famous captain in the great army of progress, but at the public table of the inn I saw a private working in the cause of conservatism, with a zeal and capacity that made me wonder. This was a supper-eater, who in order to conserve his body and soul tightly together during the night, transmitted through the portal of the human temple, his mouth, into the mysterious laboratory of life, the following articles of food, each in unstinted portions, and in the order here named:—1st course—fried potatoes, sausages, sourcrout, cold tongue; 2d course—stewed pigeon, pudding, roast pig, cheese with bread and butter. For a man with a weak digestion, it was dangerous, just before bed-time, to "assist," as the French say, at the piling up into one stomach of this huge heterogeneous bulk; for the bare image of it on his sleeping brain might be enough to cause nightmare.

—— No matter how often you may have seen the Rhine, to come upon it is always an event. The renowned river is a line of beauty traced on the globe by Nature, and embellished by man. On its shores I have dwelt so much, so pleasantly, and so profitably, that whenever I return to them they give me the glad greeting of a home.

To go back to old haunts is a reduplication of life. With the skipping actualities of the fretful present mingle the silent memories of the past, like marble statues looking upon a market-place. As we came down the Rhine, we bade the docile boat turn in again to the pier of venerable Boppart, that during the latter days of September we might tarry within the walls of the solid, familiar, roomy, old convent of Marienberg. A return to its gardens, its corridors, its terraces, we enjoyed the more, because we were not now, as in years past, to work hard for bodily salvation with aid of its healing waters.

What perverse children of Nature we are. She gives us health, we quickly set about to turn her gift into disease; she promises abundance, we choose to stay poor; she offers us palaces, we burrow in hovels. In all things we are unnatural; in eating, in drinking, in our outgoings and incomings, in our labors and our pleasures, in politics, in religion, in medicine. Under the spell of a cajoling conceit, we build up codes that are false, and then maintain them by sophistry and force. Most of our life is a kicking against the pricks. For our weal we should be always naturalists. Nature contains, is the law. Whether his work be rare or daily, high or low, Nature is every man's mistress, and teacher, and helper. From the ploughman to the poet, the task is well done in proportion as she mixes in the doing. Wherein lies the excellence of Shakspeare, of Goethe, of Burns, of Wordsworth, of Molière, as well as of Galileo and Newton, as well as of Fulton and Priesnitz? In their greater fidelity to Nature. They are deeper and broader naturalists.

The discovery of the power there is in water as a curative agent, was made by Priesnitz twenty-five years ago. Since that, the methods of its application have been scientifically improved and multiplied. Trials in acute diseases, and in all curable chronic ones, a thousand times repeated, have proved its efficacy. And yet this truth, so large and simple and fruitful, this balm-laden truth, is accepted by but a fraction of reading, reasoning white men. Custom, prejudice, interest, routine, timidity, conspire to retard its acknowledgment. The poisoning pill-box and life-draining lancet, keep on decimating and maiming the race. "Business before truth," is one of the mottoes of civilization, and so the blood-and-drug doctors continue in trade, and out of nature.

But let us seek comfort in retrospection. A hundred years ago the discovery of Priesnitz, like other discoveries that too far outrun their age, had probably died in its cradle. Men do reason more than they used to; knowledge does circulate more briskly and widely; truth has some service of the electric telegraph.

—— The choice spots of the globe for lounging, the one in winter and spring, the other in summer and early autumn, are the Boulevards of Paris and the Rhine; the one the work of man assisted by nature, the other the work of nature enriched by man; for a fog or a rain disenchants the Boulevards, and without its towns and villages and castles and man-movement on flood and shore, the Rhine were not the Rhine. In midsummer the valleys that run back draw you into their shades; later, you quit the stream for the heights; but always the zest of the walk is when you issue out again upon the river, and to saunter along its margin is what one does oftenest. If you are alone, you have company in the peasantry tilling or gathering in the precious narrow slopes between the water and the precipice, in the wayfarers on the smooth road, in the white-shining villages on either shore, in the old castles that solemnly address you from rock-founded eminences like spectres half-protruded from their tombs, in the freight-craft and the persevering horses that drag them against the swift current, in the steam-driven boats that queen it over the river they have conquered, and in the old river himself, a companion of infinite resources, of unfading freshness. Should you wish to rest, and from prudence prefer an indoor seat to one on a pile of macadamized stones, you enter the quiet inn of a village and call, not for a half-bottle of wine, but for a "spezialen." A "spezialen" is a small tumbler-full, and costs a groschen, about two and a half cents. This, for the privilege of resting, an hour if you choose, even should the chair-bottom be of walnut, is cheap,—provided you don't drink the wine. If you are thirsty, drink grapes, and I know not a more epicurean contrivance than to walk yourself into a summer thirst of a September afternoon on the Rhine, and then at sunset to be turned into a vineyard to slake it with purple bunches fast plucked with your own hand from the stalk.

> The Rhine! The Rhine! so sweet he smells
>   When buds the perfumed grape in June.
> Still dearer is his shade when swells
>   The rippling breeze at summer's noon.
> But dearest when young Autumn's Sun
>   Wipes the late dew from purpled vine,
> And pours his ripening heats upon
>   The spicy juice of pendant wine.

CHAPTER XV.

COLOGNE—DUSSELDORF—ARTISTS—LEUTZE'S WASHINGTON—FREILIGRATH.

Railroads and Commerce have put new life under the dying ribs of Cologne. The lazy, dirty old town, that fifty years ago offended the nostrils of Coleridge to the point of versification, has grown busy, and thence more cleanly. Whoever has the æsthetic sense would be robbed of a rightful enjoyment, if in passing through Cologne even for the twentieth time he were not allowed to stop, just to breathe for a few moments under the shadow of the Cathedral, the atmosphere of sublimity wherein that mighty torso of architectural art isolates itself. This is one of those great objects that so swell the mind with high emotion that possession eclipses hope. In this presence we are satisfied; our contentment with the hour is brimming; we are not driven forward or backward into time to fill the void we carry about in us. For mostly, the now is so flat and sour, that, horsed on the winged steeds of memory or of imagination, we fly to the far past or further future, to seek the pleasure we find not in the dull world we have built, and built with splendid materials, like senseless architects, who erecting a Palace should hide their marble and Mosaics in the foundation, and show above-ground only burnt clay and painted pine.

The pleasures of memory and imagination are satires on present life, which is so poor, that we are forever running away from it, and betaking ourselves to the deceased past and the unborn future. In childhood we sigh for the stature and exemptions of youth; in youth we count the years and months that bar us from the liberties of manhood; in manhood we strain forward towards age on the untiring hack, Ambition; in maturity we strive to comfort ourselves with reminiscences of youth and childhood, that come back upon us like chiding cherubs. We are always hurrying out of to-day to get into to-morrow. We would subordinate this world to the next, and we employ at great cost a numerous class to teach us to give precedence to the world to come. We drink, and smoke, and read novels, to stave off the pressing hour. We thus make time our enemy instead of our ally—time, the flapping of whose wings are the pulses of universal life, whose hours are the foot-prints of forward-marching Eternity, and mark the unresting labors of the all-sustaining God; labors, which it is our transcendent privilege to share, so prodigally, so divinely are we endowed.

—— Düsseldorf is an hour by railroad below Cologne, a neat, shady town, noted for its school of Art. A small city such as Düsseldorf, which becomes the seat of artists, pictures itself to you like one of those fine engraved heads of Poets encircled with a laurel garland. It stands in your mind crowned with the symbol of poetic triumph. The art-element, is not here, as in large capitals, an ingredient commingled and diluted with other superiorities; it reigns in sole sovereignty, a sovereignty as benignant as that of light over darkness. Here are assembled a hundred men who have dedicated themselves to Beauty. To incarnate the spirit that pervades the two worlds, the world opened to ocular sense and that revealed to the eye of the mind, this is their life's thought, aim, desire, act. Through Nature and History, through all lands and activities, through the densities of the real, and the sunny pomps of the ideal, wherever thought or sense can stretch, they range in chase of Beauty, who flies from them as the maiden from the wooer whose love she would quicken by her coyness. Wherever a high deed has been done, wherever men have sacrificed themselves for mankind, wherever the higher law has gained a victory, wherever through the impulses of generous natures poetry has become act, wherever the countenance of History is agitated by great changes, there the artists gather. From the flowers of being they suck food for the nurture of their souls, that they may fulfil their high function, which is, to second God in keeping the world replenished with beauty.

The work-rooms of artists are among the pleasant places of the earth; they are green spots in our desert of prosaic life. In them you get the repose of disinterested sensations. You are drawn out of your little self into your large self. You are, moreover, as guest, in the happiest position towards the host; you partake of a double, nay, a threefold hospitality; for the man welcomes you, and the artist entertains you, and the picture greets you, it may be with a peal of celestial clarions. Between the artist and his creation is a privileged standpoint; through you he sends his thought to his work, which on its part beams with its fullest light in its master's presence. You stand as when gazing at a dewy landscape, and behind you the rising sun that has just brought it out of darkness.

After the day's work, the painters at Düsseldorf assemble towards evening in a garden on the edge of the town. The relaxation of fencing, and archery, and tenpins, in the open air, is something; but that each one will meet a score or two of his fellows, this is the spur that, pricking each one, drives scores to the daily gathering. Men are so sociable, so human; without the rays from one another's faces they could not keep warm. Here in their club the artists chat, and drink the drink made of hops, which even on the Rhine is more relished than that from the grape, and smoke, and play at games.

"Manly games," is a phrase of universal acceptation. I deny its fitness, and affirm, that when men shall be more manly they will have no games. They will then have put away childish things. Montaigne says that "sport is the work of children." Fourier says, that for young and old, work may become sport. One of the easy miracles of scientific socialism will be to make men rejoice in labor, and drawing even children from play, lead them to seek work as the best of sports. This miracle few people will believe till they see it. The world is much more ready to accept past miracles than future.

But Montaigne is here as shrewd as ever in his observation. Children play with a worklike spirit, and indeed with them play is creative, aiding the growth of body and mind. For adults, games are utterly barren, and men with bats and cues and cards in their hands become children without the saving unconsciousness of childhood. A company of Englishmen on a lawn, spending their breath upon cricket, is no whit more respectable than a knot of Germans or Frenchmen in an *estaminet*, intent round a marble table upon a bout of dominoes. Both are excusable to that broad, unpriestly charity, that covers with the sweep of its unpaid absolution all delinquencies. You forgive them as you forgive the theft of a meal by a pauper. Under the goad of moral hunger they steal from Time and Labor, the trustful stewards of Nature and Art, the guardians and treasurers of humanity, twin partners of the Divine Architect and eternal prime Motor.

To its school Düsseldorf attracts some foreign artists, among them our countrymen, who get quickly on the scent of a good thing. A distinguished German painter told me, that of a number of young American painters whom he had known, not one was without talent, but that they did not study with due thoroughness. Structures of art to be good and durable, have as much need as cotton-factories of solid foundations. Genius can no more dispense with labor, than the eagle can with growth; the growth of genius is only through methodical application. The strokes of scientific work are the pulsations that carry nutriment to the genial germ, and make it accrescent. But genius discovers its own science, and finds often slow furtherance on the beaten roads of routine. American artists, with more boldness and freedom, carry to European academies a national impatience of delays, which may make some overleap the earlier indispensable gradations. But these are not the most gifted, for natural gifts feed themselves with the best food within their reach, as infallible in their selection as the roots of prosperous oaks. So far from being too self-reliant, genius has a quick faculty of absorbing and assimilating to itself the fruits of others' thoughts and practices. Plodding talent lags behind the pioneers and discoverers, nimble genius never. It fuses in its focal fire all things about it, so that, whether for beauty or for strength, they flow into the moulds it is fashioning.

In the studio of an American artist of high reputation in Germany as well as in America, I had one of those pleasant surprises that quicken the pulse more healthfully than a draft of old wine. On entering Leutze's spacious studio I came unexpectedly upon his fine picture of Washington crossing the Delaware. I had not heard that he was at work on such a picture. My heart was suddenly flooded with a sublime home-feeling. In Washington's majestic figure, the distant home, which he had done so much to build for me, became instantly present in a foreign land. What a bequest to his countrymen is this man's character. The great things he did are almost less than what he does. The image of him that grows into the mind of every young American, is a defence of his country as strong and steadfast now, a half-century since he died, as was in life his generalship and civil wisdom. His perpetual great presence is a national moral fortification.

Another artist who has not wrought with the pencil but with a deeper instrument, was this summer living at Düsseldorf, the Poet Freiligrath, who having dedicated his genius to the cause of German emancipation, had made himself a mark for the hate and persecution of a retrograde government.

CHAPTER XVI.

CLEANLINESS—BELGIAN PROSPERITY—STATISTICS.

PERFECT cleanliness were general perfection. A man whose body should be absolutely clean, always, without soil outwardly or inwardly, were a model man, a breathing ideal, what is often named but never seen—a perfect gentleman. Body and soul are so closely married, and so content with the bond, that strongest spiritualists and materialists, countertugging for centuries with combined might to sunder them, have not started a joint, but their interdependence and reciprocal benefactions continue unweakened, visible in all the myriad phenomena of life, their marriage being as indissoluble as that between man and woman, the which, under varying conditions, must ever be, growing freer and purer as we near the Utopia of perfect cleanliness.

But mutual dependence kills not freedom; nay, freedom is a product of mutual dependence. Thence, the body may be cleaner than the mind, and the reverse. The co-operation is not inflexibly uniform. I doubt whether the five thousand best scholars of Germany are bodily so clean, as the five thousand busiest bagmen of England. For every result there is always more than one cause. In the main, however, mental cleanliness precedes corporeal, here as elsewhere the moral element acting the masculine part, and taking the initiative.

The more animal men are, the less have they of personal cleanliness. Savages are dirtier than barbarians, whose habits again are not acceptable to educated civilizees. Ritual ablutions, like those of Mahometans, are not a full substitute for the washings that are consequent on culture. Communities or nations that are stagnant, are dirty. Movement purifies men as well as air. So soon as a man rises from lowness, and becomes progressive, he grows sweeter. The same with a people. Speaking of the practices of the Bretons in France, noted for their primitive ignorance, some one reported of them that they bring their pigs into their houses at night; "Oh! the dirty pigs," said Victor Hugo. The Brettons are supposed to be unmixed Celts, a variety of the white race not pre-eminent for cleanliness.

The English are the cleanest people of Europe, a distinction which is not shared with their fellow-subjects, Welsh, Scotch, or Irish. Next come the Dutch and Belgians, whose virtue on this side shines most, however, in their houses and streets, so that it is a satisfaction to cross from Germany or from France, into Belgium. To learn that the interior condition does not match with the outward, one has only to sojourn for a few weeks in a small Belgian town. But any advance in cleanliness is grateful and important, and a man who wears a fresh collar and bosom over a dirty shirt and an unwashed skin, is a better neighbor at table than if he had frankly exhibited his soiled linen. Nor is the Belgian neatness a false collar, it is genuine so far as it goes.

On coming into Belgium, the travellers who, witnessing the activity in Liege and in the docks of Antwerp, and beholding the spaded tillage of the fields, should talk only with the wealthy and read the *Indépendance Belge*, or the *Emancipation*, might excusably follow the common error that the Belgians are a very prosperous people. While in 1848, their neighbors of Germany and France were in hot insurrection, they remained cool; they are thriving and happy, and have nothing to gain by change.

Over nations as over men, there is in our misorganized Christendom a thick crust of hypocrisy, under which, instead of the sweet juices of what is ripe and healthful, are crudities and putrescence. Let us break this crust, and note what we find beneath it in Belgium.

The official report* of the census, taken in 1848, makes known the number of families in Belgium to be 890,566, and of inhabitants 4,337,196, being about five persons to each family.

The habitations of these 890,566 families contain 2,758,966 rooms, including cellars and inhabited garrets, giving to each family three rooms. Little enough, and less than is needful for health or comfort, or even decency. But this is the average. Many families have more than three rooms, and many therefore less. The census declares that

>154,454 families have each but one room;
>282,785 families, each two;
>453,327, three or more.

Thus 437,239 families, making almost one half of the Belgium nation, have each but one or two rooms for their whole habitation.

Over two millions of men, women, and children, every five of whom are lodged in one or two wretched rooms, badly lighted and worse ventilated, and in winter poorly warmed; this one room or two, serving as dining-room, kitchen, storeroom, cellar, work-room, sleeping-room, with rotting straw for beds, or leaves which you may see them gathering for this purpose in autumn, on the highway.

In the cities, the proportion of families that have but one or two rooms is larger than in the country. Antwerp counts 18,000 families, 11,000 of which have but one or two rooms. Brussels has 30,000 families, 13,700 of which have but a single room, and 6,800 two rooms. The medical commission of the city of Brussels, declares that the abodes of the greatest part of the laborers of

---

* See the speech of M. de Perceval, member of the Belgian Chamber of Representatives.

that city, are "living tombs whither these wretched men come to rest themselves, after twelve hours of work."

The food of these two millions is chiefly rye bread and potatoes, and a limited quantity of these. In "good times," they have meat or fish once or twice a week, but it is the refuse of the markets—liver, lungs, heart, intestines, what in America is given to dogs.

On the 30th of June, 1850, in the provinces of Flanders, out of a population of 1,415,484 there were 349,438 inscribed on the list of paupers.

The habitations of half the population of Belgium are hot-beds for the forcing of physical and moral evils. Diseases generated by bad air and bad diet sweep off annually thousands of puny children.

From these two millions what is to be looked for morally and intellectually for themselves, for the state. A man who has worked twelve hours to earn twenty cents, and then drags himself through the stenches of filthy alleys to the stale odors of a pestilential home, to find there a haggard toil-worn wife, and sad, pale, hungry children, a supper of coarse brown bread, and a bed of foul straw, what moral content, what civic strength do his slumbers replenish? He lies down without a thank for the day that is ended, he rises without a hope for the day that is beginning.

When two millions out of four and a half writhe in this unhuman degradation, the others will not have exemption from the ills of physical and moral poverty. The most favored of a community cannot so isolate themselves but that against them will react the condition of the lowest, through conductors which no strength or skill can cut. The chastest maiden, whose thoughts and sensations build round her a halo that draws the homage of the purest, cannot, on the highest social elevation, escape infection from the sickly breath of the harlot, whom she is yet too innocent to know of. It strikes like the inpalpable vapors of the pest. Unconsciously to herself her moral being is modified by the proximity of this social disease. Under Russian despotism, Belgian constitutional monarchism, American republicanism, men must form communities, they must have much in common, and cannot be rid of mutual dependence. In a higher social organization this dependence, which men now seek vainly to shake off, will be cultivated and a thousand-fold multiplied and strengthened, and with its strength will grow each man's moral and intellectual power and his freedom.

In a social or political whole, whether constructed on a sound or fragile basis, parts dovetail into parts, individuals into individuals. Connected, intermingled, interlaced with the two millions of semi-paupers of Belgium are other two millions of fellow-laborers, having more skill, many of them a little capital, earning instead of a franc, two, three, five francs, or more per day, who are most of them thus enabled to exchange often brown bread for white, and to garnish their potatoes and beans with more or less of animal nutriment. The iron hand of poverty is not on them, it is only suspended over their heads, and from them are replenished the ranks of the lowest masses, thousands annually slipping through the restless sieve of trading competition.

Of the 890,506 families not more than ninety thousand, if so many, are clear of the pressure of straitened means. Three or four hundred thousand individuals, out of four and a half millions, whose daily life is softened by the comforts of civilization, who along with spacious carpeted lodging, meats fatted and cooked with art, the luxuries as well as the utilities furnished from flax, cotton and wool, enjoy leisure for culture, exemption from over-work and the freedom of movement allowed by pecuniary ease. These favored few are the upper ranks of the "liberal professions," the bankers, merchants and large traders, the higher civil and military officers of the state, those who have inherited large capital, especially the "Noblesse," who, though now unrecognized by the state, enjoy with wealth the highest social position.

Relatively to the four millions below them, these four hundred thousand have a happy existence ; relatively to, not a hopeless ideal, but to a condition attainable within the limits of a generation by a hundred millions of living Christians, their life is barren, encumbered, slavish.

I have cited Belgium, not because its statistics present a peculiarly dark picture, but because, on the contrary, in Europe it is regarded as a shining model of national weal. Bad enough, that "Statesmanship" and Political Economy should bring nations to this pass ; worse, that they know not how to get them out of it ; worst, that they perceive not the need of getting them out of it.

CHAPTER XVII.

FRANCE—DEMOCRACY—BONAPARTE—LOUIS PHILIPPE—LOUIS BONAPARTE.

Vive la République! We have crossed the line that divides Belgium from France. Vive la République! What a promise, what a hope is in that shout! What achievements it proclaims, what consummations it prophesies! Not with the outward voice of a catching momentary fervor, bet solemnly from the depths of a soul-enkindled feeling be that stirring sound re-uttered. It is the rally-cry of Christendom. To France all Europe looks with hope. She is the centre of the new regenerating movement. Regenerating, not because it substitutes Presidents for Kings, citizen-representatives for Barons; but because it is to break down political monopoly, to make governors amenable to the governed, and, far more than this, because by giving each man a vote, it is to raise each voter to be a man.

Economy, simplicity, supplanting military by civil processes, less partiality in legislation and administration, wiser legislators and administrators (for this in the long run is the result), equality before the law, bettering of most public methods,—all these are the minor gains of republicanism, whose essential virtue is in the energizing of the primary elements, in the recognition, cultivation, refinement, enlargement of the substance out of which all forms of policy spring, and upon which they re-act, viz.: the masses of a nation, the individuals of its component multitudes, in Europe so brutified by monarchic and aristocratic despotism, as to have been lately designated by a leading "Statesman," M. Thiers, as *la vile multitude.*

Democracy is the diffusion, and at the same time the invigoration of light and organic life. It vitalizes the remotest parts; through it, generic power permeates the whole social body. It is a substitution of man for the State, of men for things, of souls for bodies. Demanding liberty, it creates what it needs; it begets the vigor whereby it is to be braced. Proclaiming the power of self-government, it develops a broader, deeper self. He who believes not in self-government is less than a democrat; he who does is more. Democracy is progressive and expansive. Its ascendency is the gain of much liberty, and the assurance of more.

Honor to France. A glory greater than that dazzling one whereby she was so long blinded is hers, the glory due to boldness and insight in social transformations. In this sphere more fruitful will be her courage than in the battle-field, although on that there may be still some last laurels for her to gather. Napier, in his History of the Peninsular War, celebrating the brilliant bravery of a French charge, notes as a characteristic of French nature, that the first fiery onslaught being repelled, their line is disheartened. They lack elasticity under defeat. Not so in that other higher field. With fresh hope and spirit they have returned to the charge under the banner of Democracy, after lying for fifty years in defeat. And again partially worsted after the triumphant onslaught of 1848, they exhibit a determination, fortitude, calmness, forbearance, that bespeak convictions matured by thought, and a confidence that cannot be broken by discomfiture.

The morning of new eras is liable to be overcast; but blinded by ignorance or fear or malignity are they who mistake this transitory obscuration for a relapse to the past darkness. A people that has in it the juices for mature strength may be retarded in its progress, but not arrested; and what seem forced retardations from without may be the natural currents of occult growth. The political revolutions of such a people can no more go back than can the planetary revolutions of the earth. Evolutions they should be called, for they are developments, however crashing may be the inaugurating acts. Democracy, or self-government, lies potentially at the heart of every people, that is, of every people of the white races. The time and manner of its emergence depend on mental constitution and outward influences. In England, where its spirit was ever strong, it took possession of the State under the Commonwealth, but it had not yet the cordial strength to impel itself arterially into all the members; and the most capable man whom it created being by nature despotic instead of generous, regal instead of Christian, principles were smothered under usurpations, so that the bastard monarchy of Cromwell was at his death easily supplanted by the legitimate monarchy of the Stuarts. Many too of the most resolute for freedom had already fled across the sea to the newly discovered Continent, there on its virgin shores, unbefouled by the tares of oligarchical egotism, to lay foundations whereon was to rise a political fabric of purely democratic architecture, whose starry flag, unfurled at the end of the 18th century, was before the middle of the 19th to challenge the regards of the world as that of a preponderating Power among Christian States. Democracy had, if not its birth, its first wide national development in America.

In France it came forth a blind Samson, and buried itself under the ruins caused by its rageful grasp. Its movement was that of the loosened lion, whose courage is made frantic by hunger and fear. Men glared on men like unchained demons in a famished hell. With insane relish they lapped blood: that was their elixir for political renovation.* But all this was transient, ex-

---

* In the massacre of St. Bartholomew, seventy thousand Frenchmen were slain, two thousand of them in Paris. During the two years of the

plosive phenomena, the agony of a great people's travail where nature had been poisoned, the convulsive writhings of an awakening giant against gyves and handcuffs. It denoted the great strength of the binding cords, and the still greater of the power that rent them. This power had at last recognized itself, and no bonds could ever again durably enthrall it. But here, as in England, the strongest child democracy had nursed, wielded the might wherewith she endowed him for the transitory ends of an impious ambition.

Bonaparte was behind his age; he was a man of the past. The value of the great modern instruments and the modern heart and growth he did not discern. He went groping in the mediæval times to find the lustreless sceptre of Charlemagne, and he saw not the paramount potency there now is in that of Faust. He was a great cannoneer, not a great builder. In the centre of Europe, from amidst the most advanced, scientific nation on earth, after nineteen centuries of Christianity, not to perceive that lead in the form of type is far more puissant than in the form of bullets; not to feel that for the head of the French nation to desire an imperial crown was as unmanly as it was disloyal, that a rivalry of rotten Austria and barbaric Russia was a despicable vanity; not to have yet learnt how much stronger ideas are than blows, principles than edicts—to be blind to all this, was to want vision, insight, wisdom. Bonaparte was not the original genius he has been vaunted; he was a vulgar copyist, and Alexander of Macedon, and Frederick of Prussia were his models. Force was his means, despotism his aim; war was his occupation, pomp his relaxation. For him the world was divided into two—his will, and those who opposed it. He acknowledged no duty, he respected no right, he flouted at integrity, he despised truth. He had no belief in man, no trust in God. In his wants he was ig-

"Reign of Terror," from '92 to '94, two thousand eight hundred and thirty-seven were executed in Paris.

noble, in his methods ignorant. He was possessed by the lust of isolated, irresponsible, boundless, heartless power, and he believed that he could found it with the sword and bind it with lies; and so, ere he began to grow old, what he had founded had already toppled, and what he had bound was loosed. He fell, and as if history would register his disgrace with a more instructive emphasis, he fell twice; and exhausted France, beleaguered by a million of armed foes, had to accept the restored imbecile Bourbons.

But that could not last a generation. For a dozen years the military boots of Napoleon had trodden down the crop of aspirations and thoughts that sprang up with the Revolution, but had not killed them. The soldier's heel cannot stamp the life out of ideas. They had lived and made roots in silence and secrecy, under the ghastly saturnalia of bloody fruitless conquests and Imperial tyrannies and ostentations. With the old men had come back the old egotisms, the old arrogances, the old inhumanities, the old feudal desires. But the old narrow forms had been shattered, the old growths cut up by the roots, and in their place were new wants, new hopes, new convictions. The old men, brought back by the enemies of France, stood isolated round the old throne. The nation was against them, and more than the nation, new truths were against them. Now was manifest the virtue of the great bloody revolution. It had engendered a new mind, broader, deeper, more earnest, higher, stronger, richer than the old one; and the young generation that entered the arena at the downfall of Napoleon, enlightened by its fire, exalted by its vigor, was the eager heir of the principles, without being contaminated by the errors, of the revolution. The propped throne was again upset, and the kingly brother of Louis XVI. was not, like him, brought to the block, but driven from France. In the "three days of July," 1830, the patchwork of the Holy Alliance was by the indignant people torn to shreds.

But a bulky old State, so deeply diseased, in order to be purged and righted, needs several crises. Its huge load of malady it can only be rid of through successive throes. France had yet to carry on her breast for some years, the imposthume of Royalty. The "Reign of Terror" was vivid in the memory of many, and its bloody image still rose up minatory whenever men directed their thoughts towards practical republicanism. The sins of that lurid epoch were not yet expiated. "Vive le Roi!" no longer a cordial cry, was still for a season to be the only one legal. Many even of the republicans accepted the project of "a throne surrounded by republican institutions." This absurdity had to be tried in order to be known. One would suppose, that the shapelessness of such a political monster would have been apparent to men's minds without the shock of practical evidence. Louis Philippe, the head of the younger branch of the Bourbons, was declared King.

This man's life, previously to his gaining the throne, was one long promise; his life on the throne, was one long lie. The bond for " republican institutions" was kept by restricting the right of voting at all to the election of the lower Chamber, and limiting the number of voters to the two hundred thousand richest men of France; by the creation of a House of Peers appointed by the King; by the most rigid centralization of all legislative and administrative power; by obstructing and gagging the Press, and withholding the right of meeting: by upholding, in so far as he could, the despotisms of Europe. Like all men who merely calculate, Louis Philippe miscalculated. In his own bosom he had naught wherewith to measure the moral force of mankind. Sordid and unscrupulous himself, he believed that all men could be bought, and that by buying a half million he could control the nation, and consolidate the throne for himself and his family. Himself and his family, this was his absorbing thought: self-aggrandizement was the end, France and Frenchmen were but his means. He was endured for eighteen long years, when France, betrayed and corrupted, wrathful at his want of faith, disgusted at his baseness, thrust him ignominiously from his perjured throne, giving him the remnant of his contemptible life to wear it out in England, where he died as he had lived, his mind teeming to the last with intrigues and hypocrisies.

Now swelled the popular heart. To claim their long sequestered rights, the millions came forth, strong in hope, strong in justice, strong with a new intelligence, strong in their forbearance, their forgiveness. The Republic was declared, and with it universal tolerance, and a many-sided freedom. But the goal of a stable liberty was not yet attained. The Royalists were routed, not annihilated. Too weak for open war, they had strength for secret mischief. The Republicans themselves were not united. Fresh convulsions ensanguined the streets of Paris, and embittered the public mind. Moreover, France had yet another expiation to make. She had to expiate the sin of pride in Napoleon and of the vanity of military glory. His spirit was to give her one more scourging. At her call, he came back in the emaciated shape of his nephew, elected through universal suffrage by an immense majority, the first President of the Republic.

Louis Bonaparte is cunning, resolute, and unscrupulous, with an ordinary intellect and an ordinary heart, and thence without principles or convictions. He is an ambitious mediocrity. His ambition being of that vulgarest kind, that springs from an intense love of self, is unleavened by any enthusiasm or expansiveness. He took the oath as President with Empire in his heart. That a man of this calibre should in the 19th century be in a position even to aspire to be Emperor of France! To gain the Imperial diadem, Napoleon did immense things; and repeated them, in order to wear it for a brief space. The largest thing the nephew will do in his lifetime, will be to have aspired to fill his uncle's seat. His dream will be his greatest deed. No spectacle is more pitiable than that of a small man in a great place. France, by offering this spectacle to the world in her first President, is expiating Napoleonism.

Napoleon, Louis Philippe, Louis Bonaparte,—here is an anticlimax of rulers. Rulers! Baffled bunglers. The day for the rule of men is passed. Even the strong Napoleon was incapable of ruling. The Christian world has outgrown individual rulers; ideas, principles now rule. He who in authority is not imbued, bemastered by these, is at most an obstruction that temporarily angers the current, which, arrested for a time, chafes and eddies, and then sweeps into the abyss all that obstructs it. The great Bonaparte was so swept down; and the wary Louis Philippe; yet now, when the stream is far deeper and stronger, the little Bonaparte would thrust forward his petty personality to divert its flooding course, to make its boiling waters back! The highest that a shrewd judgment could have devised for such as he is, had been, to float for a season the apparent helm of the State, on the ocean of Democracy.

For, Democracy, with the broad deep principles which it involves and unfolds, is henceforward to rule in France. Ideas, once rooted in a great people, cannot be uptorn. They grow until they embrace with their life every being on the soil. With their wide sun-like warmth they grasp the cold egotisms of a departed power, that vanish before them like icicles before the solstitial rays.

Over the portal of the Palace, where this soulless retrospective aspirant would already play the mimic Emperor, are largely stamped words that are to him, and to all who with him or like him plot for regal or imperial sway, a terrific writing on the wall: Liberty, Equality, Fraternity. Before these great words, illuminated by a nation's faith, they recoil stricken with dread, so committed are they to usurpation, so tethered to fraud and force, so blinded by sensuality, so hateful of what is noble and generous.

These sublime words, uttered in a mood of prophetic exaltation, proclaim the beauty and unsounded potency of the human heart. These beautiful words, the tokens of things more beautiful, reassert the Christian promise of love and peace. They are a rainbow splendor, painted on the evanescent clouds of despair by the eternal Sun of hope.*

* Since this chapter was written has come the *coup d'état* of Louis Bonaparte. This usurpation seems to dash the hopes and confound the estimates herein expressed. If the life of a nation were reckoned by months and years and not by decades and centuries, it would do so. A great Christian people cannot go back. Principles must triumph over expedients. I believe in God, not in the Devil; in the victory of good over evil.

CHAPTER XVIII.

A DAY IN PARIS.

At six in the morning of May 20th, 1851, through the tall, wide chamber-window, that lets in light from ceiling to floor, my just-awakened eyes look from my pillow upon the green plane-trees that grow in the vacant lot opposite to No. 8 *rue du Helder*. Their large foliage is shaking coolly in the morning breeze. In the centre of Paris this tree-decked void is now rare. Favored is the Parisian lodger who has such opposite neighbors. They adorn my room, and make me free in it: they are at once my curtains and my companions.

The hour of waking is a solemn hour. We have just past suddenly from darkness into light, from death to life. Unconscious babes we come crying into the world, and this matinal rebirth is a conscious daily entrance upon a scene of sorrow. It is the hour when yesterday is nearest,—yesterday that silently wrings the conscience, like the saddened gaze of a dying friend whom we have wronged. He is gone forever, and we have not been to him what we should have been. But we get hardened to these retrospective upbraidings, and thrusting yesterday behind us in thought as he is in fact, we turn in our bed,—the will not being yet enough electrified to lift us out of recumbency into uprightness,—and boldly or timorously, despondently or hopefully indifferently or cheerfully, we confront the new day that the sun has just brought to us from the mysterious East. For myself, being bent on extra work, action cuts short meditation, and I leap out of bed into water at 58 Fahrenheit,—a temperature to be recommended to those who possess the privilege of beginning every day with a cold bath.

The window unlatched, turning on double hinges like a folding door, opens its whole expanse. Fresh and sweet the morning air rolls in, untainted up here in the *Premier* (what we should call the third story) by the impurities of the pavement. The cries of Paris are in full chorus, the old-clothes men leading the peripatetic band. Opposite, a hydrant,—set running for two hours morning, noon and evening for domestic service and to gargle the gutters,— pours forth a vigorous stream, that seems to delight in its own cool gush.

—— Issuing through the *porte-cochère* into the street, a little past seven, a few steps bring us to the corner, where we surprise the *Boulevard des Italiens* in complete deshabillé. Brooms, dusters, water-pails are busy; shop-windows are disgarnished; cafés are turned out of doors to be swept; the broad sidewalks, the afternoon home for swarms of idlers, are unpeopled, save by the initiatory providers of the day, the indispensable purveyors, who could be as ill spared as the Sun with whom they rise, the bread-men and water-men and milk-men. Sad-looking women are on their way to the close hives, where a whole day's lung-and-eye-wearing stitchwork earns for them a minimum of life's first necessaries. An ice-cart, with its circular thatched roof, is at Tortoni's.—We have reached the *Boulevard Montmartre;* the shade on the east side is already welcome. Opposite, a line of cabs, mostly of royal blue with white ponies, has taken its stand of passive expectancy. Cabmen are favored: they enjoy several of the first elements of well-being. They are all day in the open air; they are never like other mortals· deserted by hope, upon which it may be said they chiefly live; they frequent the best houses, keep good company, and always ride. In return for these blessings, they are contented and civil; and if, to their small perquisite you add a *sous* or two, they on their part will add to their " merci, monsieur," a cordiality and gratitude of tone that at once make you the gainer by the gift.

The daily inaugurating act of each house in Paris is, to purge itself of the sweepings and rejected kitchen-fragments of the past twenty-four hours, which are thrown out in piles on the edge of the sidewalk, where they await the scavenger-carts that come along towards eight. But ere these can arrive squalid Poverty, pricked out of sleep by Hunger, has started from its filthy couch, and dispersed through the streets its tattered hordes. At this moment over every pile of garbage bends a hungry proletarian, seeking therein his breakfast, and it may be his dinner. Look at that man, a deep, wide-mouthed basket strapped to his back. With a short stick, hooked at one end, he rakes into the pile, drives his hook into rag or paper, delivers what he has pinned into the basket, with a rapid jerk of the stick over his shoulder, and ferrets again into the foul heap with an eye made keen by want. Here is another who has laid down the hook, and with his hands is picking out bones. I have seen a man and a dog fraternally exploring the same pile. A little further a woman is sorting, at the edge of the gutter, the rejected lemon-peels of a *café ;* the best of them,—for to poverty there is choice in lowest degrees,—she throws into her basket, and will perhaps, out of this refuse of an orgie, concoct a savory draft for her sick child. These are the *chiffoniers*, the rag-gatherers.

Seizing a moment of intermittence in the flow of carts, man-drawn as well as horse-drawn, and of lazy-looking cabs, we cross the *rue Montmartre*, one of the great arteries of Paris. We meet squads of laborers in blue *blouses*, with tools on shoulder, going to their work, distant for many of them a league or more from their homes in the *quartier St. Antoine*,—if homes those can be called where there is so little of privacy and comfort for the few hours they are in them. On the edge of the sidewalk of the *Boulevard Bonne Nouvelle* three drivers of public sprinkling-carts are lying, two of them asleep. Through the band of the broad-brimmed drab hat of each is a rosebud, shining on that coarse ground, like Beauty guarding the slumbers of Strength.

We are now at the *Porte St. Denis*. The mile that we have come on the *Boulevard* is but a small segment of this longest, broadest, freest, most commodious, most lively, most variegated, most magnificent of urban avenues in the world. The width of this queen of streets is about one hundred and thirty feet, the one half in asphalte sidewalks. The *Porte St. Denis* is a triumphal arch seventy feet high, erected more than a century since on the foundations of one of the old gates of Paris in honor of the victorious campaigns of Louis XIV. On the entablature you read in large capitals, LUDOVICO MAGNO. Monumental inscriptions that are not rescripts of the general judgment are speechless. Emphasize, begild, emblazon them as you will, they have no voice. A score of triumphal arches could not make *great* stick to Louis XIV., and this *Magno* is but an impotent ostentation.

As we retrace our steps, the Boulevard is fuller. Here a flower-woman has just taken her stand. For a bunch of rosebuds she asks ten cents and takes eight, and would probably have taken six. She is a type of all traders, great and small, whose aims, means, and whole practice may be codified into one brief precept;—buy as cheap and sell as dear as you can.—For a moment our passage is obstructed by a herd of she-asses who, with their habitual countenance of grave resignation, are coming up to the door of an invalid, to whom ass's milk has been prescribed by some doubting, dogmatic doctor. The stream of busy humanity that pours out of the *Passage Jouffroy* towards the heart of the city, deepens. Some are reading, as they walk, the morning papers, which they have just bought at a news-stall. It is nearly eight when we re-enter the gate of the *Hotel du Tibre*.

—— This is the hour for breakfast and the newspapers, both excellent; for the bread and the butter of Paris are sweet, and the newspapers are the most readable in the world. A virtue of French nature is, that it is intolerant of a bore. With Frenchmen the *style enniueux* is the only bad style. Their best pens work for the newspapers. At this moment a score of the cleverest members of the National Assembly are habitual contributors to them. Novelists, poets, men of science, critics of high name, fill daily their *feuilletons*. The Paris journals have less quantity and finer quality, less matter and more spirit, less about trade and more about taste, than those of England or America.

The French speakers and writers are sounding the depths of politics with as much ability as boldness. Their expositions throw fresh light on our practice. From several of the most marked of the Paris journals of this morning I will take a few sentences as samples of the political opinions and hopes of the day.

The *Assemblée Nationale,*—said to be under the influence of M. Guizot,—shall speak in a single sentence for all the Royalists :—" Oui, puisque la République est une nécessité du temps, de la confusion des idées et de l'abaissement des courages, subissons la avec résignation." The resignation here preached means resistance at the first opportunity; for the Royalists have understanding and will not understand, and they do sincerely believe that when they shall have gotten rid of Louis Bonaparte, they can permanently put down democracy. As wisely employed would they be in trying to put down light. Is the Sun too luminous for them, they can in no other way escape his rays than by retreating from the upper earth into cellars and caverns. Can they not bear the fertilizing heat of Democracy, let them withdraw into the wildernesses of Asiatic despotism. Europe is no place for them. For Europe, under the momentum imparted by Christianity, thought, science, instinct, is galloping into democracy.

It might be thought, that the Thiers and the Guizots, and the Broughams, being shrewd, practised men, know better, and are hypocrites when they denounce Democracy. To account for their proceeding, their sincerity need not be questioned. The intellectual vision of such men gets obscured by egotism. They commenced as light-dispensing liberals, but having within them no cordial love of truth to keep their minds warm and elastic, they have become narrowed and petrified by conceit and ambition. They never were other than political adventurers, self-seeking speculators in the market of Politics.

The *Pays* has lately come under the control of Lamartine. Writing to-day on the "Republic which best suits France," he combats the project of an Executive named by the Assembly. Here is a brick from his pile :—" Une Assemblée exécutant elle-même, sans division des pouvoirs, c'est la confusion des pouvoirs, c'est l'irrésponsabilité du gouvernment, c'est l'impunité de toutes les oppressions contre le peuple, c'est la tyrannie à mille têtes! C'est la Convention ! En voulez vous ?"

The *République*, in an article headed, " Monarchie ou République," and signed *Ad. Guéroult*, says :—" Il s'agit de choisir entre le régime paternel de l'Autriche et le gouvernement du pays par lui-même ; de retourner au moyen-age, on du continuer la Révolution Française. Qui pourra douter du résultat ?"

The *Presse*, when its proprietor, Emile de Girardin, puts his soul into it as he does just now, is the ablest journal in Christendom. It glows this morning with power. By its zeal, ability and vigor, it is the most efficient expounder of the great democratic movement in France and Europe.

To royalist papers, quarrelling about the elder and younger branches of the Bourbons, M. de Girardin says:—"Ne vous querellez pas : ni les cadets ni les ainés de la maison de Bourbon ne reviendront en France, à moins qu'il ne leur convienne d'y revenir sans autre prétension que celle de simples citoyens, électeurs et éligibles.

"Le droit commun est devenu le droit absolu ; il n'admet pas d'exceptions.

"Les Monarchistes ont tué la Monarchie en France : les fusionistes l'ont enterrée."

—— The limitations of time and space, the inexorable conditions to which he is subjected by his body and his watch pinch the stranger, who wishes to crowd into one Paris day a great variety of objects and sensations. He must hurry and be content with glimpses. But the deathless mind has no such limitations. In a second it sweeps through æons, or embraces the orbits of siderial systems. Within the compass of a few minutes, while you are passing through a Church or a Museum, long chapters of thought can write themselves upon the brain. I shall not so abuse the indulgence of the reader, who permits me to lead him about the Capital of France, as to transcribe the half of this writing. Were I to do so, instead of an hour,—he would need a day to read "a day in Paris." I spare him.

Among the cardinal objects of Paris, one of the nearest to our lodgings is the National Library, in the *rue Richelieu*, the largest in the world, containing more than a million of volumes. We arrive just as the guardians are throwing open its immense galleries at ten.

A vast compact collection of books is a table of contents of the world past and present, an epitome of human kind up to the living hour. What our predecessors on the globe have thought and done is here registered. Manuscripts, Syriac, Coptic, Arabic, fill any chasms that the briarean printing-press has not yet bridged over. From these shelves, men and nations speak and tell their story. Around you is a chronicle of your race. Those tribes whose nature and speech were too feeble to utter themselves in books, have been reported by their stronger kin.

Books denote intellectual wants satisfied; they are clasps wrought by culture to strengthen itself; they are testimonials of national character; they measure the degree of human vitality in a people. Those who have the best books will be found to be at the top of the scale, those who have none at the bottom. Recall the history of Nations, and survey a present map of the globe. Books are grains of spiritual wheat; I mean good books, such as have the life of fresh honest thought in them. A good library is a granary of thoughts; it stores up aliment for the mind; it preserves seed from all ages and countries, and, like the wheat discovered in the tombs of Egypt, this seed keeps its life for thousands of years, and if planted fructifies.

The sowing is here done broadcast, for in going the round of these gigantic halls we come upon one where, at a long table, sit a multitude of silent readers. Whoever wishes a book writes its name on a slip of paper. This the Librarian hands to one of his assistants, who perhaps has to walk through a furlong of books to fetch it. The volumes delivered to him the applicant must use in the library; he is not permitted to take them away.

Like a patriarch amidst his progeny, in the centre of one of the great halls, sits in permanent presidence, Voltaire,—Voltaire the skeptical, the witty, the versatile, the voluminous. The statue is a copy in plaster bronzed of that marvel of portrait-sculpture in the *Théatre Français*, by Houdon. The aged face sparkles with shrewdness. It is the head and face not of the wisest but of the most knowing of men. The countenance is that as of a man who had never wept. But in this it wrongs Voltaire: he was not without sympathy and kindliness. Nor was he, like Talleyrand, a man who believed in nothing but himself, and in his best moments doubted even that. Priests, whom his reason unmasked and his wit lashed, have done their worst to blacken Voltaire. With priests,—who live by creeds and credulity,—the direst offence is skepticism. But skepticism is never an original disease; it is a reaction against hypocrisy and false belief. Skepticism is the forerunner of a better belief, for men are by nature believers, and doubts are the braces of faith. The man who has never doubted is apt to be a shallow believer. To the generation that doubted with Voltaire has succeeded a generation, which, strengthened by the antecedent purgation through doubt, now believes with Béranger and with Lammenais, and with him who is the deepest and broadest believer and the most far-seeing man of his country and age, with Fourier, who came to harmonize the heart of man with the thought of God.

—— Turning to the left as we issue into the *rue Richelieu*, through the massive black portal of the Library, we soon cross the *rue neuve des Petits Champs*, and in a few paces come upon a short *passage*, by help of which, after descending a flight of stone steps, we suddenly find ourselves under an arched, open corridor, that encloses an oblong quadrangle, seven hundred feet by three hundred, planted with rows of truncated lime-trees, with grass-plots and flower-beds, fountains and statues in the centre. All round this immense corridor of two thousand feet are shops, and above it is one immense edifice, internally partitioned, horizontally as well as vertically, into hundreds of tenements, and is externally of uniform and florid architecture, with fluted pilasters and Corinthian capitals, and elaborate details of ornament. This is the *Palais Royal*, a compendium of the great Capital in whose midst it stands—a mammoth warehouse of the necessaries and the luxuries, the solids and the prettinesses, the grossnesses and the refinements of civilization. Here you may equip yourself for a journey or a ball; furnish a house or a trunk; fill your library or your larder; pass from the taciturn reading-room to the chattering *Estaminet*, to quicken time's pace by a game of billiards with *Charles* or *Romain;* wash down a twenty franc dinner with a bottle of *Clos Vougeot* at the *Trois Frères*, or a two franc one with thin *Bordeaux* at *Richard's* hard by; mount into the altitudes of Art with *Rachel*, or have *Levassor* help you digest your dinner with his side-shaking fun.

At this hour and season the spring-green leaves of the dwarfed lime-trees, which contrast harmoniously with their clean black branches, waste on the smooth gravel their rectilinear shade, not yet prized by the gossipping nurses, and less by the children that run among the legs of elderly loungers, who come to this sprightly seclusion, this palatial patch of French *rus in urbe*, to let indolence float them an hour or two down Time's lethean stream.

Besides the wealthy idle, there are in Paris thousands of people who, on incomes of from two hundred to five hundred dollars, lead a life of absolute unproductiveness. To this class, time is all pastime. Their meals are their occupations. For their attic lodgings, and other scant indispensables, they grudgingly pay their few francs daily. This is all they give; they are takers, not givers. They live on the community; that is, on what is common and open to all, which in Paris is so lively and various, that to the vacant it is as good as a fat property. In good weather they haunt the *Boulevards* and public gardens and gratis spectacles; in bad, the *cafés*, *estaminets*, auctions, passages, bazaars. Their personal relations are few. The responsibilities fed by the affections, the duties of worker, citizen, and friend, from these they emancipate themselves as fully as may be, in order to reduce existence to the minimum of care. This they call freedom, and in sadness we allow, that they are not wholly wrong; for under the civilized *régime*, such falseness is there in all relations, that he who has the fewest is the freest. What a freedom! obtained by personal isolation and moral micrification.

—— In five minutes we alight at the Church of *St. Germain l'Auxerrois*. This church has a dismal celebrity. From its belfry it was that on the 23d of August, 1572, was given the signal for the massacre of St. Bartholomew, and all through that awful night its bell tolled. Was it in penitence, or in triumph? The

Romish Church professes to be unchangeable. Are its priests then ready to re-commit that crime for which earth has no name? Did the executioners of that sacerdotal sentence afterwards bring their doings of that night to the confessional? Was the fulness of the absolution and its unction in proportion to the number of victims reported? Good God! that these godless impostors should still thrive! that men who have had opportunities and culture, men even of manly natures, should still submit themselves, their feelings and their acts, to the revision of this histrionic corporation!—But we will not stop longer on the threshold, to be embittered by the terrific retrospection, and the angry thoughts it awakens.

Within, two funeral services are going on; one in the middle of the church for a child, the other in a side chapel for an adult, and, from the tranquil acquiescent mien of the mourners, apparently, aged person. But from the group in the centre are heard the sobs of that sharp grief which cuts into the heart of the mother, and makes there a wound that never fully heals. Violence has been done, hence life-quaking sorrow; for early death, or death from any cause but decay, is against the normal law of nature. The painless death of the aged from exhaustion is the only natural death—painless to the departed, and painless, though sad, to the survivors.

In another recess an elderly priest is teaching the catechism to a large class of boys. French children in the earliest years are mostly not beautiful; they want the unconscious, untainted, selfless look, which, with a rosy transparent plumpness, makes cherubs of their little neighbors across the Channel; but among these boys, who were from ten to fourteen, there was much beauty. As we paused for a moment, the priest asked one of them to explain the mystery of the incarnation! The boy made answer according to the words of the book.

In a populous city like Paris, where there are few churches, and where so many thousands seldom visit them, except for the great sacraments, it were quite possible to hit upon an hour when, besides a funeral, there should be a marriage and a christening. As we had not this fortune, I almost regretted not to possess the gift that some reporters have, of eking out with inventions the short-comings of reality. Yet it was fitting that for this church, the image of death should stand alone in the memory.

—— Coming out, we front the east façade of the Louvre, and on the globe we could not stand on a spot from which to behold a grander architectural mass. A colonnade nearly two hundred yards long, of coupled Corinthian columns, each one thirty-eight feet high, supported on a plain basement thirty feet high, with a gallery behind pierced with windows and enriched with pilasters and festoons. But here, as in all great architectural creations, the enduring grandeur and beauty spring from the proportions. Were the basement a few feet lower, or the pairs of columns further apart, or the entablature less massive, or the central and lateral projections more prominent, the harmony would be broken, and this unique façade would have missed much of its renown. Possibly some of the details might be improved. The arching of the windows in the basement, the want of elevation in those above, the unmeaningness of the festoons over each upper window, if these are defects,—which I hardly presume to say they are,—they are merged in the splendor of effect produced by excellence of proportion among such gigantic constituents.

Those great Greeks! what a plastic genius, what a clear soul for beauty, what an infallible inward sense of form they had Look at a Corinthian column, with its wrought base, its light fluted shaft, springing with a graceful strength up to its acanthine capital, like an elastic Flora bearing a basket of flowers above her head,—what a creation it is! Imperishable from its beauty, it is an ornament to the earth forever.

—— The Quays are one of the great features of Paris. Herein

she high overrides her mightier English rival. Ten miles of quay,—five on each side of the river,—of from fifty to eighty feet wide, paved, lighted, fenced by stone balustrades, one endless terrace overlooking the Seine, the one side communicating with the other by a dozen bridges,—it is a magnificence traversing the city, such as no other city in the world can show.

Ascending the quays on the right bank of the river, we cross the *Pont Neuf* to the island, where is the original city, the primary centre, round which by successive radiations has grown in the course of more than a dozen centuries, this vast metropolis. Passing by the *Palais de Justice*, we alight in front of the huge truncated towers of *Notre Dame*, the foundations of which were laid more than eight hundred years ago.

Seldom is there in architecture a transmission of life from part to part, a quick circulation of vitality through the members, melting them into a whole. The great law of unity, predominant and transparent in every work of Nature, and therefore imperative in Art, is from weakness seldom fulfilled in its severity. Now the imposing front of the famous old Cathedral of *Notre Dame*, is not enough penetrated by this unifying essence. The parts lie one above the other strata-wise. It cannot be called heavy, yet it presses too much on the earth. The best architecture is always buoyant, lifting itself up with an intrinsic nervousness, a self-sustainment, infused by beauty; for beauty has the virtue to spiritualize the bulkiest mass.

And the exterior is the best of it. The interior is in its *ensemble* less inspired. Those stout columns, besides being not Gothic, are grossly prosaic. Instead of mounting up with alacrity to meet the down-stooped roof, and carrying it without sign of effort, they look overladen, and as though they complained of their task. But here in the transepts is a compensating pomp, two circular painted windows, opposite the one to the other, and each fifty feet in diameter. They are like the magnification of a brilliant kaleidoscope.

These Gothic cathedrals are sublime efforts made in the middle ages, to embrace God with the uplifted arms of mighty Architecture.

—— Crossing over to the left bank of the river, we traverse part of the *quartier Latin* to reach the Luxembourg. We have time but for a short turn in its spacious, shady, hospitable garden, from which we hasten up to the gallery of living French painters.

With ever new zest one re-beholds that great picture of Couture, *Les Romains de la Décadence*. A capital excellence of this masterpiece is, that it illustrates and demonstrates the limitation of the Arts. Each art has its domain within which it is sovereign, beyond which it is uncrowned. Never did artist plant himself more firmly in the very centre of his rightful dominion than does Couture in this picture. Written poetry, sculpture, music, could not with their utmost attainment, singly or united, impress upon the mind an image of the decline of Rome, so vivid, so full, so convincing, as is here done on canvass in a single view.—A Roman orgie, in a lofty banquet-hall of cool Grecian architecture; men and women reclining, standing, sitting, some with goblets in hand; and over all the languor of an irremediable satiety. In that large, graceful, recumbent, central, female figure, what fallen majesty, what spent power, what a gigantic lassitude! in those big dark orbs what a depth of fixed sadness! Never more can that countenance beam with joy. Here a male figure has climbed up to a niche and offers wine to a statue; what a fine stroke of Art to express utter satiation. On the opposite side, a woman is tearing her hair, as if suddenly seized with madness, and nobody heeds her. In the distant background, a group are tearing one another. Here there is a show of dalliance, but lacking the sting of passion. In the love there is no fire, no flavor in the wine, nor in the grapes any slaking coolness. Palate and feeling, body and soul, all is *blasé*, consumed by a heat which warms not. Those two spectators in the corner, standing indignant, like Brutus and Cassius come back, they frown in vain. Mighty Rome is fallen forever. The Latin civilization is drained to the bottom, and here are the putrid lees. It had not the soul of the highest life. The spiritual element, the higher human, the vivacious and immortal, mingled in it too feebly to project it towards an indefinite progression. Its great animal intellectual vigor, has compassed the widest orbit yet permitted to a nation. Force has run its full circle, beginning in rude strength, and ending, naturally, in voluptuousness.

But already, as Rome passed her zenith, in the East had been laid the foundations of a power, on whose immeasurable path was to be borne, not a nation, but a host of nations, and not nations merely, but better than nations, MAN. Civilized Paganism was the consecration of the State ; Christianity is the consecration of man. In Greece and Rome man was subordinated to the State ; the more the law of Christ is fulfilled, the more the State is subordinated to man. The greater the concentration and exercise of power in the State, the smaller is man. When the State is all and man nothing, as under Despotism, the instrument rules its maker, and belittles him ; for the State is of man, and man is of God. When Christianity grows strong, it strengthens man, and melts the bonds of the State. The freest nation must be the most Christian. The most unchristian power in Christendom is the Papacy.

The thoughts kindled by this great picture carry us away from the picture itself. Considering the almost unique felicity of the subject, the breadth of its purport, the intellectual beauty of its composition, the masterly richness of the execution, the high unconscious moral there is in it, this picture should rank as one of the greatest works of art in Europe. It is a canvas-compendium of Roman history. Study it, and save yourself the trouble of reading Gibbon.

—— The sun has passed the meridian, and will soon be hurrying away from us: we must hasten after him.—Coachman, drive as fast as safety and the police will let you. From the narrow, damp streets of this side the river, one issues upon the quays with a feeling of disenthralment. Turning to the left we descend the left bank. In view on the opposite shore are, the Louvre, its long gallery, the Palace, the garden of the Tuileries. On this side we drive along, first the learned quays Malaquais and Voltaire, with their book-stalls and print-shops, and the house where Voltaire died, then the Quay D'Orsay, with its imposing edifices and patrician tranquillity. Now are we crossing the *Pont de la Concorde*, from which the eye ranges up the river to be stopped two miles off by the towers of *Notre Dame*, and down, by distant foliage, then across to the *Place de la Concorde*, with its neighboring grandeurs. Flanked on the right by the massy foliage of the Tuileries, and on the left by *Elyséean* vistas under broken shade; with its two pompous fountains spouting their large expanse of clear, noisy water, between them the Obelisk of Luxor, looking in its solemn singleness like a mourner at a wedding; with its gay, bronze-gilt lamp-columns and bold statuary and incessant roll and glitter of carriages, and its magnificent environment, the *Place de la Concorde*, on every sunny day like this, wears a festal air. Now we are close upon the *Madeleine*, belted by more than fifty Corinthian columns, each one fifty feet high. For months this architectural paragon has been to me a daily joy; for, not a day but I pass it more than once, and never without fresh admiration and thankfulness. I will presume upon the privilege of having gazed at it many hundred times to find one fault in it. The pediment is not purely Grecian, but somewhat Roman, that is, a little too high. Were there a mile up the Boulevards a large specimen of pure Gothic, what termini there were to the gayest walk in Europe.

We reach the *rue du Helder* at one, most grateful for an hour's rest, which is made more refreshing by help of a mutton-chop and French roll for lunch.

—— It is half-past two when I find myself again on the other side of the river, and alighting at the corner of the Quay Voltaire, I walk into the *rue de Beaune*. No. 2 is the first gate-way on the right, entering the which I cross a broad court, ascend a few steps to the large open portal, turn to the right, and having passed through two doors in succession, have before me in a spacious, shelf-furnished room, several clerks, silently at work behind the wire netting that in French offices separates the visitor from the inmates. Invading this precinct, with interchange of salutation with the occupants, I issue out at the opposite angle, and traversing a short, dark passage, enter by a small door another capacious room with tall windows to the ground looking on a garden. At an enormous oval table in the middle of the room, covered with green baize and bestrown with newspapers, two bearded men are writing, and another is reading a journal, a sofa on one side is possessed in its full length by a recumbent fourth, while two or three others, seated before the coal embers of the large fire-place, are smoking short clay pipes. Conversation is fitful, now and then rising for a few moments into earnest continuity. This is the *sanctum* of the writers for the *Democracie Pacifique*, and the rendezvous of the Phalansterians. On the mantel-piece is a bust of Fourier.

These men believe in a new social order, to be founded on absolute justice; and they have dedicated themselves to the exposition of the laws whereby it is to be organized. Convictions of the present possibility of a more human and a more divine condition for man, contrasted with which the best he has yet had is but vanity and blight, these are the staple of their life. They live in a future, built of ideas originated by thoughtful, sympathizing genius. They themselves are not raised above their fellows by brilliancy of parts or purity of conduct; their distinction is, that, whether by the fortune of association, or by intellectual sympathy, or by æsthetic susceptibility, they have accepted the discoveries of Fourier. Providence provides that the good seed which she generates shall some of it light on soil where it can grow and fructify. They are not high on the social scale, but from the eminence of new truth they look calmly down upon the turmoil which men now call society. In the world's goods they are poor, but the incommensurable wealth of world-moulding ideas is theirs; and thus enriched, they already enjoy an inward well-being, which to flaunting grandees and bedizened officials, who think they despise them, were an incredible Utopia.

The bust of Fourier is unhappily not faithful. The artist has had the imbecile arrogance to alter God's work: he thought to improve it! He has "idealized" by squaring, enlarging, emboldening it; that is, he has annihilated Fourier, and instead of a transcript from the original head, he has given us a big, hollow, no-head. But the disciples of Fourier possess a cast from his cranium after death. This indicates a nature more distinguished for the completeness and harmony of its organization, than for any one-sided intellectual or affective superiority. I gazed at it as I had at his simple tomb in the cemetery of Montmartre, with deep emotion; for to this man I acknowledge myself to be under unspeakable obligations. He has ratified and enlightened my best intuitions; he has intellectualized my aspirations into scientific truths. His discoveries and deductions are new revelations of the greatness and goodness of God, and of the cognate power and splendor of man. "Les attractions sont proportionelles aux destinées;"—"La Série distribue les harmonies."* These two sublime formulas, into which Fourier has condensed the essence of his doctrine, and which prefigure the

---

* Attractions are proportionate to destinies;—the Series distributes the harmonies.

coming glorified condition of humanity, are as yet to the multitude cabalistic and enigmatical, and to the Pharisees what were, and continue to be to them the words of Jesus, " Love thy neighbor as thyself,"—" Be ye perfect, even as your Father which is in Heaven is perfect ;" the which sublime exhortations are still an ideal goal, shining with a star-like brilliancy, and a star-like remoteness, through the night of human enmities and imperfections. The formulas of Fourier are the vehicle wherein this high ideal shall descend to the earth, and become the reality of daily life.

—— Re-crossing the Seine by the *Pont National*, I enter the Tuileries Gardens. Trees and turf are freshly robed in the clear, clean verdure of spring. On coming into these gardens one gains a sense of freedom. The sudden salutation of Nature in mid-urban closeness were enough for this, and Art enlarges the sensation by beautifying the welcome of Nature with her own graceful courtesy. With the leaves and flower-buds children have come back. The broad alley on the *rue Rivoli* is glittering with these soul-buds, and through the joyous, busy swarm one moves slowly, imbibing spiritual peace from celestial emanations.

Quitting the Garden by the gate opposite the arch-flanked *rue Castiliogne*, in five minutes I am in the *rue Duphot*, which ascends from that of *St. Honoré* to the *Boulevard des Capucines*. At No. 12 I pass under a solid gateway over which is inscribed, *Ecole d'Equitation*, where besides the best schooling in horsemanship in a spacious covered quadrangle, good well-equipt saddle-horses are to be had by the month or day. In a few minutes I have under me a clean-limbed English blood mare, in full trot up the broad avenue of the *Champs Elysées*. A ride on a mettled horse who enjoys his own springy motion, is a cure for many of the minor ills of life.

The sight cannot escape the gigantic Triumphal Arch which

crowns the eminence at the head of this noble avenue,—by far the most massive specimen in Europe of a vain and arrogant class of edifice, and a sample of the handiwork of Napoleon, who was so great in the smaller, the material sublime, and so small in the greater, the moral sublime. Two centuries hence this monument of military achievements will by the thoughtful of that period be interpreted as a naif record,—elaborately chiselled upon the tablet of History by the " Great Captain of the age,"— of the semi-barbarism of the nineteenth century, whereof himself was the most shining exemplification.

Leaving this monster* on the right, I join the current which, on the cushioned seats of coach or saddle, sets at this hour up the avenue of St. Cloud towards the *Bois de Boulogne*. This sandy area, about seven miles in circuit, covered for the most part by a stunted growth, chiefly of oaks and birch, is intersected throughout by numerous straight avenues that run across from edge to edge and cut one another at all angles. There is but one meandering path, running through the middle, and much frequented by equestrians. This is a pleasure-ground for that portion of Parisian idlers who can afford the daily luxury of horses. On Sundays all the hackney-carriages of Paris are in request to transport thither a fraction of the *Bourgeoisie*. But even hacks are beyond the reach of the mechanical and other hard-working classes. Those on whose broad, steadfast labor Society rests as her foundation, she dooms to exclusion even from the meagre relaxations which in her penury she doles out. In her diabolic perversity she honors most the least creative, those who consume much and produce nothing.

Here comes, on a stout sleek horse, a stout well-tailored man, with groom to match. His square fleshy face is sallow, his eye egotistic and unhappy. He looks like a rich sensualist hopelessly

---

* It cost two millions of dollars. For his own magnification, the Corsican spent the gold of Frenchmen as lightly as their blood.

riding for an appetite. In passing, he scans me, as though by my look he would measure my worldly importance. In a button-hole of his coat he has a red ribbon, and on his overcoat the same. Medals round the necks of children are hateful to me. They are mostly a falsehood, as not expressing the absolute relative merits of the wearers to their mates. They are often a testimonial of only apparent excellence; they are always a bait to draw vanity to the surface, and are therefore stimulants of a morbid emulation. They demoralize the child. On an adult they are disgusting, a stain on his manhood, a badge of his subjugation. A man to have a bit of ribbon pinned to his breast by another man, in token of superiority over his fellows! The degradation is the deeper for its unconsciousness. The tone of manliness is so chronically lowered on the Continent of Europe by the habit of submission to arbitrary state-power, that men of honorable nature are insensible to the dishonor that intrinsically attaches to the wearing of these " decorations," of which they therefore make a peacock-like parade.

The joyous music of young women's laughter, accompanying the martial tramp of numerous strong hoofs in quick gallop, sounds close through the leaves, and I have barely time to yield the better half of the road, when two English girls, superbly mounted, spring by at an Amazonian speed. Their fun seems to be to distance their cavaliers, who strain after them in loud glee. "I say, Harry," cries one of these, evidently enjoying the sport almost as much as a fox-chase, "this is devilish hard work." Four women out of five that one meets on horseback are in swift gallop. Our masculine imaginations make the steed look proud of his beautiful burthen; but for all that, I pity a woman's horse

Adopting the feminine pace, from the centre of the wood I reach the *Boulevards* in thirty minutes.

—— It is past five when, on my way homeward from the stable, I cross the *Place Vendôme,* where is another of Napoleon's military monuments, the column made of brass cannon taken from the Austrians and Russians in 1805, surmounted by a colossal statue of the Imperial Artilleryman. This column, like most of its author's works, is an imitation of a bad model. In keeping with its borrowed form, the inscription on the base, telling why it was erected, is in Latin. This latinity serves a purpose; for the heartiest admirers of the monument being the ignorant, the unknown tongue, while it sharpens their sense of their own ignorance, will quicken their admiration; and thus, Napoleon is elevated in proportion to their abasement,—which is just as it should be.

Even the cultivated are somewhat imposed upon by Greek or Latin words. These have a big oracular look. The imagination is aroused by the sight of them ere they have spoken. A voice sounding across twenty centuries must be freighted with import. Thus we are apt to infuse into a quotation from those languages a deeper meaning than it ever had; partly too because, no one ever thoroughly understanding a language that he has not learnt through the ear as well as the eye, the imagination, with its practised self-confidence, fills up the void.

—— Nothing exhibits more flagrantly the injustice inherent in civilization than the inequality among the dinners served up to her children; and Paris, by the superlative degree to which she stretches this inequality, deserves the title she assumes of being the capital of the civilized world. Out of her million of inhabitants, more than half can hardly be said to dine at all. In their dark, unfurnished, crowded, infectious lodgings, or, far away from these wretched homes, resting at noon from work, the mechanic and day-laborer appease the gross cravings of hunger with a stinted portion of the plainest, and often unwholesome, innutritious, refuse food. The solace, physical and moral, of a leisurely, abundant repast,—due to every man by Nature, and which Nature is willing and anxious to pay,—this they never have. When two out of three of all who are buried in Paris are so at public cost, and one third die in the hospitals, no especial skill in statistical arithmetic is needed to estimate, without other data, how many of the living daily uphold life by what may be called a dinner; that is a wholesome, sufficing meal. When I put down the dinnerless at six hundred thousand, I am within bounds; and scores of thousands among these would on many days utter in vain the prayer, " Give us this day our daily bread."

Of the remaining four hundred thousand, two consist of small shop-keepers, best-paid mechanics, clerks at low salaries, the inferior class of artists, and others, who although they sit down with a table-cloth, and even napkins, and wine (at 8 cents a bottle), live in the daily habit,—without the virtue,—of obedience to the hygienic prescription of rising from dinner with an appetite.

To make up the million there are two hundred thousand left, comprising capitalists who live on their incomes, computed to be about seven per cent. of the whole population of Paris, the wealthier professional and literary men and artists, the upper *Bourgeoisie*, bankers, traders and large shop-keepers, and the higher office-holders. These are the true diners, the elect (epicureanly speaking), for whom capons were discovered and *riz de veau à la financière*, for whom turbot and oysters of Ostend are brought in ice from the sea, and truffles from the south, and asparagus and strawberries are forced, and *Chambertin* and *Lafitte* exhale their *bouquet*,—men for whom cooks are educated and sauces invented, whose forks come from Potosi and their napkins from Silesia, men who, in our present up-side-down world, stand on that immeasurable height up to which their brother-men gaze with an intensely human longing, and an intensely unchristian sensation,—that predominating eminence, where they are so far above their fellows and the low cares of bread-nourished life, that, without fear of to-morrow, they can to-day spend five to ten francs, and some even twenty or fifty, for a dinner.

To these may be added forty or fifty thousand strangers, permanent and transient; and these are a main stay of the *Restaurants*.

Turning to the left as I issue out of the *rue du Helder* towards six, and walking up the *Boulevard des Italiens* a few hundred yards, I am surrounded by some of the best *Restaurants* of Paris, the *Café de Paris*, the *Maison Dorée*, the *Café Riche*, and on the other side, the *Café Anglais*. At any one of these, at any hour, may be had an impromptu dinner of succulent substantials or of wholesome delicacies, the first course of which will be served, to a man in a hungry hurry, by the time that he has chosen his wine. To-day I disregard their solicitations, and entering the *rue Richelieu* pass under the gateway of No. 112, ascend a short broad stone stairway, and opening a door with the inscription *Cercle de la Conversation*, find myself in the apartment that twenty years ago was widely known as the Frascati gambling-rooms, now occupied by a club, many of whose members are men of letters and artists. Here every day at six a table is laid for twelve or fourteen at three francs and a half, a good French *bourgeois* dinner. Here at a private concert, opened by a witty poem from the spirituel *Mery*, I have heard *Godefroi* on the harp, *Lacombe* on the piano, and *Hermann* on the violin.

This Club deserves its name, being the only one in Paris where there is enough of geniality and of intellectual sociability to create the need of cultivated conversation. In tongue-skirmishing, as in that on the field, the French are rapid and brilliant. Their minds lie near the surface; they dart in and out with a sparkling agility that quickens the wits of all listeners. Just after Lamartine had assumed the control of the journal, *Le Pays*, I asked at dinner a Legitimist opposite (the Legitimists all hate Lamartine)* " Est ce que Monsieur Lamartine a acheté *Le Pays?*" Without the

---

* "Has M. Lamartine bought the *Pays?*"—"No, the *Pays* has bought M. Lamartine."—"Capefigue has a great depth of learning."—"You mean thickness."

pause of a semi-colon he answered, "Non, c'est *Le Pays* qui a acheté M. Lamartine." Some one saying of *Capefigue*, a second-rate historical and political writer, that he had " une grande profondeur de connaissance."—" Vous voulez dire épaisseur," rejoined the same gentleman. I have here heard a French poet conclude a graphic picture of the opening of the battle of Trafalgar by declaring that the signal there thrown out by Nelson,— " England expects every man to do his duty,"—was one of the most sublime incidents in History. I have heard the military infallibility of Napoleon questioned and his tactics criticized, and the pre-eminence of Shakspeare acknowledged. The French have expanded out of their old self-sufficiency; within fifty years they have learnt much from their neighbors and from adversity; from the latter they are just now learning very fast.

Frenchmen are charged with vanity; themselves hardly deny the charge. But this is one cause of their cheerfulness, and of their conversational vivacity; for vanity is a great weaver of cords of connection, which, if not the strongest, are for that the more numerous, and being short and taught, wonderfully enliven superficial personal relations. A man who wishes to attract your regards upon himself, will try to please. That vanity does not necessarily make a man agreeable, and is often a large ingredient in a thoroughly selfish character, we need not go to France to learn. The impulse whereof it is the overgrown fruit, has no root in the heart, it is purely self-seeking; nevertheless, in the composite movement of associated humanity, it plays a functional part To judge of the heart of a Frenchman, or other man, Paris is not a fair place, for nowhere are men more dwarfed by the pressure of the heartless motto of civilized life—" Every man for himself, and God for us all." This is another testimony in favor of the claim of Paris to be the capital of civilization.

It is not far from eight, when, dinner being some time over, I break off from a pleasant after-chat, and take leave of the Club.

—— * I was introduced to this Club by my friend Henry S. Sanford, Secretary of the United States Legation in Paris. An act of personal kindness I should not thus publish, were not so many of his countrymen under like obligations to Mr. Sanford, that an acknowledgment of them here seems not unbecoming, and will, I am sure, be acceptable to hundreds of Americans, who in the past three or four years have profited by his kindly services.

And here let me add a few words in regard to what is expected of American Legations in Europe.

Some citizens of the United States suppose, that their citizenship entitles them in Europe to the acquaintance and attention of the United States envoys. This is a mistake. A diplomatic agent is a public, not a private servant. So long as the American traveller has no complaint against the public authorities for ill-usage (and even then in most cases the Consul is the proper functionary of whom to seek redress), his claim upon the Envoy has no stronger basis than that upon other American residents in foreign capitals. Equally with the private resident, the Envoy retains the right of expanding or contracting his circle of acquaintance, of choosing his companions, according to his taste or his calculations. If, through inclination or policy, he "entertains," from the greater facility of obtaining introduction to a public than to a private person, a large number of his countrymen will be his guests. But his hospitality lies within the bounds of his reserved private domain. Whether he lives "like a hermit," or "like a prince," is of no concern to any but the small circle to whom the closeness or the openness of his house, is a private loss or a private profit. Princely living was wisely not included in the diplomatic duties of American ministers, by those who established

---

* These remarks on American Legations, commenced as a note, have stretched so much beyond the expected length, that I have thought it best to include them in the text.

their salaries, and Americans have, as such, no claims on them for balls, dinners, or cards.

What they have a right to expect from them is, that not only should they in their official business, which is little and intermittent, maintain the rights and interests of the United States,—and this they do; but that also in their daily bearing, their habits, tone, conversation, that is, in their unofficial conduct, which is much and not intermittent, they should uphold the principles to which the United States owe their birth, being, and matchless welfare, the principles of political justice, of civic equality, of republican freedom,—and this they do not.

European diplomatic agents in America set an example, which American diplomatic agents in Europe should follow. With rarely an exception, the representatives of foreign governments resident in this country, are unanimous in their condemnation of our institutions, and of all our democratic principles and processes. These feelings of distaste and of oppugnancy to democracy are not concealed: they need not be. These gentlemen represent monarchies and despotisms: their governments are conducted on principles directly hostile to those which rule us. In their opinions, conversation, habits, they manifest the hostility. Hereby their official relations are in no manner obstructed or embittered. They are true to their masters: we acknowledge and respect their right to be so. They keep themselves as European and aristocratic as they can; nobody objects or takes offence.

Now on the contrary, the American diplomatic agent in Europe, instead of keeping American and republican, is no sooner installed, but he sets about to Europeanize and aristocratize himself as much as he can. He bedaubs his carriage with armorial bearings (if not inherited, *improviséd*); claps livery on his servants; begilds his outside often with more than the official lace;*

---

* A court-dress with modest gold-lace trimmings, is prescribed by our Government. This should be done away with, as being at war with our

finds as many virtues as possible in the royal family where he is accredited; submits to condescensions from his or her Majesty, or Royal Highness, and even feels himself thereby elevated; affects titled society, and with self-gratulation takes the place which his credentials provide for him as a member of the profligate, arrogant, brazen, soulless, godless circle that surrounds every throne in Europe. But for all his obsequiousness, he and his are admitted no further than the outer halls of this Temple of Belial. Aristocracy is always exclusive, scornful, relentless, as close as freemasonry; and to obtain from it the grasp of fellowship, one must have other credentials than those received from the President of a Democracy.

How different, and how much more consistent, is the bearing of a European envoy. He makes no secret of being bored by people and things, public and private, at Washington. So far from seeking virtues in the Executive body, he scans it with satirical malice; he picks as many holes as he can in the character and intellect of our "great men;" he quizzes our fashion; he sneers at our pretension; and when he quits us, he rejoices in his departure as the end of an exile. The offspring of Monarchy and Aristocracy, he detests our politics and hates our people.

The offspring of Democracy, if true in like manner to his birth and breeding, should regard every Christian king as an usurper, every hereditary privilege as a robbery; and in the presence of royalty and nobility, bedizened in court-tinsel, should feel his moral sense offended, just as is the immoral sense of the diplomatic scion of nobility in presence of the sovereign people in America. The citizen of the United States who has not something of this feeling, is a spurious offspring of the Republic. However he may vaunt his republican home, he has not a discerning, logical appreciation of the blessings he is born to, and is

universal usage in civil costume. Our Legations should be ordered to appear at foreign courts in plain ungilded republican dress.

not fit fully to represent this great self-governing country in
prince-ridden Europe. Too many of our envoys have been thus
disqualified; and from the commanding position we have now
reached as the one great Democracy in the world, hostilely arrayed (in sentiment at least) against the despotisms of Europe,—
and the object of their fears, their machinations, their hate,—this
disqualification is become the more discreditable to us, and the
more hurtful to our true interests. The old and the new are face
to face in deadly defiance. We are the new, and whoever represents us in old Europe, should fully feel the nature and significance of this antagonism, and act throughout accordingly.

Instead of living the simple, manly life of hearty republicans,
encompassed but not defiled, by aristocratic carnalities; seeking
intercourse with those who are at once the ornaments and pillars
of a country and the best bonds between their own and other
lands, the men of science and culture, and large sympathies;
breathing encouragement or consolation into the hearts of the
bleeding workers for truth and humanity; instead of this honorable, appropriate, elevated part, which courts by its very heartiness
the representatives of the only great Republic in the world, too
many American legations are false to their high mission, and,
by adopting the thoughts and associations of the implacable foes
of freedom, lower the American name in Europe. Aping and
otherwise flattering haughty aristocrats, who patronize and sneer
at them, and but for the gigantic uplifted arm of Democracy behind, would despise them, they eagerly rush, with the shallow
and the idle, into the whirl of oligarchic fashion, and there circle
round on the outskirts of the dance of frivolity and vanity, until
too soon a change of administration sounds the knell of their recall; when, sighing over the loss of so many Lords, Counts, and
Barons, with whom they have sipped champagne and nibbled
boned turkey, and sighing still deeper to think, that in exchange
for these beribboned and betitled Dons, their associates henceforth

are to be militia Colonels and county court Judges, they sadly return home to hog and homony, or pork and molasses.

Leaving the Club,* I drive far up the *Boulevard Poissonnière*, and then turning into a street to the right soon alight at a Café. To one familiar with Cafés on the Boulevards, the plainness of furniture is all that is at first noticeable. There is the usual sprinkling of small tables, brilliant gas-light, and on one side of a long room, the raised desk where presides the universal feminine Divinity, who fingers the cash and deals out sugar and orders. But on calling for beer and segars, to pay for entrance, we find cut on the glasses a red triangle, emblematic of the tripple-phrased republican device. It is a cheap democratic Café where mechanics and laborers meet in the evening for dominos and gossip, and where for a few sous they get a glass of wine or beer with tobacco. This is one of the *salons* of the poor. There are to-day not many visitors, and so after putting into the box, modestly presented by the waiter, a small contribution for imprisoned and exiled democrats, my companion and I withdraw.—In the *marais*, a quarter in the direction of the Faubourg St. Antoine, we alight at another. Here in one large hall are ten billiard tables, nearly all occupied. The players are probably small clerks, journeymen-tailors, and others, whose sedentary vocations earning for them from three to five francs a day, they come here to buy an hour's exercise with that portion of their incomes which continental people, rich and poor, appropriate to amusement. Round the best players are groups of pipe-smoking spectators, and dominos are clattering in other parts of the hall. There is nothing boisterous or rude; an air even of refinement pervades the place. The inmates seem to be thankfully enjoying a rest after the day's work.

* The name and composition of this Club have since been changed, it being now called *Cercle des deux Mondes*, and counting among its members a large number of Americans.

—— It is past nine, when having driven back down the Boulevards, I enter the *Théâtre des Variétés*, and take possession of a *stalle d'orchestre* with that pleasant cachinnatory expectation wherewith one seats oneself in a Parisian Comic Theatre.

Flanked by Music and Painting the Histrionic Art here assails the spectator with batteries of fun and pleasantry. The *Théâtre Français*, where Molière and Corneille, and the Opera, where Mozart and Bellini preside, live in the high region of æsthetics. But the *Variétés* and its kindred are mostly in their aims too superficial to reach the æsthetic sphere. They deal with facts not with feelings; and their facts are from that omnivorous but uninspired receptacle, the absurd. Though not themselves expressing the profound, their representations have depth of significance. Just beneath the surface where the ridiculous plays its antics, lies a ground of seriousness and sadness. The fantastic figures of the Comic are at times but the flickering flames that shoot through the crust from an intense tragic fire that consumes the core. The absurd is the child of the illogical. The nonconformity to reason and divine law in the fundamental relations of men causes the discords and complications out of which the comic spins its motley web. The truth of comedy is often a demonstration of the falsehood of sober life. Many a spectator here joins in the laugh at a sally, whose piquancy is the crack of the whip wherewith his domestic peace is lashed to death.

At these theatres three or four pieces are given. When the Parisian *Bourgeois* pays for a box, he wishes to spend in it the whole evening, and a long one. The second piece was nearly over when I entered. The third, the beginning whereof was not very sprightly, had proceeded half an hour, when a sudden roar in my ears made me start:—I had fallen asleep, and an electric burst of merriment had waked me. I strove hard to keep my ears alert for the next *double entendre*, but my eyes refusing to back them, I retreated, with the reflection, that a theatre is not the place for one who has worked hard all day. The crowd that I left so wide awake and in a mood so susceptible to fun, had risen late and worked by routine, or not at all.

My day was ended, whether I would or not.

CHAPTER XIX.

A WALK IN THE LOUVRE.

To-day, the 26th of July, 1851, I will take one of my last walks in the Louvre.

Cane or umbrella you surrender in the vestibule, in the basement dedicated to ancient sculpture. Marble walls, marble columns, marble floor, marble statues in spacious lofty halls, overtopped by a palace and enfolded by four feet depth of stone. Here is a Temple consecrated to coolness. The dog-days stay outside with the umbrellas. Correspondent to the physical temperature, the moral air is sedative. A man enraged would quickly subside here : before these empedestalled ghosts he would be ashamed of heat. But you are not depressed, you are tranquillized, you are elevated. Sculpture is serious, not sad ; ideal, not servile. The silence, whiteness, solidity, induce meditation. The calm of these figures imparts itself to the beholder ; their pensiveness is catching. They stand circumfused, and you with them, by the atmosphere of the world's early days. Vivid and youthful they come from the dim, dead past. They have the weight and dignity of age without its weakness. They are fresh from the heart of Antiquity.

I always go first right through to the Gladiator. For two thousand years those marble limbs have glowed with the splendor of the perfect manly form. In presence of the living human body in this marvellous completeness, your delight in its power, and beauty almost passes into awe ; and then, the intensity of sensation is relieved by thoughts on the power and beauty of the human mind that could thus reproduce its own body.

Art is a projection of man out of himself, under the momentum of an effort to appease his yearning for beauty. This creative warmth, when it results, as in this great sculpture, in the reproduction of nature in her selectest proportions and expressions, implies mental elevation and intensity. High Art is the offspring of the craving for perfection—a most noble parentage.

Close by is the Venus of Milo, mutilated of the arms, in whose erect body, sinking as it were into itself, there is as much sleeping strength as voluptuousness. In the head and face, and especially in the mouth, is a world of power. And herein this Venus is higher and truer than the famed one of Cleomenes in the Tribune at Florence. It is a degradation of divine love to present its ideal in a rich body with a poor mental organization. This is to shorten its wings, to materialize its flame, to sensualize it too much. Where the head is so small, as in the statue of the Tribune, all the passions are limited, straitened, belittled. There is no channel for the voluminous flood of love, for its exuberant ardors, no scope for a wide play of its kindling influence, for its deep impregnation of the whole large being with its fire. That it be unfolded in its full richness, it should inflame a glowing strong nature, such as is indicated by this head of the Louvre. In that wealthy mouth there is capacity for more than one passion, and the one that predominates is by this opulence ennobled.

What is the source of the unique perfection in the Grecian type of head ? It is, that the brain—itself well proportioned—has generated the face. All the features are finely married to one another and to the forehead. The Grecian face is subordinated to the forehead. Thus the nose is a continuation of the line of the brow, from which it has the air of being directly descended. A Grecian nose pre-supposes a good brow.

The mouth and chin are predominated by the nose ; they neither coarsely project nor weakly retreat. The same with the cheek bones, which are kept back by the intellectual, sensuous superiorities of the forehead, nose and eyes. To say that, in a word, all the parts of head and face are in harmony, were not enough ; for the essence of the Greek ideal is a harmony growing out of the dominance of the superior parts. The Grecian face is not of necessity eminently intellectual, but it cannot be animal. There may be harmony out of the Grecian type, as there may be and is great beauty without prevalence of the Grecian characteristics.

In the Grecian ideal the brow, the lower range of the forehead, is always full, the Greek mind being highly sensuous. In heads and faces the furthest removed from the Greek type, there is no subordination of face to forehead, and no smooth union among the features, nor between them and the brow. Cheek-bones are prominent, or nose and chin independent, or nose is scornful of its neighbors, acknowledging no pre-eminence in the forehead above it, making between itself and the brow a chasm over which it petulantly leaps without the aid of a bridge, or springing out conceitedly from the rest of the face and going on its own hook.

The renowned Diana, sister of the Apollo Belvidere, is here ; but the warm mood which one brings from the Venus is not that most favorable to appreciating the cold beauty of the man-shunning goddess. So, amid marbles less divinely touched, we will pass on to the stairway that leads to the galleries above.

Architecture holds out her magnificent jewelled hand to conduct us from the halls of sculpture to those of painting. The ascent of this grand stairway is an enjoyment like that of gazing at a sculptured or painted masterpiece.

Crossing the graceful, enmarbled Rotunda, at the head of the stairway, we traverse a gorgeous hall more than one hundred feet long, where decorative art has lavished its wealth of gildings and mouldings, and from whose upper end we issue directly into the great octagon room, on the lofty walls whereof are piled up many of the masterpieces of the collection, choice works of the columnar men of Art. Here we cannot now tarry ; this is to be the luxurious dessert of our day's feast ; so, walking resolutely through this treasure-house, we enter the long gallery, which, being arranged chronologically, opens with the painters of the 14th and 15th centuries, whose greatest merit it is that they were the predecessors and teachers of Leonardo and Raphael. Had they not had such followers, their works would have been unknown. The light from the creations of their great pupils draws them out of darkness. Due honor to them as having made the dawn of an unequalled meridian splendor ; but we have not now come to study the development of the art, but to enjoy the products of its ripeness.

In our walk we shall stop before those that in frequent visits have oftenest arrested us ; not learnedly to comment on them, but to yield ourselves to the sentiment they awaken, attempting at most to account for the impression made on us, without aiming at critical precision or technical accuracy. Some of unquestionable excellence we shall pass by, and where we do pause, we shall not always have the most words for those we most prize. We go down on the right side.

In the Fine Arts a sentiment, or incident, or person, or passion, must be conveyed into the mind by beauty. If it has not beauty for its vehicle it does not reach the inmost soul, but rests for a time near the surface, whence it is soon effaced. Only in the beautiful is the divine idea vividly present, and therefore only by the beautiful is the human soul deeply wrought and fertilized. To feel this, first stop before this youthful head by the great Leonardo da Vinci, with auburn tresses thickly matted. Without deadening, three centuries have shadowed that beaming brow. Your admiring gaze is met by clear, full, soul-softened eyes. Through a rich smile the closed ample mouth speaks joy, which the eyes second. The up-pointing finger leads your eye to a thin, dim cross held in the other hand, and tells you that you are looking at St. John, whom, but for this emblem you would have taken for a paragon woman, so womanly are the head and face in their contour, benignant expression, and superlative beauty. Drink deeply of this countenance, and carry away as much of it as you can; the whole Empire of Art offers scarcely anything more inspired.

Here is Francis I., by Titian. The large sensuous, sensual head of the luxurious King is in profile, and you at once perceive that this was the best view of him, as it always is of a man of his organization and temperament. This head is charged with electricity; it scintillates with life.

By the side of another superb portrait of Titian is the head of Tintoret, by himself, earnest, grizzly, vigorous.

Artists being the servants of Beauty, which is the twin-sister of Hope, should be hopeful when saddest: they should be optimists. Tragic subjects treated in this transfiguring spirit are rare. Hence I avoid Crucifixions; but it is impossible to pass this small one by Paul Veronese, it stands out in such ghastly clearness against that sickly sky. Only strong genius is equal to this awful theme, so that by the grandeur of the treatment Art bemasters the tragic with the sublime. Even the great Rubens hardly does this; his Crucifixion in the Museum at Antwerp is too terrific. His masterpiece is the Descent from the cross, by some deemed the masterpiece of the world. In a Descent, the agony being over, the heart is not lacerated, and yet the whole feeling of the divine tragedy is brought home.

Venus and Mars, with attendant Cupids, by Lucca Giordano. This little picture is buoyed up by the warmth of its coloring; it seems almost to float on the air. Mark the little Cupids, one of them with a dog, how intent they are on their own play, as if their work was done, and they were taking a holiday.

Cast a glance at the Canalettos and Guardis, with whom canal and ivory, marble and water, fluid and solid, are but accessories to exhibit the transparence of a Venitian atmosphere.

We have arrived at the Holy Family, by Murillo, before which we would fain distend our faculty of admiration. The mother is seated, the child Jesus standing on her knee, taking hold of the cross held by the child St. John below, the lamb is on the ground before St. John's feet, the dove over the head of Jesus, and the Father is bending over all from the clouds in an attitude of love and benediction. A rosy freshness with harmony of color, perfect grouping, and an expression from the whole of religious serenity and holy sweetness, hold you before this picture in a state which proves to you the exalting power of Art. The absence of a shining ideal in the heads is made up for by depth of feeling, simplicity, naturalness, and grace.

Hanging next it is a landscape by Collantes, full of Southern richness and Spanish passion.

Here is a Salvator Rosa that would whet an assassin's lust for blood. I don't mean the grand battle-piece, but the stormy landscape, the rock-fronted desolation, with corseletted bandits perched on a precipice.

Walk on until you are stopped by the light which breaks as through a window, from a Holy Family resting in their flight by Albani. Not the first one, but the second, No. 6. [In the first one, No. 5, the landscape is the best.] Winged Angels are offering flowers to the Child, who leans forward from his mother's lap to take them. The landscape looks illuminated by the holy travellers. The figures are wrought with miniature fineness, without weakness. Two Cherubs flying down with a basket of flowers, is a picture within a picture.

We are now in the Rubens' Gallery. This series of colossal canvas exhibits the boundless conception and invention of Rubens. But his hands could not gather up all the wealth that his brain shook down.

Teniers exemplifies the force of truth. Vividly reproduce Nature in full moments, and without your seeking it the electric light of beauty will radiate from your canvas. The Temptation of the Anchorite is such a picture as Burns would have painted, had he worked with pencil. It is sparkling with strength and fun. And so brilliantly executed, such a transparency of light and shade, such reality and vivacity of comic effects. The bearded head of the Anchorite is grand.

Gerard Dow, Ostade, Mieris, express the delight there is in the artistic reproduction of simple, homely objects. With them, Art concentrates itself into microscopic fidelity. But there is something more than this. Look at the Seller of game, by Mieris; it is ideal as well as real, so select is each object, and wrought with such fineness of texture, which fineness is itself a phasis of the beautiful.

At the end of this compartment are the Vandykes. The best one is on the other side. If you wish to be spoken to by a picture, put yourself face to face with the portrait next to the column, the gentleman with open collar and dark velvet doublet.

Before coming upon Wouvermans, there is a single Moucheron, a strip of French elegant rurality, with vases and an orange sky, a glorious segment cut out by genius from Nature's wide landscape.

Two Boths, with skies that are active with life. Whoso can paint the air in motion with sun in it is a master of landscape. That is the key; the rest may by many be acquired; that is the gift. In a picture, as in nature, good air is the first necessary; it vitalizes each tiniest part.

A few steps further is a small Heus, a gem of tone, color, delicacy and truth; warm and happy.

Here is a Cuyp, with shepherds and cows, which warms the whole of the broad canvas it covers. It has the virtue of cheerfulness.

Then we have a wealth of Ruysdaels, Van Bergens, and one Hobbema,* who is the painter of coolness. The Van Bergen next to it glows in contrast with pleasant summer heat.

We pass a number of good Dujardins to get to the better Berghems. There are eight or nine of them, all with sleek cattle and shepherdesses, and all full of health and content. Cattle tell of home and sufficiency. We like to see them thus honored by Art; it pays part of our debt to them.

Amid them is a large Wynants, strong enough to stand its ground in such proximity. Let us not overlook a Vintrank over the last Berghem. It is a sample of modest merit.

We have reached the French department, beginning with a long line of landscapes by Poussin. His pictures want freedom and lightness, and especially they want atmosphere, whereby their grace of composition is blurred. He has been called the learned Poussin. He could never be called the inspired. His pictures are faded; and even the cheerful subjects have a sad look.

The glory of French art is Claude Lorrain, the lustrous, as he might be termed. He has visited the sun, and brought away the secret of its light. His pictures are heated by so natural a fervor, that it seems supernatural. It looks not like art, but intuition. But besides this there is an unfading grace in his forms, whether of hill, tree, bridge or building. His water is luminous.

Go to the end of the gallery for the sake of a head by Lefevre. In this head is the mystery of all great portraits. The features and flesh are transparent, by means of a light burning within, which makes the blood tingle to the surface.

We have walked fourteen hundred feet in a straight line; we will return on the other side.

Pass the long, stiff, uniform regiment of lifeless Lesueurs, and

---

* My friend, Thomas J. Bryan, of Philadelphia, for many years a resident of Paris, has in his collection a Hobbema of higher quality than this one.

only stop for a moment before a head by Ferdinand Bol, in which students of Harvard of a quarter of a century back will recognize good President Kirkland energized.

A few steps further is the exquisite Vanderfelde, an evening cattle-piece, with the purple-tinted sky reflected in the glassy water.

We skip a long file to get to a portrait before which I always linger longer than before any other in the Louvre, No. 389, by Phillipe de Champagne. The lips are slightly parted, for there is more life within than could be supported by breathing through one inlet. From the polish on the hair to the dew of the eye, there is everywhere inflation of life. The flesh has the pulpy look that belongs to an in-door man, and the transparent hand knows of no rough handlings. Pause here still to wonder at the vivifying power there is in the fingers of man when moved by a genial brain.

Next we have three landscapes by Pynaker, three graces. Here are skies as warm and lively as Claude Lorrain's; not so dazzling, because freshened by more northern clouds and less expansive. Every object is rounded by the mellow ripening air. Clover is growing sweeter every hour, and peaches more juicy. The distances are as true as an Indian's sight.

Stop before a fruit-piece by Mignon, the one with the melon and the red Indian corn, and the summer ripeness and luxuriance. To judge from a glimpse we get through a leaf-darkened arch, the landscape beyond is fine, but is shut out by overgrowth of August foliage.

Six naked children dancing in a ring, hand in hand, to music by a maiden on a triangle, by Giraud de Lairesse. The treatment is not equal to the conception and composition, and to the sensibility denoted by the choice of subject.

Three landscapes by Asselyn, which might serve as pendants to those of Pynaker.

Next to these is a nest of Poelembergs, who should be styled the pearly. A practised discernment might, one would think, in the characteristics of the work, detect those of the artist. Yet the engraved portrait of Poelemberg is not at all wanting in boldness and virility, while his pictures look as though the hand that painted them had been as soft as that of a petted woman.

I am not attracted by architectural pictures, but I cannot pass by Pannini's interior of St. Peter's at Rome, painted on a canvas about seven feet by five. The elevation, the vastness, the richness, the spaciousness, the play of light through gigantic arches, the grandeur and gorgeousness of the marble world, all is there.

It is wearing late, and the large hall awaits us. We must hasten by the Carraccis and the Guidos, the tears in the eyes of whose upturned feminine faces are drops distilled from the serenest depths of Heaven. But here is a countenance we can never pass without a greeting. Look at that youthful, mild, thoughtful, beardless, beautiful, womanly, profound face. Coleridge somewhere says that high poetic genius is largely feminine. The mind of universal sympathies has twofold elements. The type and exponent of humanity, it partakes of woman's as well as man's nature. The truth of this is exemplified in the picture before us, and in the character of him of whom it is the portrait. It is that of the youthful Raphael, .

—— that beaming face,
Where intellect is wed to grace.

Now we are back to the octagon Hall, seated before the vast renowned Paul Veronese, the Feast of Cana. This picture represents not a solemn miracle, but a pleasant festival; it is agreeable, not great. Its merits are in coloring and individualities; as a whole it is prosaic. Neither the head nor the position of Jesus is predominant. But for the glory, it would hardly be recognized. The foreground is filled by the musicians, who should be nowhere visible. The two wings of the table pull the eyes from one to the other across the wide canvas. In a sacred subject such gross anachronisms of costume and architecture are not allowable. Take away the Christ, and the picture becomes more satisfactory. It has not the elevation and holiness which that subduing presence should shed, whatever the subject.

Two hours of standing and walking, with eyes and brain stretched before scores of differing mind-moving objects, drain the nervous reservoir. It has just replenished itself by a delicious slumber of twenty minutes, whereto the deep, springy, soft-backed ottoman was accessory. A day-sleep I never enjoyed more than this, and rise up re-animated to finish my grateful task.

The master is shown by the selection of subjects, and then by his mastery in treatment over a good choice. Capability of grace is the highest test of a pictorial subject. The artist having the insight and sensibility to appreciate this test, his next step is to make the most of this capability in his execution. Look at the Correggio on the left of the Supper of Cana. Here is grace in forms, in attitude, in grouping, in expression.

Beauty does not necessarily involve grace. Grace is the matrix of beauty, but the offspring sometimes neglects the parent. Grace is the finer essence, an emanation or a movement which is more than corporeal beauty. "The beautiful," says Plato, "is the splendor of the true." The graceful may be called the spirit of the beautiful. Grace is always beautiful, but beauty is not always graceful.

Contrast with this divine Correggio the Giorgione next to it. Those two nude female figures look as though they had been fatted for roasting.

Talent cannot reveal, it can only perceive what is already revealed; new things it invests with old forms. Genius not only reveals, but to old things it gives a new face. See that Raphael, the winged St. Michael descending, spear-pointed, upon the prostrated Devil. Here is grandeur magnified, simplicity ennobled, by grace. What lightness in the down-flashing angel, and at the same time what power; how strength is spiritualized by beauty. The wings here give impetus to the blow. Wings help a descending figure; but when the figure ascends, their inadequacy to lift the human body will mingle in and weaken the effect. The wings idealize the combat, which without them would be prosaic, like all combats, the which are therefore subordinate subjects of Art. The cultivated sensibility, which in health rejects real horrors, digests easily the factitious when handled in this style. In Raphael as in Shakspeare instinct and judgment work together.

The Correggio opposite, Antiope and Jupiter in form of a satyr, with its glittering beauty in the head and limbs of Antiope, falls short of perfection from the ungraceful foreshortened position of the body.

The comic dispenses with grace, or rather it veils it with a playful mask. In the corner is an Ostade, wherein is more of the comic than probably the artist intended. It is a schoolroom, with urchins at anything but their books, and presents a quiet rich contrast between pedagogy and nature, between compulsion and liberty, the teacher being the most compelled. What transparence, individuality, reality. The light goes into every corner, and the shadows too are everywhere. You can measure the dimensions of the room.

Further to the left is a Solario, a Mother suckling her child, before the which you can commit no extravagance of praise, such a clustering of beauties is there. You think the mother's face the most beautiful you ever saw, so beaming is it with maternal joy. Then fix your look on the infant, holding, in the playful fulness of life, one foot in his hand. After you have wondered at the creative efficacy of Art, cap your admiration with a gaze into his half-closed eye. I know not what is the judgment of traditional criticism on this picture, but to me it is one of the master-works of the Louvre.

We pass a female head of Rembrandt, glowing in the golden mist that he steeps his heads in, and pause before a Raphael beside it, another maternal incarnation, and we let the breath of genius inflate enthusiasm till it floods. Here is a rainbow of expression whose feet are the countenances of the ecstatic St. John and the sleeping child, and its arch that of the benignant mother.

Next is another woman. But here is no deep emotion inspiring the countenance. There is no sparkling flush of feeling on the surface. The soul is not out on the face, it sleeps behind. Gaze, and you will become aware of it, and at the same time not wish it more revealed. The power of beauty here suffices; its excess is its inspiration. Anything more were too much, and would overcome the artist. This is beauty in its calm splendor, in its dazzling ripeness. It is " Titian's Mistress."

Beauty in Art, itself the highest artistic creation, is in turn creative, inbreeding in the beholder new thoughts, dilating him into a higher, happier susceptibility.

CHAPTER XX.

FRAGMENTS.

In one of the "Latter Day Pamphlets," Mr. Carlyle asks tauntingly, what have the Americans done?—We have abolished Monarchy, we have abolished Aristocracy; we have sundered Church and State; we have so wrought with our English inheritance, that most Englishmen better their condition by quitting the old home and coming to the new. We have consolidated a State, under whose disinterested guardianship the cabined and straitened of the old world find enlargement and prosperity. We have suppressed standing armies; we have decentralized government to an extent that before our experiment was deemed hopeless; we have grown with such a dream-like rapidity, as to stand, after little more than a half-century of national existence, prominent on the earth among the nations; and this, through the wisdom of political organization, whereby such scope is given to industry and invention, that not only are our native means profitably developed, but the great influx of Europeans is healthfully absorbed. We have in fifty years put between the Atlantic and the Pacific an Empire of twenty-five millions, who work more than any twenty-five millions on earth, and read more than any other fifty millions. We have built a State at once so solid and flexible, that it protects all without oppressing any. Our land is a hope and a refuge to the king-crushed laborers of Europe, and from the eminence above all other lands to which it has ascended, by our forecast, vigor, and freedom, it is to the thinker a demonstration of the upward movement of Christendom, and a justification of hopes that look to still higher elevations.

Mr. Carlyle's sneers at our lack of heroism would be unworthy of him, from their very silliness, were they not more so from their sour injustice. Let any People recite its heroic deeds, on flood or field, since we were a nation, and we will match every one of them. And in the private sphere, where self-sacrifice, devotion, courage, find such scope for heroic virtues, our social life is warm with them. But this is no theme for words. For his unworthy ones, we deem well enough of Mr. Carlyle to believe, that, when disengaged from the morbidly subjective, and therefore blinding and demoralizing moods, to which he is liable, he is ashamed of having printed them. It looks somewhat as though this passage had been written just to give us an opportunity of victorious retort, or to tempt us into an exhibition of our national propensity to brag,—a propensity, be it said, which is national in every nation we know anything of, whether English, French, German, or Italian. We only beat them in bragging, just as we beat them in ploughs and statues, in clippers and steamboats, in whalemen and electric telegraphs, in cheap newspapers and cheap government. They all do their best at bragging, and so do we,—and we beat them.

The mummies of Egypt are a type of conservatism,—a childish effort to perpetuate corporeal bulk, to eternize the perishable, to subordinate essence to form, to deny death. The result is a mummy.

It were hard to say, whether in this "villainous world" there is more of malignant censure, or of unclean praise.

Hereditary aristocrats are puppets to whom motion is imparted by wires, inserted under ground into the dead bones of their fore-fathers.

In England, money is the only means wherewith to get what is called a "good education." The best is poor enough, to be sure. For want of culture, the minds and souls of the masses stagnate in a brutish obscurity, or blindly stir in a chaotic twilight. Thus are the noblest and highest faculties in man dependent for their unfolding and growth, on gold,—gold, which in our present society, is ever obtained by accident, by self-immolation, or by fraud. The treasure of God is in the keeping of Mammon.—With us, public schools greatly assuage this evil.

In civilized life,—which is a universal battle,—truth forms the reserve, and is only brought up at critical junctures.

There are spiritual egotists, people who self-complacently assume to be the elected of God. The humility of such is a weed nourished in the rank soil of pride; their belief is mostly an induration on the fancy of a shallow nature.

Many of the self-righteous are not only proud of their supposed nearness to God, but assume towards him patronizing airs; so monstrous are the effects of pride in combination with religion.

Music is a marriage of the sensual with the spiritual. Each is merged in the other. In perfect harmony there will be neither sensual nor spiritual, but the two will be made one in the fulness of life and purity.

One has at times the desire to cast away one's personality, with all the petty memories and imaginations that cling around self, and to bound off into the empyrium of the Universal. Thus disencumbered, the Intellect and Soul might make great discoveries. Is not this the secret of the far-seeing glances of some of the mesmerized, that they are emancipated from the bonds of self, and for the time lifted out of the obscurities of fleshly life, into the translucent sphere of the disembodied?

Galileo calls doubt the father of inventions.

The practical might imparted by integrity is seldom fully valued. Hence Washington is underrated by some men, who judge him by his intellect and prudence.

Our habitation, the Earth, is not self-subsisting; it moves in dependence on a heavenly body far distant. The Sun's light helps to feed the breath of our bodies; and shall we from the soil beneath our feet, from the dust into which our bodies dissolve, draw the breath of our souls? If millions of miles off is one of the chief sustainers of our flesh, where should we look for the source of the spirit we feel within us?

When a man's conversation consists chiefly of reminiscence, he may be said to talk backwards.

People in high places who are not beneficent, are out of place on an elevation.

When there have been great examples of virtue, revealing the capabilities of human nature, crime in the powerful is more criminal than in earlier inexperienced times. The selfishness of Napoleon is more repugnant than that of Cæsar.

In many cases when people speak of their conscience, conceit is mistaken for conscience

When man is young, the whence he is and the mysteriousness of his being possess his nascent thoughts. Later, he occupies himself about the object and ends of his existence. Hence the religious dreams of nations in their youth ; and the philosophies of nations that are cultivated.

———

Preaching is in these days not unlike shovelling sand with a pitchfork.

———

Men whose masterly vigor was the servant of expediency not of principle, self-seekers not truth-seekers, liars in act and in thought, were Cromwell and Bonaparte.

———

The Hebrews mounted to the idea of unity ; but their God was revengeful, " a jealous God," and therefore false and sub-human.

The Greeks were more intellectual and much more æsthetic than the Hebrews ; yet one cannot conceive of Christianity originating in polytheistic Greece, it could only spring up in monotheistic Judea.

———

To the opinions and creeds they have received from their fathers men hold as to the houses and lands they have inherited. Conservatism is a sort of materialism, men confounding the spiritual with the material, and treating him who takes away their opinions like him who steals their cattle ; in their density not perceiving that, instead of a theft, the destruction of their opinions is a barter whereby they may gain a hundred-fold. Thoughts are subject to higher laws than things.

———

Beliefs imply non-beliefs. Creeds are compounded mainly of negations.

———

The remedy for England is to turn, not her waste lands to use, but her waste mind, her waste intellect and feeling. This, the most precious domain she possesses, is half tilled in patches.

Good rhetoric is a good thing in a good cause.

By continuous breach of the moral law, men forfeit mental growth. Napoleon and Cromwell grew not wiser as they grew older. Their minds did not ripen, they petrified.

On the Continent of Europe it looks as though government had been made first, and man afterwards.

The great recent discoveries of Gall, of Fourier, of Priesnitz, all combine to make apparent the resources, the incalculable vigors, the inborn sufficiency of man.

In England so many people look as though they were waiting for my lord.

That with all the mind's achievements, practical and poetical, its conquests in science, its Christian and intellectual development, its many enlargements and emancipations, there still should be so much evil, so much misery, proves how wide a swing mankind must make to fulfil its destiny. Hereby are denoted opulence, and depth, and complexity of power.

In this light, evil is a whip to urge moral effort up to high tension. Society perfects itself through tribulation. Man may be figured as at first lying in the low places of life, with but dim sparse glimmerings into upper fields. Out of a night of animal being, little by little he struggles into the day of a wider humanity, his struggles getting fiercer as he rises. As feeling and thought unfold themselves, his inward conflicts grow warmer and deeper. The grandeurs of his nature loom out as much in endurance as in action. The terrible, the pathetic, the sublime, are the great offspring of his throes, the tokens of his splendor and his resources. Through this stormy region, darkened by chasms and abysses, he ascends to one more serene, where, under influences wrought out by his higher self, he breathes an atmosphere predominated by spiritual elements. He grows in intellect by working with Nature in her richest fields; and with his heart purified by beauty, and enlarged and strengthened into freer communion with God, he attains at last to a blessed activity, a creative calm.

Shakspeare's words, when boldest and richest, are but ambassadors, behind whom there is a greater than themselves. Racine's and Afieri's, though not so erect and gorgeous, are the Kings themselves, and thus leave nothing untold, and feed not the imagination.

To see things as they are, one must have sympathy with the Spirit of God, whence all things come. Then can be discerned to what degree there is remoteness from original design, and thus actual conditions be rightly judged.

In the style of Shakspeare there is an oceanic undulation. In that of Corneille and Racine the surface is level, or if broken, it is with furrows, not with billows.

In poetry, much of the meaning is conveyed by the sound. Transpose the words of a fine passage, and you impair its import.

You may gather a rainbow out of one of Rubens's great pictures.

A sonnet should be like a spring, in being clear and deep in proportion to its surface; and like a whirlpool, in a certain silent self-involved movement.

The mind is defiled that comments habitually on the vices of others. One that is undefiled, cannot long endure the fumes that arise from the stirring of moral filth.

When a man readily gives ear to a calumny, he betrays fellow-feeling with the malignity whence it sprang.

Forms soon waste the substance they are designed to hold. Thus ceremony and hypocritical corporeal salutations get to be a substitute for genuine politeness; religion is crushed under a burthen of ritual observances; paper-money drives out metal, to represent which, it was invented.

Some of Wordsworth's poetry is, like his person, too gaunt; it wants a fuller clothing of flesh.

Many of the old monasteries were founded by repentant reprobates; and the early sins of their founders seem to have borne fuller crops, than their latter virtues.

Every now and then a woman sallies boldly into our territory; as if she wanted to make reprisals on the tailors.

When you build selfishly, you build frailly. When your acts are hostile to the broad interests of your fellow-men, they are seed which will one day come up weeds, to choke your own harvest-field.

A man with wounded feelings walks into the country, and there the perfumes and sweet aspects of Nature accost his heart with consolation.

Rhymes should sit as lightly on verse, as flowers on plants.

Poetry is not put into verse to please the ear; it is in verse because it is the offspring of a spirit akin to that which dwells ever in hearing of the music of the spheres. To poetry, rhythm is as natural, as symmetry to a beautiful face. Genuine verse pleases the ear, because like the voice of childhood or of woman, it is in itself delightful. The setting sun, a lively landscape, a noble deed, give pleasure, because they speak to and are in harmony with our higher being; and so is poetry, and therefore it too gives pleasure. But to say, that the object of poetry is to give pleasure, is to rank it with the shallow inventions of the showman.

In the drama, the incidents should all grow out of the characters. Individual characterization is the mystery of the drama. He who does not unlock this mystery, fails to achieve a genuine drama, whatever may be his other excellencies.

The strong genius who rules, as strong genius always does, his fellows, feeds them from the common springs of humanity, with evil or with good, through the vast channels of his own mind. If himself evil, the evil of his time sways his contemporaries through him. Into himself he collects the black vapors of falsehood, and blasts them forth over the world or his country, with a tempestuous power, before which the good and the true shrink for a time into privacy and silence. But what he does, however stupendous, lacks life; for evil cannot create, it can only obstruct or arrest creative good.

The poet is the pupil of truth; for the false can never be poetry.

The dramatic writer, says Lessing, as his production is to be seen as well as heard, is somewhat under the restrictions of the painter.

Lessing, who may almost be called the father of modern criticism, thinks that the chief cause of the inferiority of the Romans in tragedy, was their gladiatorial combats. In the words of De Quincey, who has adopted this opinion, "the amphitheatre extinguished the theatre."

In sunny, fruitful, populous Italy, naught is so alive as the voice of the long-dead Dante. Sick at heart, the Italian, prince-ridden and priest-ridden, goes to his home, saddened by the execution, or imprisonment, or exile of a son or brother, and there, to fly from the present, he opens his Dante;—and soon his pulse beats strong again, and his eye glistens, and he gains assurance of his own manhood, and he hopes and he dares.

Where in English Prose is there a diction so copious, apt, forceful, as Carlyle's, at once so transparent with poetic light and so compact with a home-driving, idiomatic solidity, doing the errand of a thoughtful fervent nature with such fulness and emphasis?

Possibly the mind cannot, in its most far-piercing imaginations, outrun its capabilities. Were it a law of being, that the brightest flowers, unfolded in the sun of the heart's warmest day-dreams, contain the seeds of substantial realities?

Just ideas are the only source of healthy moral life; by them are institutions moulded, and to uphold institutions which ideas have outgrown, is to be destructive, not conservative. They are the highest benefactors of their race who can discern and apply the deepest ideas; and thus the boldest reformer may be the truest conservative.

The Greeks and the English seem to be the only two nations possessing enough sap and vigor and fulness of nature, to reproduce themselves in distant soils, through colonists that swarmed off from the parent hive.

What power there is in belief, and what power in falsehood, in our sensual organization of society, that sinful, semi-pagan Rome is still the so-called spiritual head of the half of Christendom.

———

In Italy the living is clewed to the dead : the carcass of the past lies athwart the legs of the present.

———

The increasing delight in Natural Scenery is one of the proofs that man is growing nearer to God.

———

We talk of this man's style and that man's, when, rightly speaking, neither of them has a style. Style implies a substantial body of self-evolved thought. The mode and quality of the clothing in words and phrases to this original body constitutes style. Now, from so few minds come fresh emanations, that most writings are but old matter re-worded, current thought re-dressed. Each one's individual mode of re-wording and re-dressing is, and should be called, his *manner*, not his *style*. In Writing as in Painting, every man, the weakest as well as the strongest, must have a manner, but few can have a style.

———

To be sought and cherished is the man whose mind is too large to be filled by creeds and systems, and too generous to close itself against any wants of humanity. The mental home of the true man is among principles, and principles are infinitely expansive.

———

People nominally worship God one day in the week, and really worship Mammon seven.

———

The grand and sublime are in the exuberance of rudimental energy. Heaving and glowing with creative power, they stand apart, too stern to coalesce, too overbearing for harmony. They are Strength not yet married to Grace. Hence they generally precede the beautiful. Phidias came before Praxitiles, Michael Angelo before Raphael, Æschylus before Sophocles.

1st Boy (tauntingly). Who was that man with your father?
2d Boy. That man's worth more than your father.
1st Boy. He was drunk, anyhow.
2d Boy. He's worth two houses.
1st Boy (worsted). Ho, I guess my father's worth two houses, too. (Street dialogue, Newport, R. I., Jan. 26, 1848.)

St. Augustine calls Homer, "Sweet liar."

The Bible should be studied with activity of spirit. Its great heart will not beat but to the throbbing of yours. Just to read it passively, traditionally, dulls the very susceptibility through which it is to be taken in. Not thus will you find God in the Bible. Who has not first sought him in his own heart and in the life around him, will scarcely find him there at all. God is not locked up in the Bible: he is at all times around, within us. Strive with Jesus to feel his presence. Then you may hope for purification, for inspiration: then your heart may produce biblical chapters. For what is in the Bible came out of the human soul, touched to inspired utterances by the awakened inward divinity.

The Priests of Rome discourage intercourse with God through the Bible, which is already at one remove. Themselves they constitute the sole interpreters of the divine, the sole medium of communication between God and man. The divine essence they would first distil through the foul alembic of their brazen egotism. Hence, where they long dominate, religion becomes materialized, and for uplifting, soul-purging knowledge of God, is substituted abasing, sensual submission to priesthood.

Widely and kindly around us must we look as well as inwardly and upwardly, or we leave untenanted some of the heart's best chambers. Our breasts are large enough to entertain multitudes, and only when thus filled is our daily life a full blessing.

Our poor social organization engenders vacuums, which are apt to fill with wind. Hence, most of Northern " abolitionism," and other pseudo-philanthropies. Many people are not comfortable without pets or hobbies. It is not the poor African that is the pet,—would that it were,—but a something abstract, an ideal formula, a pet of the mind. That it cannot become concrete, is its chief qualification as a hobby. It can be ridden the more showily and at the same time safely. Snuffing perfume from the fields sown by a philanthropized imagination, the rider careers along with a plethoric self-complacency, and really believes that he is doing something. And so he is, in truth, but something different from what he believes. This class of people have discovered the secret of making virtue easy.

An ape is a creature who has approached the gates of reason, and stands there grinning and jabbering in tragi-comical ignorance of his nearness to the regal palace.

Religious humility is apt to be accompanied by personal arrogance.

So luminous and creative is the mind, that what is brought to it through the imagination is often more stirring than the same presented by the senses. Hence, some scenes are more exciting if well told, than if actually beheld. The mind magnifies and adorns them in its immeasurable chambers.

We seek happiness by heaping on our puny selves all we can, each one building, according to the joint force of his intellect and selfishness, a reversed pyramid, under the which the higher it rises the lower he is crushed on the small spot his small self can fill.

We are capable of life-long joy. Continuous, varied enjoyment might be the sum of earthly existence. If our lives will not bring out this sum, it is because men have misplaced, or mislaid, or overlooked, or misreckoned with some of the counters.

When we sow the best fields of life with our appetites, we cannot but reap hates and fears. Blighting disappointment comes from thwarted greeds, from frustrated self-seeking.

A fit ideal embodiment of the artist were a countenance upraised, beaming, eager, joyful, moulded with somewhat of feminine mobility.

Goethe goes out of himself into the being of natural objects. Wordsworth takes their being up into himself. These two poets illustrate sharply the difference between the *objective* and the *subjective*.

Envy, like venomous reptiles, can only strike at short distances.

There is no deeper law of nature than that of change.

A book should be a distillation.

Everything that we do being a cause, he is the most sagacious who so does that each cause shall have its good effect. This practical long sightedness is wisdom, the want of it foolishness. To-days are all fathers of to-morrows, but like many other fathers, they sadly neglect their paternal duties. To-day, if it thinks at all, thinks of itself, and leaves to-morrow to take care of itself. Life is a daily laying of eggs, some to be hatched to-morrow, some next month, some next year, some next century. Many are not hatched at all, but rot or are broken; many come prematurely out of the shell, and perish from debility; and thus that much life is wasted. Charity is long-sighted, selfishness is short-sighted. And yet, so defective is our social constitution, that a man may be long-sighted in using his neighbor for his own ends. Thus doctors,—who are short-sighted when they take their own physic, which they seldom do,—are long-sighted when they give it to their patients; for the more of it these take, the oftener the doctor is called. It were a mistake to suppose that parsons are long-sighted because they set their minds so much upon the next world; their long-sightedness consists in directing other people's thoughts to that quarter, while from the super-mundane spectators they draw the wherewithal to be content with this.—Lawyers are short-sighted when they encourage litigation; the long-sighted know that the perverted passions of civilized men will bring grist enough to their mill without their stir.—Tailors intend to be long-sighted when they stitch on your buttons instead of sewing them.—The man who sells rum is short-sighted, but less so than he who drinks it.—Authors are very short-sighted when they write to please the public, instead of writing to please the truth.—Expedients are short-sighted, principles long-sighted; and notwithstanding the apparent prosperity of some liars, nothing is so long-sighted as truth.

In the plainest of Wordsworth's many hundred sonnets there is more or less of the fragrant essence of high humanity.

To write a good book on any subject requires the "instinct of the beautiful."

"You cannot serve God and Mammon:" nay, you cannot serve yourself and Mammon.

To weave the wondrous form wherewith life invests itself in humanity, the heart works ceaselessly, and every organ, member, part and particle of the living frame works, each joyfully in its sphere, in unison with the heart, for the maintenance of the common fabric. But a continuation and extension of the unconscious labor of the heart and lungs is the conscious work of the head and hand of man, whose end is, to feed, to clothe, to lodge, to develop, to delight his body and his mind. All labor, the unconscious and the conscious, is but life methodized, that is, life made more living, more intelligent, and thence more productive. And thus labor, which is the condition and result of life, becomes the means of its perpetuation, its extension, its elevation. All labor may be delightful; and as, the healthier the body is, the more joyfully and thoroughly the heart and its allies perform their unconscious work, so in a healthy social organization all labor, the greatest and the least, ceasing to be repulsive and becoming attractive and delightful, would be proportionately productive. A consummation this not barely most devoutly to be wished, but most surely to be accomplished, by that high labor which the intellect exalted by love and faith is equal to performing.

The ideas of eternity and infinity are innate in the human mind as attractions towards perfection, as indications and promises of incalculable elevation.

The subjects of old European Monarchies inherit from the past such a load of debt, of slow-paced customs, of lazy monopolies, and other cold drawbacks from behind, that they cannot move forward. Instead of briskly turning the now, the to-day, to rich account, they have to work first against yesterday, to stave it off with its manifold pressure. Hence, half the laborers of England, Germany, France, earn not for themselves food, clothing and lodging enough to keep out hunger and cold. Their hands are mortgaged to the past. Their existence has no new life in it; it is a lingering perpetuation of the past. Whereas we of democratic America let not the past accumulate upon us. For us, sufficient for the day is the evil thereof. We make clean work as we go. We keep the present lively, because we are ever snatching a new present from across the confines of the future. We are always "going ahead;" that is, building up the Future out of itself and not out of the past. We don't wait for the Future, we rush in pursuit of it.

The higher the sphere the greater the freedom. Mineral, vegetable, animal; zoophite, reptile, quadruped, man; savage, barbarian, civilized. Each of these series is an ascension towards freedom, the highest being the freest.

Religion, above all things, needs to be steadied and purified by science and culture.

Classification is the highest function of intellect; it brings order out of chaos. It is both analysis and synthesis. The higher the department of universal life, the keener of course must be the intellectual insight that could detect its organic law. To order minerals is feebler work than to order morals. The man who classes, needs to have a kind of creative mastery over his material. He intellectually recreates it. The savage, who has mastery over nothing, but is a brute serf of Nature, has scarcely any power of classification.

Thought is ever unfolding. A good thinker keeps thinking.

As with the body 'tis a sign of derangement, if the action of any organ makes itself felt, the motions of the heart, for example, or the laboring of the stomach; so too with the mind, the protracted consciousness of any feeling is unhealthy, whether it be the religious sentiment or the lust of revenge.

Who fears the forces of Nature? We use them for our profit: the stronger they are, the more profitable we make them. The passions of man, all his feelings, impulses and motives to action, are similarly innocent and available. They are the strongest forces and instruments in Nature. We must learn only to use them.

We must be realists, not dreamers; we must found our convictions on facts, not on imaginations which are dream-like. Nothing is nobler than facts. Facts are God's; imaginations are man's, and are only then god-like, when they enfold coming or possible facts, or adorn existing ones.

The spokes of the wheel are helpless until bound together by the rim.

Christianity promises such moral splendors, that men, refusing to credit these as an earthly possibility, translate its consummations to the super-mundane sphere. Priestcraft has always fostered this incredulity, which opens to it the imagination as its work-field, where the tillage is much lighter than on a tangible soil. It is easier to saw air than to saw wood; easier to put the wretched off with sanctimonious assurances of celestial compensations, than to wrestle with earthly ills, and by wisely opposing, end them; easier to preach of Heaven to come, than to put hand to work to drive off a present hell. The conscientious pastor knows, how almost fruitless a task it is, when, not content with stale ritual repetitions and wordy exhortations, he labors practically to purge and vivify his flock. With all his toil he brings little to pass. His theological tools are dull; what steel there ever was in them is worn off.

Nature rejects with contempt an hereditary aristocracy.

In our present mis-organized society, helplessness is the condition, not of nine in ten, but of all. The wisest and wealthiest are encompassed by exposure, dangers, calamity. Against earthly troubles, resignation and ultra-terrene expectation are a poor resource, as illogical as meagre. What is done on earth is of our own making or allowing. Heaven is just, and inflicts naught. It lets us do for our good or evil, and when we help ourselves, helps us. Put we our shoulders to the wheel, the Hercules is instantly at our side. We make the beds we lie in; not you or I, but you and I, and all the you's and I's that surround us. Against our needs and woes, you *or* I can do little, but you *and* I, everything. Association, which has made railroads and banks, can do much better and higher.

As its roots spread and strike down, the tree expands and mounts. Thoughts and aims are only then sound, when their roots are firm in the earth. The rest is brain-sick fancy, conceited delusion. The earth and our bodies are for the mind and heart to grow and revel in. When we would sacrifice the God-given earth and its joys to a tinsel manufacture which we miscall Heaven, we stigmatize Providence, and supplant it with our puling fantasies.

But people do not so sacrifice; they only make themselves bootlessly wretched by vainly striving to do so. This short-sighted effort is for the behoof of the priest, who, three times in four, is but a broker who drives a belly-filling business by exchanging drafts on the next world for coin that buys the comforts of this.

There is nothing that some people are more ignorant of, than their own ignorance.

The classification of England's inhabitants into nobility, gentry, shop-keepers, mechanics, laborers, paupers, is as consonant to nature as would be the classing of animals according to weight and color.

Fourier undertakes to make all men honest. No wonder that he is looked upon as a visionary, who promises so stupendous a revolution in human affairs.

An unsightly object is an old face haunted by the vices of youth.

Credulity is a characteristic of weakness. Imagination precedes Reason. Fancies are a loose substitute for knowledge. Hence the unreasonable creeds of young nations, fastened upon them by priestcraft, whose criminal practice it has been, and is still, by terrifying the imagination to subjugate the reason. The first-born of priestcraft was the Devil.

Priests are ever shuffling over the leaves of old books: the life there may be in these they petrify with their own hardness: they seek God in traditions and hearsays, and the dim utterances of the livers of old: they abide by the outgivings of obsolete mystics: they re-assert the beliefs of antiquated seers: the ecstasies of feverish hallucination they endorse as imperative dogmas. They grovel and grope in the darkness and dawn, to find stakes planted by the crude beginners of the world, to the which, by grossest cords, they would bind to the past our forward-reaching souls. The future, too, they suborn and would monopolize: with their contemptible Heavens and ridiculous Hells, they would captivate our hopes and our fears. Out of imaginations that are shallow, unhallowed, meagre, foul, they impudently construct both the past and the future. That they may be paid for furnishing rush-lights, they cultivate darkness, and be-curtain with creeds and dogmas the human tabernacle against the sun of truth. Those who appeal to the God of light, and to the upright soul of man, against their sophistications and usurpations, they crucify. Audaciously they dub themselves the ministers of God, they who are especially not God's ministers but men's. Spiritual insight, moral elevation, rich sympathies, these are the tokens whereby the divinely ordained are signalized. Are candidates for any priesthood admitted or rejected by these signs? Not by inborn superiorities of sensibility, but by acquired proficiencies, by intellectual adoptions are they tested. This creed, these articles, this ritual,—do they accept these, then are they accepted. To be learned in humanity, a living learning, which the large heart imbibes without labor, this is not their title; but to be learned in theology, a lifeless learning, which the small head can acquire by methodical effort. They would live and make others live by the dead letter, and not by the living law. The dead letter is the carcass of what has been, or what is imagined to have been. The living law is what is: it is not written, it is forever being written on the heart of man by the hand of God.

What by defect of harmonious organization Christendom waste of nervous power would vitalize a planet.

Machinery and the useful Arts are man's inventions for industrial helps. The Fine Arts he creates for æsthetic helps.

Disproportion is disqualification. Too much is unwieldy: too little is feebleness. A giant is of no more use than a dwarf. A man seven feet high finds his extra foot a daily incumbrance. A man of more head than heart is dangerous: a man of more heart than head is a victim.

Every deed of man is preceded by a thought. In the most trivial movement, immaterial action is the antecedent and producer of the material. Every result brought about by human contrivance and will is an embodied finishing whose beginning is a spiritual seed sown in the brain. No grossest act but existed first in thought before it took body. Without thinking, a man would go without his dinner. Every act proves a precedent thought. This is an absolute law of the mind. As all human acts pre-suppose human thought, so superhuman acts pre-suppose superhuman thought. A man is a superhuman act, and the existence of a man demonstrates the pre-existence of God.

THE END.

SCENES AND THOUGHTS IN EUROPE

AMBLESIDE, WESTMORELAND COUNTY, ENGLAND,
July 29th, 1840, Wednesday Evening

MY DEAR ———:

Three weeks since, I was in America: I am now writing to you from an English village, distant but a mile from the dwelling of Wordsworth. Between noon and evening we have come to-day ninety miles; first by railroad from Liverpool to Lancaster, where we took outside seats on a coach to Kendall, and thence by postchaise fourteen miles to Ambleside. An American just landed in England wants more than his two eyes to look at the beautiful, green "old country." For several miles the road lay along the bank of Lake Windermere, sleeping in the evening shadows at the feet of its mountains, whose peaks were shrouded in mist, except that of Nabscar, on whose southern side near its base stands the Poet's house.

So soon as we were established in the clean little inn, I walked out, about eight o'clock, on the road that passes Wordsworth's door. Meeting a countryman, when I had been afoot ten or fifteen minutes, I asked him,—"How far is it to Mr. Wordsworth's?" "Only a quarter of a mile." The wood-skirted road wound among gentle hills, that on one side ran quickly up into mountains, so that the house was not in view; and having resolved not to seek him till to-morrow, I turned back with the tall laborer, who told me he was working at Wordsworth's. We passed a lady and gentleman on foot, who both gave a friendly salutation to my companion. "That," said he, "is Mr. Wordsworth's daughter."

Thursday Evening.

This morning, at ten, Nabscar still wore his nightcap of mist, but as the wind then hauled, in sailor's phrase, to the north from the southwest, which is the rainy quarter here, he was robed before noon in sunshine, to welcome on his breast a far-travelled homager.

I spent an hour to-day with Wordsworth. His look, talk, and bearing, are just what a lover of his works would wish to find them. His manner is simple, earnest, manly. The noble head, large Roman nose, deep voice, and tall spare figure, make up an exterior that well befits him. He talked freely on topics that naturally came up on the occasion. He proposed that we should walk out into his grounds. What a site for a poet's abode! One more beautiful the earth could scarcely offer. A few acres give shifting views of the Paradise about him, embracing the two lakes of Windermere and Grasmere. Would that you could have heard him sum up in hearty English the characteristics of the bounteous scene! We passed a small field of newly-cut hay, which laborers were turning;—"I have been at work there this morning," said Wordsworth, "and heated myself more than was prudent." In the garden a blackbird ran across our path: "I like birds better than fruit," said he; "they eat up my fruit, but repay me with their songs." By those who, like you, appreciate Wordsworth, these trifles will be prized as significant of his habits. I would not record them, did I believe that himself,— with knowledge of the feelings which to us make them valuable,— would regard the record as a violation of the sacred privacy of his home. A literary caterer might have seized upon much that would better have served a gossiping hireling's purpose.

SATURDAY, August 1st, 1840.

Yesterday evening we spent three hours at Rydal Mount, the name not of the mountain near whose base is Wordsworth's dwelling, but of the dwelling itself. We went, by invitation, early. Wordsworth, soon after we arrived, familiarly took me through the back gate of his enclosure, to point out the path by which I might ascend to the top of Nabscar,—a feat I purposed attempting the next day. On our return, he proposed a visit to Rydal Fall, a few hundred yards from his door in Rydal Park. On learning that five weeks since we had stood before Niagara, an exclamation burst from his lips, as if the sublime spectacle were suddenly brought near to him. "But, come," said he, after a moment, "I am not afraid to show you Rydal Fall, though you have so lately seen Niagara." As for part of the way he walked before us in his thick shoes, his large head somewhat inclined forward, occasionally calling our looks to tree or shrub, I had him, as he doubtless is in his solitary rambles for hours daily, in habitual meditation, greeting as he passes many a flower and sounding bough, and pausing at times from self-communion, to bare his mind to the glories of sky and earth which ennoble his chosen abode.

At the end of our walk a short descent brought us to the door of a small, stone, wood-embowered structure, the vestibule, as it were, to the temple. Entering, the waterfall was before us, beheld through a large regular oblong opening or window which made a frame to the natural picture. The fall was not of more than twenty-five feet, and the stream only a large brook, but from the happiest conjunction of water, rock and foliage; of color, form, sound and silvan still life; resulted a scene, decked by nature so choicely, and with such delicate harmony, that you felt yourself in one of Beauty's most perfect abiding-places. The deep voice of Wordsworth mingled at intervals with the sound of the fall. We left the spot to return to his house. The evening was calm and sunny; we were in an English Park in the bosom of mountains; we had come from a spot sanctified by Beauty, and Wordsworth walked beside us.

The walls of the drawing-room and library, connected by a door, in which, with the affable kindness of a refined gentlewoman, Mrs. Wordsworth received ourselves and a few other guests, were covered with books and pictures. Wordsworth showed me many editions of the British Poets. He put into my hands a copy of the first edition of Paradise Lost, given him by Charles Lamb. He spoke copiously, and in terms of admiration, of Alston, whom he had known well. In connection with Alston, he mentioned his "friend Coleridge." The opportunity thus offered of leading him to speak of his great compeer, was marred by one of the company giving another turn to the conversation. Wordsworth, throughout the evening, was in a fine mood. His talk was clear and animated; at times humorous or narrative. He narrated several lively incidents with excellent effect. We sat in the long English twilight till past nine o'clock.

Sunday Morning, August 2d, 1840.

Yesterday was pleasantly filled in making an excursion to Colistone Lake, in rowing on Windermere, and in strolling in the evening through the meadows around Ambleside. At every pause in our walk, the aspect of the landscape varied, under the control of the chief feature of the scenery, the encircling mountains with their vast company of shadows, which, as unconsciously changing your position you shift the point of view, open or close gorges and valleys, and hide or reveal their own tops, producing the effect of a moving panorama.

But a week since, we were on the ocean,—a month since, in the new world,—now, on the beaten sod of the old, young Americans enjoying old England. Every object within sight, raised by the hand of man, looks touched with antiquity; the grey stone wall with its coping of moss, the cottage ivy-screened, the Saxon church tower. Even what is new, hasn't a new look. The modern mansion is mellowed by architecture and tint into keeping with its older neighbors. To be old here, is to be respectable, and time-honored is the epithet most coveted. You see no sign of the doings of yesterday or yesteryear: the new is careful of obtruding itself, and comes into the world under matronage of the old. But the footprint of age is not traced in rust and decay. We are in free and thriving England, where Time's accumulations are shaped by a busy, confident, sagacious hand, man co-working with Nature at the "ceaseless loom of Time," so that little be wasted and little misspent. The English have a strong sympathy with rural nature. The capabilities of the landscape are developed and assisted with a loving and judicious eye, and the beautiful effects are visible not merely in the lordly domain or secluded pleasure-ground, where a single mind brings about a pre-determined end, but in the general aspect of the land. The hatched cottage, the broad castle, the simple lawn, the luxurious park, the scattered hamlet, the compact borough, all the features which make up the physiognomy of woody, mossy, rain-washed, England, harmonize with nature and with one another.

Sunday Afternoon, 2 o'clock.

We walked this morning to Rydal Church, which is within almost a stone's throw of Wordsworth's dwelling. Through a cloudless sky and the Sabbath stillness, the green landscape looked like a corner of Eden. In the small simple church there were not more than sixty persons, the congregation, as Wordsworth told us afterwards, consisting of fourteen families. When the service was over, Wordsworth, taking us one under each arm, led us up to his house. After a short visit we took our final leave.

In these three days, I have spent several hours at different times with Wordsworth. I have listened to his free and cordial talk, walked with him, beheld the beautiful landscape of Westmoreland with the aidance of his familiar eye, and have been the object of his hospitality, more grateful to me than would be that of his sovereign. The purpose of our visit to Ambleside being accomplished, we leave this in half an hour.

OXFORD, WEDNESDAY MORNING, August 5th, 1840.

A glance at the map of England will show you what a flight we've made since Sunday. For most of the way 't was literally a flight, being chiefly by steam. Yet have we had time to tarry on the road, and give ourselves up tranquilly without hurry to deep and gentle impressions.

Leaving Ambleside on Sunday afternoon, our road ran for ten miles along the eastern shore of Lake Windermere, which lay shining at our side, or sparkling through the foliage that shades the neat dwellings on its border. From the mountains of the lake region we passed suddenly into the flats of Lancashire, and at dark reached Lancaster, too late to get a good view of, what we had however seen as we went up from Liverpool, the castle, founded by

"Old John of Gaunt, time-honored Lancaster."

Between nine and three o'clock on Monday, a railroad bore us from Lancaster, on the north-west coast, to Coventry (which Falstaff marched through) in Warwickshire, the very heart of England. We passed through, but did not stop at Birmingham. The sight and thought of these great overworked underfed workshops are oppressive. An invalid has not the nerves to confront the gaunt monster, Poverty, that dragging along its ghastly offspring, Squalor and Hunger, stalks so strangely through this abundant land.

There is nothing like a "locomotive" for giving one a first vivid view of a country. Those few hours left on my brain a clear full image of the face of England, such as can be had by no other means. Town, river, village, cottage, castle, set all in their native verdure, are so approximated by rapidity of movement, as to be easily enclosed by the memory in one frame. The ten miles between Coventry and Warwick, a stage-coach carried us on its top, passing through Kenilworth village, and giving us a glimpse of the famous ruins.

Beautiful to behold is England on a sunny summer's day ; so clean, so verdant, so full of quiet life, so fresh, wearing so lightly the garland of age. What a tree ;—that cottage, how fragrant it looks through its flowers ;—the turf about that church has been green for ages. Here is a thatched hamlet, its open doors lighted with rosy faces at the sound of our wheels ;—this avenue of oaks sets the imagination to building a mansion at the end of it. What town is that clustered around yon huge square tower ? and the ear welcomes a familiar name, endeared by genius to the American heart. Such is a half hour of one's progress through time-enriched England, the mother of Shakspeare and Cromwell, of Milton and Newton.

Yesterday morning we walked to Warwick Castle, which lies just without the town. There stands the magnificent feudal giant, shorn of its terrors ; its high embattled turrets disarmed by Time's transmuting inventions ; its grim frowns converted to graceful lineaments ; its hoarse challenges to gentle greetings ; there it stands, grand and venerable, on the soft green bank of Avon, guarded by man's protecting arm against the levelling blasts of antiquity, not less a token of present grandeur than a monument of former glories. As slowly as the impatient attendant would let us, we loitered through the broad lofty halls and comfortable apartments, from whose walls flash the bright heads of Vandyke. Through the deep windows you look down into the Avon, which flows by the castle and through the noble park. We lingered on the green lawn, enclosed within the castle walls, and in the smooth grounds without them, and we hung about the towers of the dark old pile until noon, when we walked back to the inn, having enjoyed without drawback, and with more than fulfilment of cherished expectations, one of the grandest spectacles old Europe has to offer.

At one we were approaching Stratford on Avon, distant eight miles from Warwick. Fifteen years since I was on the same ground. But Shakspeare was to me then but a man, to whom greatness had been decreed by the world's judgment. I was not of an age to have verified for myself his titles: I had not realized by contemplation the immensity of his power: my soul had not been fortified by direct sympathy with his mighty nature. But now I felt that I was near the most sacred spot in Europe, and I was disappointed at the absence of emotion in my mind. Here Shakspeare was born, and here he lies buried. We stood above his bones: on the marble slab at our feet, we read the lines touching their rest, invoking a curse on him who should disturb them. We sat down on a bench within a few feet of the sacred dust. We walked out by a near door past tomb-stones to the edge of the Avon. The day was serene and bright. We returned, and gazed again on the simple slab. 'Twas not till we had quitted the church, and were about to pass out of the yard, that a full consciousness of the holiness of the place arose in me. For an instant I seemed to feel the presence of Shakspeare. We walked slowly back towards the inn. In this path he has walked; at that sunny corner he has lounged;—but 'twas like clutching at corporeal substance in a dream, to try to call up a familiar image of Shakspeare. Objects around looked unsubstantial; what the senses beheld wore the aspect of a vision; the only reality was the thought of Shakspeare, which wrapped the mind in a vague magical sensation.

Between three and four o'clock we were on the way to Oxford, smoothly rolling over an undulating road, under a cloudless sky, through the teeming, tree-studded fields. We passed through Woodstock, and for several miles skirted the Park of Blenheim. 'Twas dark ere we entered Oxford. The coach whirled us past square upon square of majestic piles and imposing shapes, and we alighted at the inn, suddenly and strongly impressed with the architectural magnificence of Oxford. We are going out to get a view by sunlight ere we set off for London, which we are to reach before night.

London, August 10th, 1840.

From the top of the coach, which carried us eight miles to the Great Western Railroad, I looked back upon the majestic crown of towers and spires, wherewith,—as if to honor by a unique prodigality of its gifts, the high, long enduring seat of learning,—the genius of architecture has encircled the brow of Oxford. At a speed of thirty to forty-five miles an hour, we shot down to Windsor, where we again quitted the railroad for a post-chaise, wishing to enter London more tranquilly than by steam.

By the road from Windsor it is hard to say when you do enter London, being encased by houses miles before you reach Piccadilly. Some cities are begirt with walls, some with public walks, some merely with water; but London, it may be said without solecism, is surrounded by houses. At last the "West End" opens grandly to view through Hyde Park. What a look of vastness, of wealth, of solid grandeur! We are passing the house of Wellington, and there to the right, across the Green Park and St. James's, are the towers of Westminster Abbey. We are in the largest and wealthiest city of the world, the capital of the most vast and powerful empire the earth has ever known.

We can now give but a few days to London, barely enough to get a notion of its material dimensions and outward aspects. Size, activity, power, opulence, fill with confused images the wearied brain when the stranger's laborious day is over. The streets of London seem interminable; its private palaces are countless; its population consists of many multitudes. Through its avenues flow in counter-currents, from morn till midnight, the streams which send and receive from the ends of the earth, the life-blood of a commerce, which all climes and continents nourish. From within its precincts issue words, that, sped to the four quarters of the globe, are laws to more than one hundred millions of men. Thither are the ears of states directed; and when in the Senate, that for ages has had its seat in this still growing capital, the prime minister of England speaks, all the nations hearken. Of the wealth, strength, bulk, grandeur of the realm, London is the centre and palpable evidence. See the docks in the morning, and drive round the Parks in the afternoon, and you behold the might and magnificence of Britain.

From this endless throng I was withdrawn yesterday to a scene, a sketch of which will, I know, have for you especial interest. I drove to Highgate Hill, and alighted at the house of Mr. Gilman. From the servant who opened the door I learnt that he had been dead several months. Mrs. Gilman was at home. I was shown into a neat back drawing-room, where sat an elderly lady in deep mourning. I apologized for having come to her house: it was my only means of getting tidings of one I had known well many years before in Göttingen, and who, I was aware, had been a friend and pupil of Mr. Coleridge during his stay under her roof. She made a sign to the servant to withdraw, and then gave way to her emotion. " All gone, all gone !" were the only words she could at first utter. My friend had been dead many years, then Coleridge, and lastly her husband. I was much moved. Mr. —— had been a son to her: to have been intimate with him was a favorable introduction to herself. She showed me several of Mr. Gilman's books, filled with notes in Coleridge's handwriting, from which are taken many passages of the " Remains." In another room was his bust; and in another a fine picture by Alston, given by him to his great friend. She put into my hands a sonnet in manuscript, written and sent to her by

Alston, on the death of Coleridge,—the most beautiful thing of the kind I ever read.

In the third story is the chamber opened by the most cordial and honorable friendship to the illustrious sufferer, and by him occupied for many years. There was the bed whereon he died. From the window I looked out over a valley upon Caen Wood. Here, his lustrous eyes fixed in devout meditation, Coleridge was wont to behold the sunset. Mrs. Gilman tired not of talking of him, nor I of listening. I thought, how happy, with all his chagrins and disappointments, he had been in finding such friends. You recollect with what affection and hearty thankfulness he speaks of them. They could sympathize with the philosopher and the poet, as well as with the man. Mrs. Gilman's talk told of converse with one of England's richest minds. To me it was a bright hour, and with feelings of more than esteem for its lonely inmate, I quitted the roof where, in his afflicted old age, the author of Christabel had found a loving shelter. In a few moments I was again in the whirl of the vast metropolis. I shall bear away from it no more vivid or grateful recollection than that of yesterday's visit. Few men have had more genius than Coleridge, more learning, or more uprightness, and in the writings of none is there more soul. His poetry will live with his language. As a prose writer, he is a conscientious seeker of truth, a luminous expounder of the mysteries of life; and the earnest student of his pages, without accepting in full either his Theology, or his Philosophy, or his Politics, finds himself warmed, instructed and exalted.

LEAMINGTON, September, 1840.

The day after the date of my last, we left London for Leamington in Warwickshire, where we have been for a month. There are times when one can neither write nor even read I begin to fear that I shall not have many moods for work in Europe. To say nothing of health, one's mind is constantly beset by superficial temptations. All kinds of trifling novelties importune the attention. And even when settled for weeks in the same lodging, one is ever possessed by the feeling of instability.

My reading at Leamington has been chiefly of newspapers. From them, however, something may be learnt by a stranger. They reflect the surface of society; and as surfaces mostly take their shape and hue from depths beneath them, one may read in newspapers somewhat more than they are paid for printing. Even the London "Satirist," that rankest sewer of licentiousness, has a social and political significance. It could only live in the shade of an Aristocracy. The stomach of omnivorous scandal were alone insufficient to digest its gross facts and fabrications. The Peer is dragged through a horse-pond for the sport of the plebeian. The artisan chuckles to see Princes and Nobles wallowing in dirt, in print. The high are brought so low that the lowest can laugh at them: the proud, who live on contempt, are pulled down to where themselves can be scorned by the basest. The wit consists chiefly in the contrast between the elevation of the game and the filthiness of the ammunition wherewith it is assailed; between the brilliancy of the mark and the obscurity of the marksman. A register is kept of Bishops, Peeresses, Dukes, Ambassadors, charged with being swindlers, adulterers, buffoons, panders, sycophants; and this is one way of keeping Englishmen in mind that all men are brothers. It is a weekly sermon, suited to some of the circumstances of the times and people, on the text— "But many that are first shall be last."

England looks everywhere aristocratical. A dominant idea in English life is possession by inheritance. Property and privilege are nailed by law to names. A man, by force of mind, rises from lowliness to a Dukedom: the man dies, but the Dukedom lives, and lifts into eminence a dullard perhaps, or a reprobate. The soul has departed, and the body is unburied. Counter to the order of nature, the external confers instead of receiving life; and whereas at first a man made the Dukedom, afterwards 'tis the Dukedom that makes the man. Merit rises, but leaves behind it generations of the unmeritorious not only to feed on its gains, but to possess places that should never be filled but by the deserving. In an hereditary aristocracy the noble families form knots on the trunk of a nation, drawing to themselves sap which, for the public health, should be equally distributed. Law and custom attach power and influence to names and lands: whoso own these, govern, and so rigid and cherished are primogeniture and entail, that much of them is possessed without an effort or a natural claim. The possessor's whole right is arbitrary and artificial.

To ascribe the short-comings of England to the aristocratic principle, were as shallow as to claim for it her many glories. In her development it has played its part according to her constitutional temperament; but her development has been richer and healthier than that of her neighbors, because her aristocracy has had its roots in the people, or rather because (a false aristocracy having been hitherto in Europe unavoidable) her people have been manly and democratic enough not to suffer one distinct in blood to rear itself among them. Compare English with any other aristocracy, and this in it is notable and unique; it does not form a caste. It is not, like the German, or Russian, or Italian, a distinct breed from that of the rest of the nation; nay, its blood is ever renewed from the veins of the people. This is the spring of its life; this has kept it in vigor; this strengthens it against degeneracy. It sucks at the breast of the mighty multitude. Hence at bottom it is, that the English Peer is in any part of the world a higher personage than the German Count or Italian Prince. He cannot show pedigrees with them, and this, a cause of mortification to his pride, is the very source of his superiority.

From this cause, English Aristocracy is less far removed than any other in Europe from a genuine Aristocracy, or government of the Best, of which, however, it is still but a mockery. It is not true that all the talent in the realm gravitates towards the House of Lords, but some of it does; and as such talent is, of course, in alliance with worldly ambition, the *novi homines* in Parliament are apt not to be so eminent for principle as for intellect. Until men shall be much purer than they have yet been, no nation will, under any form of polity, throw up its best men into high places. The working of the representative system with us has revealed the fact, that with free choice a community chooses in the long run men who accurately represent itself. Should therefore Utopia lie embosomed in our future, instead of the present very mixed assemblage, our remote posterity may look for a Congress that will present a shining level of various excellence. Only, that should so blessed an era be in store, Congresses and all other cunning contrivances called governments will be superfluous. In England, in legislation and in social life, most of the best places are filled by men whose ancestors earned them, and not themselves. These block the way to those who, like their ancestors, are capable in a fair field of winning eminence. By inheritance are enjoyed posts demanding talent, liberality, refinement—qualities not transmissible. It is subjecting the spiritual to the corporeal. It is setting the work of man, Earls and Bishops, over the work of God, men. The world is ever prone to put itself in bondage to the external: laws should aim to counteract the tendency. Here this bondage is methodized and legalized. The body politic has got to be but feebly organic. Men are obliged in every direction to conform rigidly to old forms; to reach their end by mechanical routine. A man on entering life finds himself fenced in between ancient walls. Every Englishman is free relatively to every other living Englishman, but is a slave to his forefathers. He must put his neck under the yoke of prescription. The life of every child in England is too rigorously predestined. To him may be addressed the words of Goethe, in Faust :—

> Es erben sich Gesetz' und Rechte
> Wie eine ew'ge Krankheit fort;
> Sie schleppen von Geschlecht sich zum Geschlechte,
> Und rücken sacht von Ort zu Ort.
> Vernunft wird Unsinn, Wohlthat Plage;
> Weh dir dass du ein Enkel bist!
> Vom Rechte, das mit uns geboren ist,
> Von dem ist leider! nie die Frage.*

This is a rich theme, which I have merely touched. It is pregnant too with comfort to us with our unbridled democracy. May it ever remain unbridled.

PARIS, November, 1840.

On the way from Leamington to France we were again two days in London, where I then saw at his house one of the master spirits of the age, Mr. Carlyle. His countenance is fresh, his bearing simple, and his frequent laugh most hearty. He has a wealth of talk, and is shrewd in speech as in print in detecting the truth in spite of concealments, and letting the air out of a *windbeutel.* Like the first meeting across the seas with a bountiful worldly benefactor,—except that the feeling is much finer, and admits of no gross admixture,—is that with a man to whom you have long been under intellectual obligations. It is one of the heartiest moments a stranger can have abroad. The spirit that has been so much with him, has taken flesh and voice. He grasps for the first time the hand of an old friend. When in

---

* Laws and rights are inherited like an everlasting disease; they drag themselves along from generation to generation, and quietly move from place to place. Reason becomes nonsense, blessings become curses; woe to thee that thou art a grandchild! Of the right that is born with us, of this, alas! there is no thought

London before, I had a good view of the Duke of Wellington, as he rode up to his house, at the corner of Hyde Park, and dismounted; so that I have seen England's three foremost living men, Wordsworth, Wellington, Carlyle.

On Friday afternoon September 11th, at three o'clock, we left London by railroad for Southampton, which we reached at six, and crossing the channel by steamboat in the night, entered the port of Havre at ten the next morning. The town looked dirty at a distance, and is dirtier than it looked. The small craft we passed in the harbor were unclean and unwieldy. The streets ran filth to a degree that offended both eyes and nose. Knots of idle shabby men were standing at corners, gossipping, and looking at parrots and monkeys exposed for sale. The inn we got into, commended as one of the best, was so dirty, that we could not bear to face the prospect of a night in it. We hired a carriage and started at four with post-horses for Rouen, which we reached at midnight. Here we spent Sunday. Rouen is finely placed, on the Seine, with lofty hills about it. In the *Diligence*, in which we started early on Monday, to overtake fifteen miles up the river, the steamboat to St. Germain, I heard a Frenchman say to a Frenchwoman, "Rouen est le pot-de-chambre de la Normandie." You know of the Cathedral at Rouen and of the Maid of Orleans' execution, but this is probably in all respects new to you. To me it was also new and satisfactory, being an indication that some of the dwellers in this region have a consciousness of the presence of stenches. We entered Paris in a hard rain at ten o'clock on Monday night.

The French claim for Paris that it is the most beautiful city in the world. From a point on the right bank of the Seine, near the bridge leading from the *Place de la Concorde*, is the finest, and truly a noble panoramic view. Standing with your back to the river, right before you is the *Place* itself, with its glittering fountains and Egyptian Obelisk. Directly across it, the eye rests on two imposing *façades*, which form a grand portal to the *Rue Royale*, at the end whereof, less than half a mile distant, the Church of the Madeleine presents its majestic front of Corinthian columns. On the right the eye runs down the long façade of the *Rue Rivoli*, cut at right angles by the Palace of the Tuileries, peering above the trees of the Tuileries garden which, with its deep shade and wide walks, lies between you and the Palace. To the right now of the garden the view sweeps up the river, with its bridges and miles of broad *quais*, and ends in a distant labyrinth of building, out of which rises the dark head of *Notre Dame de Paris*. Near you on the opposite, that is, the left bank of the Seine, and face to face to the Madeleine, is the imposing *Palais des Elisées Bourbons*, now the Hall of the Deputies. To the right the gardens attached to the *Elisées Bourbons* and the grounds of the *Hotel des Invalides* fill the space near the river on the left bank, and the *Champs Elisées*, at one corner of which you stand, press upon its shore on this side, while the view directly down the stream stretches into the country. Back now through a full circle to your first position, and with the Madeleine again in front, on your left are the *Champs Elisées*, at the other extremity of which, more than a mile off, just out of the Neuilly Gate, towers the gigantic Imperial Arch of Triumph built by Napoleon. But to get the best view of this magnificent Colossus, you must advance to the centre of the *Place de la Concorde*, where, from the foot of the Obelisk, with your back to the Tuileries, you behold it closing the chief Avenue of the Champs Elisées, and, by the elevation of the ground and its own loftiness, standing alone, the grandest monument of the French Capital.

A rare and most effective combination this, of objects and aspects. From no other city can there be embraced from a single point an equal extent, variety and grandeur. There are similar but less striking views from several other open spots.

From the general deficiency of good architecture, large cities show best when, from the banks of a river or broad open squares, they can be beheld in long distant masses. Paris gains hereby especially, as, from the habits of the people, not only are the streets dirtier than need be, but the basements are mostly unsightly and often disgusting; and the faces generally, even of massive buildings, with architectural pretensions, have an unwashed and ragged look.

Paris, March, 1841.

A Frenchman, more than other men, is dependent upon things without himself. Nature and his own mind, with domestic interests and recreations, are not enough to complete his daily circle. For his best enjoyment he must have a succession of factitious excitements. Out of this want Paris has grown to be the capital of the world for superficial amusements. Here are the appliances,—multiplied and diversified with the keenest refinement of sensual ingenuity,—for keeping the mind busy without labor and fascinated without sensibility. The senses are beset with piquant baits. Whoever has money in his purse, and can satisfy through gold his chief wants, need have little thought of the day or the year. He finds a life all prepared for him, and selects it, as he does his dinner from the voluminous *carte* of the Restaurant. To live, is for him as easy as to make music on a hand-organ: with but slight physical effort from himself, he is borne along from week to week and from season to season on an unresting current of diversions. Here the sensual can pass years without satiety, and the slothful without ennui. Paris is the Elysium of the idler, and for barren minds a Paradise.

When I first arrived, I went almost nightly to some one of the many theatres. I soon tired of the smaller where, mostly, licentious intrigue and fabulous liberality alternate with farce to keep the attention awake through two or three acts of commonplace. At the *Théatre Français*, I saw Molière and Rachel. It is no disparagement of Molière to call him a truncated Shakspeare. The naturalness, vigor, comic sense, practical insight and scenic life of Shakspeare he has; without Shakspeare's purple glow, his reach of imagination and ample intellectual grasp, which latter supreme qualities shoot light down into the former subordinate ones, and thus impart to Shakspeare's comic and lowest personages a poetic soul, which raises and refines them, the want whereof in Molière makes his low characters border on farce and his highest prosaic.

Rachel is wonderful. She is on the stage an embodied radiance. Her body seems inwardly illuminated. Conceive a Greek statue endued with speech and mobility, for the purpose of giving utterance to a profound soul stirred to its depths, and you have an image of the magic union in her personations of fervor and grace. Till I heard her, I never fully valued the might of elocution. She goes right to the heart by dint of intonation; just as, with his arm ever steady, the fencer deals or parries death by the mere motion of his wrist. Phrases, words, syllables, grow plastic, swell or contract, come pulsing with life, as they issue from her lips. Her head is superb; oval, full, large, compact, powerful. She cannot be said to have beauty of face or figure; yet the most beautiful woman were powerless to divert from her the eyes of the spectator. Her spiritual beauty is there more bewitching than can be the corporeal. When in the *Horaces* she utters the curse, it is as though the whole electricity of a tempest played through her arteries. It is not Corneille's *Camille*, or Racine's *Hermione*, solely that you behold, it is a dazzling incarnation of a human soul.

Through Rachel I have seen the chefs-d'œuvre of Corneille and Racine, reproduced by her on the French stage, whence, since the death of Talma, they had been banished.

Without creation of character, there is no genuine drama. So vivid and individual should be the personages, that out of their feelings and acts the drama evolves itself, under the guidance of judgment and the purification of poetry. Without such individuality and productive vitality in the characters, poetry, sentiment, action, fail of their effect in the dramatic form. The personages of the French Theatre are not creations, they are transplantations. Corneille and Racine took in hand the tragic subjects of antiquity, but they did not re-animate them. Agamemnon and Augustus owe nothing to their Gallic parents: their souls are not swelled with thoughts beyond a Greek or Roman age. Measure them with Shakspeare's Coriolanus, or Anthony, or Brutus, and they are marrowless. Shakspeare has so vivified his Romans, that the pages of history, whence they are taken, pale by the side of them.

The French appear not to have had depth enough to produce an original tragic Drama. The tragic material,—whereof sentiment is as essential an element as passion,—is meagre in them, compared with the Germans or English; hence the possibility and even necessity of a simpler plot and a measured regularity. Corneille or Racine could not have wrought a tragedy out of a tradition or a modern fable: they require a familiarized historical subject. The nature of French Tragedy, compared with English, is happily illustrated by the Hamlet of Ducis, which I have seen played at the *Théâtre Français*. The title of the piece is, " Hamlet, Tragedie en 5 acts, imitée de l'Anglais par Ducis." A fitter title were, " Hamlet, with the part of Hamlet left out, by particular desire of French taste." It is as much an imitation of Shakspeare, as straight walks and parallel lines of trees are an imitation of Nature. Hamlet is resolved into a tender-hearted affectionate son. He has not been put aside, but is king. Ophelia does anything but go mad. The mother is overwhelmed with remorse for the murder, which she confesses to a confidant. The heart of Hamlet's mystery is plucked out. The poetry is flattened into phrases. The billowy sea of Shakspeare is belittled to a smooth pond, in every part whereof you can touch bottom. It is not deep enough to dive in.

It is the nature of high poetry to bind the individual to the universal. Corneille and Racine live in a middle atmosphere between the two. They have not the rich sensibility, which, united on the one hand to high reason, reveals to the poet the primal laws of being, and on the other with powers of minute observation, imparts liveliness to his embodiments. They are neither minute nor comprehensive; hence their personages are vague and prosaic. The highest quality of their tragedies is a refined and skilful rhetoric. Their verse is like bas-relief; the parts follow one another in a graceful well-joined sequence; but there is no perspective, no deep vistas, breeding as you pass them suggestions and subtle sensations. Their personages leave nothing to your imagination; they are terrible egotists; they do most thoroughly "unpack their souls with words;" they give measured speech to feelings which at most should find but broken utterance.

French Tragedy is not primitive. With laborious skill their tragic writers re-cast old materials. In *Polyeucte* Corneille throws a deeper line, but attains to no greater individuality of characterization, nor is he less declamatory than in his Roman pieces. Both he and Racine are more epic than dramatic. The French language, moulded by the mental character of a nation wanting in depth of sensibility, is not a medium for the highest species of poetry, and had Corneille and Racine been poets of the first order, they would either have re-fused the language, so that it would have flowed readily into all the forms forged by the concurrent action of sensibility and thought, or, failing in that, they would, like Rabelais, have betaken themselves to more obedient prose. Molière had not a highly poetic mind, and he wrote verse evidently with uncommon ease; and, nevertheless, I doubt not that even to him the Alexandrine was a shackle; and although Corneille and

Racine cannot be rated among the first class of poets, I think too well of them not to believe, that by it their flight was greatly circumscribed. French verse, which requires a delicate attention to metre or the mechanical constituent, affords little scope for rhythm, and is therefore a hindrance rather than a furtherance to the true poet. In other cultivated languages the form meets the substance half-way—is, as it were, on the watch for it; so that the English, or Italian, or German poet, far from being impeded by the versification of his thoughts as they rise, finds himself thereby facilitated, the metre embracing the poetic matter with such closeness and alacrity as to encourage and accelerate its production and utterance. Hence in French literature the poets are not the highest names. Homer, Dante, Shakspeare, Goethe, are supreme in their respective lands; not so Corneille or Racine.

The Frenchman who, as thinker and creator, may best claim to rank with the poet-thinkers of other nations, did not write in verse. Rabelais was a master-mind. His buffoonery and smut are justified by Coleridge, as being a necessary vehicle in his age for the conveyance of truth. As it was, he is said to have owed his liberty and even life to the favor of Francis I. I suspect that he was naturally so constructed as to wear willingly such a mask. His great work presents a whole of the most grotesque humor, which may be defined, the shadow caused by the light of the spiritual falling on the animal through the medium of the comic. Rabelais's full animal nature and broad understanding presented a solid and variegated mass of the low and corporeal for the sun of his searching reason and high spirituality to shine upon, and the shadows resulting are broad and deep. The two natures of beast and man seem in him to measure their strength, for the entertainment of the Comic, which stands by and sets them on.

Pascal is the only French writer I know in whom there is the greatness that results from purity and depth, the contact wherewith lifts one up and kindles emotions which possess the soul like a heavenly visitation, banishing for a time whatever there is in one of little or unworthy.

Carlyle calls Voltaire the most French of Frenchmen. I will not do the French the injustice to call him the greatest, though doubtless most of his contemporaries so esteemed him. He was the leader of a generation whose necessary calling was to deny and destroy. His country panted under a monstrous accumulation of spiritual and civil usurpations: he wielded the sharpest axe in the humane work of demolition. His powers were great and his labors immense; and yet there were in him such deficiencies, as to defeat the attainment of completeness in any one of his various literary undertakings. Voltaire had not soul enough to put him in direct communication with the heart of the Universe. Whatever implied emotion, came to him at second-hand, through his intellect. He was not a great poet, a creator; he was a great demolisher. Let him have thanks for much that he did in that capacity.

I record with diffidence these brief judgments, for I have made no wide and thorough study of French Literature. It does not take hold of me: it lacks soul. Of the present generation of writers I am still less qualified to speak, having read but partially of any one of them. They don't draw me into intimacy. It is a peculiarly grateful state of mind when, on laying down a fresh volume, you resolve to possess yourself of all that its author has written. You feel like one who has found a new friend. I have not yet met with the French writer who gives me assurance of this permanent enjoyment. I refer more particularly to works belonging to the provinces of creation and criticism, else I should mention *Thierry*, whose volume entitled *Lettres sur l'Histoire de la France* seems to me a masterpiece of historical research and political acuteness. The authors whose names have lately most sounded abroad, Guizot, Cousin, Villemain, want vitality. Their writings, to use a phrase of Dr. Johnson, come from reservoirs, not springs. Thierry is of a higher order. In La Mennais is the will and noble aim, without the power and accomplishment. The romantic dramas of Hugo and others, simmering with black lawless passion, are opaque as well as shallow, and empty of poetry. They have much more sound than substance, more fury than force. The new French Literature is yet to come into being.

The French beat the world in milliners, in tailors, in porcelain, in upholstery, in furniture; their *or molu* is unrivalled, so are their mousselines and silks; but not so is their painting, or their sculpture, or their music, or their poetry. In the ornamental they are unequalled, but not in the creative. Their sphere is the artificial and conventional: their sympathy with nature is not direct and intense. Their Ideal in Art is not the result of a warm embrace with nature, but of a methodical study of established masters. With their poets and artists the aim and motive in labor is too much the approval of Paris, where humanity is so bedizened by artifice, that the smile and melody of nature are scarce discernible.

I saw Napoleon's funeral, a showy martial pageant, befitting the Imperial soldier. The escort was a hundred thousand armed men; the followers, half a million of both sexes. For hours, the broad long avenue of the Champs Elisées was choked with the moving throng. It was a solemn moment when the funeral car came slowly by. There, within a few feet, lay the body of the man, the tramp of whose legions had been mournfully heard in every great capital of the continent; whose words had been more than the breath of a dozen kings. His shrivelled dust passed through triumphal arches and columns, emblazoned with the record of his hundred conquests. Of them, there was nothing left to France but the name,—of him, nothing but those cold remains. Not even a living member of his line was present, sadly to share in this tardy show of honor. The day was cold and so were the hearts of the multitude. Those bones, let out of their ocean prison, brought with them no hope for the nation. When they are buried, there will be an end of Napoleon. His name will hereafter be but a gorgeous emptiness: his memory is not vitalized by a principle. In his aims there lay no deep hope, whence his fellow men, battling for rights, might for ever draw courage and strength. While he still lived, his schemes were baffled, and what he founded had already passed away. His plans were all for himself, and hence with himself they fell, and left scarce a trace behind. He gave birth to no great Ideas, that, fructifying among men, would have built for him in their souls an everlasting home. He saw not into the depths of truth, and he knew not its unequalled might. Therefore, with all his power he was weak: naught of what he wished came to pass, and what he did with such fiery vehemence, with still more startling swiftness was undone. His thoughts were not in harmony with the counsels of God, and so they perished with himself. The Emperor will have his conspicuous place in History, but the man will not live in the minds of men. For the most potent king of the Earth, what is he, if he be a false man? That one so false could so rule, is a token of the confusion of the times.

One looks almost in vain for the spots that were the centres of the terrific doings of the Revolution. They are mostly so transformed as to have lost their identity. Time has been quick in wiping out the bloody stains. Whoever wishes to bring before his mind, on the ground itself, the place of execution, will need an imagination intense enough to close the avenues of his senses against the garish sights and sounds of the most brilliant public square of this gayest of capitals; for what is now the *Place de la Concorde*, with its lively gilt fountains and rattling equipages, was once the *Place de la Revolution*, where blood streamed daily under the axe of the headsman. If, then, he can succeed in calling up the Guillotine, with its pale victims and exulting throng of savage spectators, it will be easier for the timid to shudder at its butcheries, than for the thinker to solve the problem of their permission. Through the tears and woes of man, the deep laws of Providence march on to their mysterious fulfilment. One may believe, that to a people so brutified by tyranny, so despoiled of natural rights, was needed the swiftest sweep of authority, the broadest exhibition of power, the grossest verification of escape from bondage, in order to vindicate at last and for ever their human claim to a will.

The French people, according to report of those who have known them in both periods, are more earnest and substantial than they were two generations back. They think and feel more, and talk less. There must be hope for a nation that could erect itself as this did, scatter with a tempest the rooted rubbish of ages, overturn half the thrones of Europe, and though re-conquered through the very spirit of freedom that at first had made itself invincible, once more at the end of a half century, rend the old re-imposed fetters and stand firmly on a blood-purchased ground of liberty,—liberty, in comparison with its civil and social condition sixty years ago. For neither was the second Revolution any more than the first the beginning of popular rule: it was the end of unpopular misrule. The mass of the French people have still no direct agency in the government. One of the two legislative bodies, as you are aware, the Chamber of Deputies, is chosen by about two hundred thousand electors out of a population that numbers five millions of male adults; the other, the Chamber of Peers, is created by the king,—a monstrous anomaly, and an insulting mockery. If the revolution of the three days was a protest against monarchical predominance and military coercion, Louis Philippe misrepresents it most flagrantly. By the army is he upheld, not by the nation. I have seen him, going to open the session of the legislature, closely guarded by twenty thousand bayonets. What the purpose is of the fortification of Paris, will become palpable in some future revolution. If the tens of millions buried under this vast cincture, destined to be levelled by popular wrath, had been expended upon railroads radiating from the capital (not to mention higher national wants), Paris would have been rendered impregnable, and France greatly forwarded in wealth and civilisation. The "throne surrounded by republican institutions," promised by Lafayette when he made Louis Philippe king, was the groundless hope of a veteran patriot, too single-minded to have forgotten the dream of his youth, and too short-sighted to discern how far it was then from realization. The fulfilment of the promise he confided to one, whose mental construction was the very opposite of his own, as well intellectually as morally.

The present is a government of bayonets tempered by the Press. The Press, though not quite free, is an immense power, and its growth is a measure of French progress in sixty years. The people, though far yet from that maturity which self-government implies, do not require the semi-military rule of the Orleans Dynasty. Yet are their bonds not so heavy and tight but that they have in some directions quite a wide range of movement. And they have a healthful abiding consciousness of their power to pull down the state, if ever again it should become grossly oppressive. It is utterly incalculable, what, by two such triumphant efforts as their two revolutions, a people gains in self-respect, and self-reliance, and hopeful self-trust, the basis of all moral superstructure, and therefore of all permanent self-government.

ANTWERP, June, 1841.

In France there is little rural beauty. The country looks bald and meagre and lifeless. No clumps of trees, nor rose-sweetened cottages, nor shady hamlets, betokening snug firesides and a quiet sympathy with nature. 'Twas cheering to get into Belgium. Here were the marks of a deeper order and more intelligent labor. On all sides cleanliness and thrift. The sightly, compact towns looked full of well-husbanded resources. From Courtrai, near the borders of France, to Antwerp, we passed, by railroad, for sixty miles through what seemed a fair rich garden, so smooth and minute is the tillage. The soil looked grateful to its working.

It would almost appear that there had been a defeat of Nature's intent in this quarter of Europe; a territory has been split, which was so naturally adapted for unity. One cannot help thinking it a pity the Burgundian sovereignty had not lasted. Where there are now discordant French, Belgians, and Dutch, there might have been one homogeneous people of eight or ten millions, with breadth of territory, and strength and variety of resources, sufficient for an ample national development. Just at the period, towards the end of the fifteenth century, when a nation was forming and about to be knit together by Literature and the Arts,—for which it exhibited such aptitude,—the whole country, by the marriage of the heiress of the last of the Burgundians, passed into the hands of Austria, and thence by Charles V. was left to his son, Philip II. of Spain. The high spirit of the people would not brook the cruelties of this tyrant and his creature Alba, who wished to establish among them the Inquisition, that masterpiece of Satan's most inventive mood. In the famous revolt, only the northern provinces were successful. Belgium remained under the dominion of Spain a century longer, when it was re-transferred to Austria, from which it was finally wrested in the French Revolution, to be first incorporated into France, and then by the Congress of Vienna reunited, after a divorce of more than two centuries, to Holland. But during that long separation, the two, living under totally different influences, had naturally contracted habits that were reciprocally hostile. Holland was Protestant, Belgium, Catholic; and the language, which, under a permanent union, might have been unfolded by the wants of a vigorous nation to take rank by the side of the cognate German, was broken into dialects, that of Holland becoming cultivated enough to be the medium of some literature, that of Belgium remaining the half-grown speech of the peasants and Bourgeois, and giving place in *salons* and palaces to the more refined tongue of its overshadowing Southern neighbor. It was now too late to make one nation of the Netherlands, and so, the marriage, brought about by neighbors through persuasions too well backed by power to be withstood, was soon dissolved, and Belgium was erected into an independent monarchy, under a new king, by the side of Holland, or, I should say, a separate monarchy; for when united, they had not the strength for independence, and now of course will even the more readily fall victims of greedy neighbors, whenever the beam of that very unsteady fixture called the balance of power shall be kicked.

Antwerp has still much of the wealth and beauty it inherited from the olden time, when, with its two hundred thousand inhabitants, it was, in commerce and opulence, the first among the cities of Europe; and its merchant princes built up cathedrals and squares and palaces, for Rubens and Vandyke to people out of their procreative brains. The population is reduced now to seventy or eighty thousand, the port is content with a hundred vessels at a time instead of two thousand; but the broad clean streets bordered with stately mansions are still here, and the cathedral, whose spire alone is a dower for a province; and the inhabitants, yet rich in fat lands and well-filled coffers, are still richer in the possession of some of the fairest offspring of their great fellow-townsman's genius. The potency of genius and art is here most forcibly exemplified. Take away Rubens and the Cathedral, and Antwerp would not be Antwerp. This tower, steadfast, light, fretted with delicate tracery, springing nearly four hundred feet from the ground, which it seems to touch no more heavily than a swan about to take flight, is an unfading beauty shining daily on the hearts of the people, while the memory of Rubens and his presence in his gigantic handiwork are a perpetual image of greatness. To the passing stranger they are an adornment to the land, but to the natives a stay and brace to the very mind itself, keeping ever before them the reality of beauty and power, and fortifying them with the consciousness of kindred with genius and greatness.

Antwerp has at this time high artists, Jacobs, Keyser, Waeppers, who sit under the transparent shadow of this marvellous tower, and whose art attains a more juicy maturity in the sun of Rubens's genius. Their works sell at high prices as fast as they produce them. Love of art, blended in the hearts of the people with religion, is an element of their nature. The creations of their great painters illuminate the churches, and through the incense that ascends from the altar, beam upon the upturned countenance of the worshipper. In the public Museum are preserved some of the best works of Rubens and Vandyke; and in private dwellings are seen family portraits from their hands, fresh from the embalming touch of genius, twice-prized,—by personal and by national pride.

In a rich private collection of old books and pictures, I have seen a set of engravings, bound up into several huge tomes of the greater part of Rubens's works. To behold thus at a single view, the collected product of such a spirit's life, is to have in one's hand a key to much of the mystery of the painter's art. This man's mind was an ever-teeming womb of light-dyed forms. These were the spontaneous absorbing growth of his brain. With him, existence could only be enjoyed, fulfilled, by delivering himself of this urgent brood of brain-engendered pictures. What a wealth of invention and inexhaustible vigor! What fertility, and boldness, and breadth and fire! What opulence and grandeur of imagination! What skill in the marshalling of his legions!

What life in each head, in each figure, in each group! And what a flood of beauty in his coloring! 'Tis as if, for his great pictures, he had gathered into his brain the hues of a gorgeous sunset, and poured them upon the canvas.

Among the features wherein old Europe differs from young America, none is more prominent than the large number of idlers in Europe. Capital being wanting in the United States, almost the universal energy is busied in supplying it; in Europe it is abundant, and many live in industrial unproductiveness upon its moderate dividends. With us, it is hardly respectable to be idle; here, only they who are so, enjoy the highest consideration. With us, gentility is confined to those who addict themselves to certain kinds of labor; in Europe it excludes all who labor at all, except in the highest offices of the State. In "good society" here, you meet with neither lawyer, nor merchant, nor physician, not even with the clergy, for in Belgium, priests are drawn from the peasant and bourgeois classes, and their consecration is not believed to confer upon them nobility. Birth has hitherto been an almost indispensable passport into the highest circles, but money, aided by the stealthy progress of democratic ideas, is making breaches in the aristocratic entrenchments, and ere many generations, " good society" in Europe will present somethinglike the motley concourse that it does with us, where, the social arrangements having no support from the political, old families go down and new ones come up, and the power of a man on 'Change is often the measure of his position in fashionable drawing-rooms. This is but the chaos of transition: the soul will in time assert its transcendant privileges.

In Europe, notwithstanding occasional intermarriages, the aristocratic prestige still prevails against plebeian merit. In social longer than in political life, the nobility naturally retain a predominance, that is of course exercised despotically. Although, since the invention of printing, the expansion of commerce, and the rapid development of industry and science, knowledge and wealth, the sources of the highest power in communities, have been passing out of the hands of the privileged few, still, social advantages, depending upon deep-rooted ideas, are the last to be forfeited, and the nobility throughout Europe, long after their exclusion from the high posts in the State, will look down upon the herd of plebeian aspirants to *ton*, just as the *ancienne noblesse* of France did upon the military upstarts of Napoleon, and do still upon the Court of Louis Philippe. And this from a real superiority of position.

The nobility of Europe,—the early, and at first the rightful sole possessors of power as the originally strong men; the acknowledged monopolists of social elevations; the dispensers of place and patronage; the recipients and in turn the fountains of honor; in short, the controllers with kings of all high interests and lords of etiquette and manners,—acquired, by the cultivation of the stateliness growing out of courtly usages and the tone contracted from conscious superiority, an easy commanding style of bearing and intercourse, which was of a natural inward growth, the unforced expression of their social rank and being. Now, as this social rank and being is no longer attainable by others, so neither are the modes of life, the style of manners, the segregation from the people, which were its natural products. All attempts therefore on the part of those, who, since the breaking up of the monopolies of knowledge and wealth, are now sharing their possession with the old nobility, to assume too their bearing and style, are and must be a bare assumption, a hollow imitation; and not merely as such an inevitable failure, but one tainted with vulgarity, the essence of which is false pretension. So long as another standard than the feudal aristocratic is not set up as the measure of social position, there will be war between the old *régime*, which in its sphere was a genuine true thing, and the new, which being an apery of it, is a false thing. In the end, the old, no longer upheld by law, impoverished by idleness and debilitated by generations of luxurious inactivity, will have to succumb, and become socially extinct, or absorbed into the triumphant new, and pedigrees will grow confused, and the imagination cease to invest birth with virtue.

In this conflict will for a time be aggravated the most repulsive quality of aristocratic life. The feeling of superiority over one's fellows, mere personal pride, will be still more cherished. Their children are already bred up to look upon themselves as better than all other children. Towards their fellow-men a sentiment rather of repulsion than sympathy is generated in the members of a privileged class. Instead of keeping their hearts open with liberal susceptibility to worth and excellence, they are ever on the alert to fend off all others from contact with themselves. They form a narrow circle, living to themselves on sympathies of selfishness. These feelings, latent while their rank was undisputed, become active against plebeian encroachment; while their plebeian rivals and imitators cultivate the same feeling as well from imitation, as to strengthen their new state against the aspiring multitude still below them. An offspring too of this conflict is Fashion, which is an effort to outvie exclusiveness, to be more tonish than *haut ton* itself. Fashion is a wingless aspiration after elegance; a brazen usurpation; a baseless pretension kept alive by quick changes of aspect; an impertinent substitution of personality for principle; an imposition of effrontery upon weakness; a caricature of beauty; a restless prosaic straining for an ideal; a mock flower, bloomless, odorless and seedless.

Although, in the large cities, the mimicry of European ways evolves out of our prosaic citizens an unavoidable portion of vulgarity, the corrective of republican self-respect is ever active; and amidst much false aim and shallow endeavor, there is perceptible a growing appreciation of the genuine and true. Already the aspiring *nouveau riche* feels that culture and taste are the essence of social excellence, and hastens to give his children the advantages himself has missed. Where there is natural susceptibility of polish, education and republican self-reliance tell at once upon the second generation, and at times,—such is the richness of nature,—a man springs up from the workshop, and while by talent he attains to affluence, attains to grace and courteous propriety by native refinement and generosity; and totally devoid of the grimaces, the sleek well-tailored outside, the money-jingling vulgarity of the *parvenu*, he takes his place as a gentleman without the English ordeal of three generations. We apply a practical test to know what is good blood, and soon recognize him for what he is. Evidence is constantly thrown out of a tendency towards higher things. The intellectual lift up the tastes, and the spiritual the desires, for other wants than for furniture and equipages.

As inequality in mental faculties among men is a law of nature, the idea of a "best society" is real, and will go on manifesting itself more and more distinctly, working constantly upward through impure materials. The mind will by degrees straighten itself into better proportions. Factitious and grossly-bottomed distinctions will be effaced. In our country we have compassed a vantage-ground of liberty, whence to ascend to higher platforms of social condition. Grossly do they underrate the worth of liberty, who regard security of person and property, equality before the law, freedom of speech and of printing, as its ripe fruit. These are but the foundation for a broader and more beautiful structure. Through them the mind will brace its wings and sharpen its vision for wider sweeps into the domain of the possible; and expanding with unrestricted inter-communion, grow in brightness and beneficence. Proofs of this progress are discernible in the easier emancipation from soul-smothering customs, and in the longings and hopes of the freest minds. In this higher organization the gentleman will of course not be wanting; for no well-developed society could be without him, in whom, as Spenser sings,

"The gentle mind by gentle deed is known."

Let those who regret the decay of the old-fashioned gentleman, because the new-fashioned one, being a coarse imitation of him, is, like all imitations, a failure, take hope, that there is one of a higher fashion possible and already forming, in whom politeness, being the offspring of love and beauty, shall cease borrowing of falsehood; in whom refinement shall not be the superficial show of conventional discipline, but a spontaneous emanation from the purified mind; courtesy be free from pride, and elevation be enjoyed by right neither of pedigree nor Plutus, but solely by natural endowment, be acknowledged as ungrudgingly as difference of stature, and sit on the possessor as unconsciously as flowers on stalks, and like them dispense beauty all around.

Boppart, on the Rhine, July, 1841.

After spending six weeks most pleasantly at Antwerp, we turned our steps towards the Rhine, stopping but a day in Brussels, to get a glimpse of the pictures in the Museum, a look at the painted windows of the Church of St. Gudule, and some insight into the manufacture of Brussels lace. We didn't care to see Palaces. We had been paced through those of Paris and its neighborhood, and Palaces are all alike; on the outside, huge, overgrown, depopulated-looking edifices, and in the inside, suite upon suite of lofty rooms and halls, where upholstery, with its glittering gildings and silks, keeps repeating its short circle of adornment. Brussels is a cheerful, sunny city, but it is always associated in my mind with its little ambition of being a little Paris, and with its sub-population of questionable and vulgar English, that taint its atmosphere. I was told at Antwerp of an Englishman and his family, who came there to live, although a dull town compared with Brussels, because, as he said, he had a good name at home, and he wouldn't have it blasted by a residence at Brussels.

From Brussels steam carried us in a few hours through the fat, well-tilled land to Liege, the Sheffield of Belgium. The railroad not being finished beyond Liege, we there took post-horses. The country all about Liege lifts itself briskly up into hills, and the road thence to Aix-la-Chapelle offers lively landscapes to the traveller's eye. Before reaching Aix we passed the Prussian frontier. After fifteen years I found myself again in Germany. the strong, rich tones of the language came back familiarly to my ears. They came laden with memories of kindness, and enjoyments, and profit. My re-entrance into Germany was one of the happiest hours of the journey; nor was it marred by vexations at the Prussian custom-house, through which we were allowed to pass after a nominal search. It is one of the important events in a traveller's career, the crossing of a boundary. Another variety of the species man, with new fixtures and environments. Another people, another language, another look to the land and everything on it. Other sights and other sounds to the freshly busied senses; and to the interior mind,—alive in each region with its peculiar heroes and benefactors,—other inmates. History unrolls another leaf of her illuminated testament, and we tell over again another treasure she has bequeathed us.

In Aix-la-Chapelle, the birth and burial place of Charlemagne, famous since the Romans for its sulphur baths, we spent but a night, and continued our way to strike the Rhine at Cologne. Thence to Göttingen was, by the nearest route through Westphalia, hardly more than a two days' journey. It would have been but a melancholy pleasure to re-visit the noble old University, now made ignoble by the base-mindedness of her rulers. What a fall, with her seven hundred students, from her palmy state in 1824–25, when she counted over fifteen hundred; and when, drawn from all quarters of the globe by her high renown, we sometimes assembled together under the *Cathedra* of a single Professor, listeners from North America and from South America, from England and from Italy, from France and from Sweden, from Russia and from Switzerland, from Poland and from every State in Germany. The galaxy of teachers she then had, the successors of others as eminent, the cowardly policy since pursued towards her, has prevented from being renewed. Göttingen has ceased to be what Napoleon called her, "l'Université de l'Europe." She has dwindled into provincialism.—And beyond was Weimar, enwreathed to all cultivated imaginations with a unique glory. In his youth, the Grand Duke Charles Augustus,—a natural leader among men, for fifty years the companion of Goethe,—belted his little Capital round with the brightest stars of German genius. During his long life they illuminated and refined his court, and were a blessing to his people; and since his death, their sparkling names form a diadem round his, that outshines the crowns of haughty Kings. At the time of my visit in 1825, the Grand Duke and his congenial Duchess, and the greatest of his poetic band, Goethe, were still alive; and over the hospitalities of the Palace, the remarkable beauty of the ladies of his court threw a fascination that made it like a fairy castle.— Still further was Dresden, with its natural charms and its treasures of Art. But I was not now to behold those well remembered spots. Our destiny rules us most despotically when our will seems freest.

We arrived at Cologne early enough in the afternoon to go out and look at the Cathedral, which, finished, would have been, as well from its size as its beauty, the foremost among Gothic Churches. Most of the Gothic Cathedrals are, like this, unfinished. The conceptions of their artists were loftier than the power or will of those who supplied the means for their execution. Their incompleteness is symbolical of the short-comings of the noblest minds in their aspirations. Our road now lay up the Rhine, but the river only enjoys the embrace of its hills, and the animating company of the old castles that crown them, between

Bonn and Mayence. Bonn is twelve miles above Cologne. Here, on my way from Göttingen fifteen years before, coming down the Rhine, partly on foot, before the day of steamboats in Germany, I had stopped, with an English fellow-traveller and student, to see Niebuhr and A. W. Schlegel, who were Professors in the University of Bonn. Schlegel kept us waiting some time in a neat drawing-room, where hung a portrait of Madame de Stael. He then came in hurriedly, adjusting the tie of his cravat. He was affable and lively, and in his dress, bearing and conversation, seemed anxious to sink the Professor and appear the man of the world. Niebuhr was out, but came in an hour to the Hotel to see us. He was a tall, striking, man and spoke English perfectly. The sight of an American seemed to excite his mind. He plied me with questions about our institutions and customs. Doubtless his thoughts were often busied and puzzled with the new historical phenomenon of the great Republic, whose huge bulk was heaving itself up portentously in the far west. But Niebuhr was not the man to seize its significance or embrace its grandeur. His mind was exegetical and critical, rather than constructive and prophetic.

We are now in the heart of Rhenish Prussia. The civil government of Prussia is after the military model. The king is the commander-in-chief of the nation, and the schoolmaster is his drill-sergeant. The boys are taught in such a way that the men shall fall readily into the ranks of obedience. A uniform is put upon their minds, and, as with the rank and file of a regiment, the uniformity is more looked to than the fitness. The government does all it can to save men the pain of thought and choice, and if it could would do everything. The officers of administration having the intelligence and industry of the cultivated German mind, and these being everywhere the German solidity and honesty, the system bears some good fruit, such virtue is there in order and method, though only of the mechanical sort. Prussia is a well-managed estate, not a well-governed country; for good government implies a recognition of the high nature of humanity, the first want of which is freedom. The only basis whereon the moral being of man can be built up is individual independence. To reach that higher condition of freedom, where he shall be emancipated from the tyranny of self, of his own passions, he needs first of all to be free from that of his fellows. The one freedom is only possible through the other.

That the Germans are a breed that can keep pace with the best in the development of civilisation, they have given manifold proof in achievements by word and deed. They are a strong-brained, deep-hearted race. What creative power have they not exhibited in letters, in science, in Art! With what soul and steadfastness they backed their mighty Luther, in his great strife for mental independence! How they rose, like a giant from his sleep, against French usurpation, and with Leipzic paid Napoleon for Jena! The conditions were reversed. At Jena, Napoleon, though with dementing egotism he had set a crown upon his head, was still the leader of a freshly emancipated people warring against old tyrannies: at Leipzic he was the hardened despot, with no instruments but his legions, and no props to his vulgar throne but force and fear; while the monarchs of Germany and Russia were upborne on the hearts of the liberty-seeking people. The sceptred weaklings, whose capitals had been a prey to the conqueror, became suddenly strong with the strength of wrath-swollen multitudes. This wrath is ever ready to be rekindled. Its next outburst will not be against foreign oppressors.

At Bonn we stopped but to change horses. Now it is that the Rhine discloses its treasures. Two or three miles above Bonn, we passed under the ancient Castle of Godesberg; a little further that of Rolandseck; opposite, on the other side of the water, the Drachenfels gives life to the "Seven Mountains;" and midway between them, lying softly in the low river, is the Island with the old Convent of Nonnenwerth. Around are green valleys, and plentiful fields, and grape-mantled steeps, and frequent villages and compact towns. And thus, the whole way from Bonn to Mayence, you drive through a double population. Above, the sides of the castle-crowned hills are alive with mailed cavalcades, bugles are winding from the turrets, fair ladies are leaning over parapets waving their sweet welcomes and farewells; while below, through the tranquil movements of a secure industry, the noiseless labors of tillage, the hum of busy towns, you roll smoothly forward on a macadamized road, and try to stir up your phlegmatic postillion to a race with a steamboat abreast of you on the river. To eyes at all open to natural beauty, this region, unpeopled, rude and naked, were a feast; but twice-touched as it is by the productive hand of man, the broken shadows of ancient strongholds checkering the turfed flanks of the cannon-guarded fortress; the images of spires, of cottages, of wooded heights, of ruins, of rocky precipices, of palaces, all playing together in the ripple of the sinuous stream; the old river, fresh and lively as in the days of Arminius, with its legends, its history, and its warm present life; senses, thought, imagination, all addressed at once amid scenes steeped in beauty;—'tis a region unmatched, and worth a long journey to behold.

As we approached Coblentz, Ehrenbreitstein, the Gibraltar of Germany, lifted high its armed head, frowning towards France. The next morning we were again on the enchanted road, and in two hours reached Boppart. Turning up hill to the right, just on entering the town, we ascended to a large substantial old pile directly behind and above it. This was formerly the convent of Marienberg, for noble ladies, most solidly and commodiously built for a household of two hundred; seated in a valley between hills, with shady walks, and springs, and fountains, and broad terraces, whence you look over the old town, founded by Drusus, into the river, now enlivened almost hourly with sociable steam.

boats. The convent has been converted into a water-cure establishment. While at Antwerp several small works on the water-cure had fallen into my hands, and impressed my mind at once almost to conviction with the truth of its principles. I will endeavor to give you a sketch of what it is and what it does. I cannot better begin than with an account of my own daily proceeding.

At five in the morning I am waked up by a bath-attendant. Having stripped the narrow bed, he lays on the bare mattress a thick blanket, wherein he wraps me closely from neck to heels; then another blanket doubled is laid on and tightly tucked in, and then another, and then a light feather bed. This is fitly called being packed up. In about an hour I begin to perspire; whereupon the window is opened to let in fresh air, and half a tumbler of cold water is administered, which draught, repeated every quarter of an hour, promotes perspiration. After perspiring for forty or fifty minutes, I am unpacked, get streaming out of the blankets into an empty bath-tub at the bed-side, when instantly a couple of large buckets of cold water are poured over my head and shoulders. For a minute or two my hands and the attendant's are swiftly plied all over the surface, as if to rub in the water. Then comes a thorough dry rubbing with a coarse linen sheet, and after dressing quickly, a walk abroad for half an hour or more to support and hasten re-action, drinking the while from the fountain two or three glasses of water. On the breakfast-table are wheat and rye bread, butter, milk, and water, and fruit for those who choose it; no tea, nor coffee, nor anything warm. Between eleven and twelve I take a sitting-bath of from fifteen to twenty minutes' duration, on coming out of which I go up to the top of the hills as if the muscles that had been immersed were turned into wings. Two or three more tumblers of water are drunk during the exercise. Dinner, at one, is never smoking hot, and consists for the most part of beef, mutton, and fowls roasted or boiled, with vegetables, followed by a simple dessert. No spices are used in cooking, and water is the only beverage. Bathing re-commences about four, a long interval being prescribed after each meal. My afternoon bath is generally what is called a *staub-bad*, literally, a dust-bath, which is in fact a shower-bath, except that the shower, instead of falling from above, comes laterally from circular tubes in the midst of which you stand, and which, the moment the water is let on, pour upon you a thousand fine streams. Resolution must be well seconded by quick friction with the hands, to keep you within this refrigerating circle two or three minutes. After this is the best time for a long stroll over the hills or along the shores of the Rhine. Supper, between six and seven, is much the same as breakfast; nothing hot, nothing stimulating. All meals are alike in the voracity of appetite with which they are eaten. I wear all day over the stomach a waterband or compress,—a double fold of coarse linen, six or seven inches wide and about twenty long, half wrung out in cold water, over which is tied a dry one of the same material and thickness, a little broader and meeting round the body. This, excluding the air, prevents evaporation from the wet bandage, and keeps it always warm. The compress is re-wet every two or three hours. Its effect is, to draw more life into the weakened stomach.

A similar course is daily followed by the rest of the inmates. Instead of the affusion from buckets, most plunge directly into the full-bath after the sweating in the morning. Some are wrapt in a wet sheet, within the blankets, in which they lie about an hour. Then there is the potent *douche*, a stream of two to four inches diameter, falling from ten to twenty feet perpendicularly, which is taken when the body has become invigorated and the skin opened by the other applications. There are, moreover, local baths; foot-baths, head-baths, eye-baths.

The number of patients in this establishment at present is about eighty, with all kinds of chronic maladies,—gout, rheumatism, neuralgia, dyspepsia, deafness, lameness, paralysis, &c. Fill up the &c. with every name that has been coined to express the bodily afflictions of man, and not one that is curable, but can be cured by means of water. By *means of water*, note that; for water can cure no disease; it can but help or force the body itself to cure it. What more does medical Art profess to do? No intelligent physician aims at aught but so to rouse or direct the *vis medicatrix naturæ*, the curative force of nature, that it may throw off disease. To his lancet, his purgatives, his emetics, his narcotics, his stimulants, he ascribes a purely secondary agency, that of touching the spring of life in a way that it shall rebound against the evil that presses it. All his appliances and efforts and doses have but one single aim, namely, to act on the vital force. In awakening, seconding, guiding this, consists his whole skill. Herein, then, the water and drug systems are alike. Most unlike are they in the innocence and efficacy of their means, and in the success of their endeavors.

Patients are here, as at mineral watering places, on account of chronic diseases, that is, diseases that have taken up their abode in the body, because the body has not vigor left to eject them. These complaints the Faculty hardly ever profess to eradicate. In most patients so afflicted, disease and the Doctor have a joint life-estate. Change of air, temperance, quiet, diet, are the alleviating prescriptions to some. Permanent restoration is seldom promised by the upright physician. Priesnitz and his disciples undertake to cure, and do cure, many such; and by means of water nearly all are curable, where there is constitutional vitality enough for re-action, and no organic lesion. The process is as simple as nature's laws. The world will soon wonder, as it has done at other revelations of genius, why it was so long undiscovered. Priesnitz has revealed the power there is in water. With this one agent he can co-work with all the processes and movements of nature in the human organism. He can draw the vital stream from one part to another; he can unload the congested blood-vessels; he can quicken or slacken the action of the heart; he can elevate or depress the nervous energy. And his agent, in this at once subtle and powerful co-operation, is not a poison, as is almost every drug, never weakens, as does every bleeding, but is a pure nourishing element, as precious to the body as the vital air itself, and having with its every texture such sympathy, that four parts out of five of the constituents of the blood are water. In this consists much of its virtue as a curative means. It is not enough that it be cold: Priesnitz rejects all mineral waters, and even salt sea-water.

The first step towards a restoration of health is a re-subjection of the body to natural laws, as regards food, drink, air, and exercise. Further; as the vital energy is the final source of restoration, it is necessary, when disease has become fixed in the body, that this energy be directed against it with undivided aim. Hence, there must be withdrawal from business and care and serious mental occupation; and therefore it is, that the cure of chronic complaints can, in most cases, only be undertaken with hope of success at a water-cure establishment. These first conditions being satisfied, under which the body begins at once to feel fresh vigor, the next step is, to accelerate this invigoration. The fortifying effects of cold bathing are universally known. Without considering now the various forms of its application, devised by the sagacity of Priesnitz, the mere loss of caloric in a cold bath necessarily stimulates the appetite. More food is called for to supply the lost heat. The quickened respiration in the bath and during the rapid exercise it provokes, supply a correspondent increase of oxygen. As Liebig simply and beautifully explains, animal heat is the result of the combination within the body between the oxygen brought in through the lungs, and the carbon and hydrogen in the food. The oxygen consumes, literally burns up, the waste of the body, the dead particles that have served their purpose of nourishing the vital activity. The fire burns more briskly. By the increase of food, fresh material is furnished more rapidly; the burning of the old keeps pace through the increased influx of oxygen; and thus the transformations in the body, the source and index of health, go on with increased quickness, and the strength grows in proportion. A man with a good fund of vitality left, who takes three or four cold baths and drinks a dozen glasses of cold water daily, will eat just double his usual quantity, and that of the plainest fare, and with a relish that he never felt at the costliest banquet, and a sweetness and fulness of flavor, that recall the time of his fast-growing boyhood.

'Tis a familiar fact, that if a fragment of bone, for instance, in case of fracture, be left loose and unknit up when the fracture heals, it will be thrown out to the surface by the vital force. Where there is life enough, the same self-purifying, self-protecting effort will be made against whatever arrests or disturbs the vital process, against every form of disease therefore. The third step in the proceeding of Priesnitz is, to encourage and assist this tendency by more specific means than the mere addition of strength by cold bathing.

How is the determination from the centre to the surface to be promoted?

By action on the skin through the sweating in blankets, and the soaking in the wet sheet inclosed by blankets. The power of these applications cannot be conceived but by one who has seen them, I may add, felt them. An activity is awakened in the skin unknown to it before, and this without any foreign or hostile appliances. Under the air-tight blankets softly oozes out the perspiration; the wet sheet sucks at the whole surface, like a gentle all-embracing poultice. The skin is in a glow—a glow which it owes to no heat but that beneath it. The life of the whole body is drawn to and towards it. In this state of heightened animation it re-acts against the cold bath with alacrity. One or other of these processes—according to the disease, condition or temperament of the patient—repeated daily, keeps the currents, so to speak, always setting outwardly. The skin, that great auxiliary of the lungs, grows elastic, regains its functions, that had become lamed by the destructive practice of swathing in flannel, and the neglect of cold ablutions, needed daily for the whole surface as much as for the face. Chronic congestions and inflammations are thus gradually relieved; the system feels lightened. Morbific matter is expelled. That it is morbific, is often known by its odor and color. Frequently, too, what medicines have been taken, sometimes years before, is discovered by the odor of the perspiration; as valerian, iodine, assafœtida, sulphur, mercury.

The sitting bath performs the important part of drawing the blood from the brain, and of invigorating the great nerves of the stomach and bowels, which in nearly all chronic complaints have become weakened by drugs, heating food and drinks, and sedentary habits. When, by the sweating or the wet sheet, the sitting bath, and copious daily draughts of cold water, the skin has been opened and animated, the internal skin—the lining membrane of the lungs and digestive organs—stimulated, and all the functions invigorated, so that the system is restored in a degree to its pristine power of resistance, then is applied the most vigorous of all the water agents, the douche, which rouses to the utmost the nervous energy, and thus contributes much towards putting the body in a state to cope with its foe.

Now the aim of all these purifying energizing processes is, to bring on a *crisis*, that is, an effort of the system to rid itself of the disease which obstructs and oppresses it. The *crisis* is, in fact, in strong cases, an acute attack, taking the form of diarrhœa, more or less active or prolonged, or of vomiting, or cutaneous eruption, or fever. Sometimes these symptoms come one after the other, or even several at once. With knowledge and judgment, the **crisis is guided surely to a cure.** When the disease is not of long standing, the functional derangement not being firmly established, the cure is effected of course much more quickly and often without apparent crisis. On the other hand, in aggravated cases, when the body, in the phrase of Priesnitz, is very full of bad stuff, the patient may have to go through two or three crises, before his system is perfectly purged of disease. Once through the crisis, the patient is cured, cured effectually, radically, not apparently and temporarily, but permanently and absolutely. The nervous energy is renovated, the skin is restored to the full performance of its important functions, the digestive apparatus works perfectly, the blood flows actively and impartially, no morbid condition lurks in any of the tissues, the transformations go on briskly and smoothly, life plays lightly and evenly through the whole organism; the man is well. With healthy habits he can keep so all his days, and end them with an easy natural death, not the hard unnatural one that most are doomed to, dying of disease and the Doctor.

Visitors are astonished at the cheerfulness of the inmates. A merrier company is not to be found on the joyous Rhine. Such a happy Hospital is a phenomenon. No brilliant balls, nor luxurious lounges, nor dainty viands, nor fragrant wines, nor gambling saloons, are needed here as at the neighboring Ems and Wiesbaden, to charm away ennui and make the day endurable. Noon drives away morning, and evening noon, ere we have done with them; and when we lay our heads down at night, so quick and dream-tight is sleep, that morning is upon us again as if he had but waited for the closing of our lids, and nature had compressed hours into moments that they might lie weightless on our brains. Such is the virtue of water, which at once soothes and exhilarates. It must be remembered, too, that the invalids here are all outcasts, unfortunates sentenced by Doctors' edicts to perpetual banishment from the realm of health. Hence the slowness of the cure, which few who have the time have the perseverance to complete. Most of us are impatient if complaints of years' standing are not washed out in a few weeks. Thus, but a small number earn the full benefit of a radical cure; more are partially relieved of their pains; the rest, and largest proportion, only get strength and habits wherewith the better to bear them.

But it is in acute diseases, that the triumphs of the water-cure are most signal and astounding. Here its results look like miracles, so rapid are they, so regenerative, so complete.

I have said, that the *crisis* is an acute attack. On the other hand, an acute disease is but a *crisis* brought about by the vital force of nature, unexalted by the water-processes. Priesnitz cures all such, rapidly, with ease, with certainty. What he is always striving to produce, is here brought to his hand. An acute disease being a strenuous effort that the organism makes to throw out the enemy, Priesnitz comes in helpfully, by cooling the skin and opening its pores. This sounds very simple and easy. Is there in Christendom a physician who can cool the skin and open the pores at will in a burning fever? Not all the schools and systems of all countries through long ages of experiment and woe, have discovered the nature of fevers and the art of treating them. In spite of his tonics, his diaphoretics, his antiphlogistics, his lancet, Death strides past the Doctor, and seizes upon the young and the robust, as boldly and surely now as a thousand years ago. Let the world, then, rejoice. Glad tidings have come from Graeffenberg. Some of the scourges of mankind are stayed. The cholera, the scarlet-fever, the small-pox, are shorn of their terrors. At this proclamation some will smile, some will chide, the most will ejaculate incredulous. Facts upon facts are there, and thousands have witnessed them and spread afar the news of the blessing, and those who have looked at them studiously, know why they are and that they must be. Inflammations and fevers are perfectly manageable by Priesnitz and his pupils. What is the glory of Harvey and Jenner to that of the German peasant?

From the times of Hippocrates and Galen, down to those of

Currie and Hoffman, many are the Doctors, as set forth in the books brought out by Priesnitz's doings, who have cured diseases with water. But the shrewdest of them had only glimpses of its power. Nature, as is her way, has constantly thrown out hints to them, and temptations with facts; but not in one of them before Priesnitz did the facts inbreed thoughts, that, wrought upon by the awakened spirit of research, led it on to the detection of the laws, whereby this one element becomes a curative means of an efficacy beyond the liveliest hopes of medical enthusiasts. Still, "the Faculty" say, forsooth, there is nothing new in Priesnitz's pretended discoveries. Is there nothing new in putting a patient daily for months through four or five cold baths, one or two of them while his skin is dripping with perspiration produced by his own warmth, and thereby curing him radically of the gout? Is it not new to thrust a man delirious into a cold shallow bath, and there keep him for nine hours with constant friction on his legs and pouring of cold water on his head, and thus to restore him in twenty-four hours? Who ever before put a child with a brain fever through forty wet sheets in as many successive half hours, and by so doing completely subdued in three days a disease, whose cure would have been doubtful with drugs, in three weeks. This magical wet-sheet itself, what a discovery! Is it not a stupendous novelty to regard fevers as, in all cases, but the manifestation of the struggle going on within between the vital principle and a disease which threatens it? And is it not a new feeling, in the summoned healer, to approach the fever-heated patient with clearest confidence, looking on the fever as a sign of vital activity, which with a single agent he can uphold and helpfully direct to a rapid and safe issue? instead of going to work against the vital principle with his drugs,—which draw it off from its struggle with the disease to fight themselves,— and with his life-tapping lancet, inwardly trembling,—if he be clear-headed and conscientious,—for the slow result, doubting of his whole procedure, coming back daily for weeks with the trepidation of one who is tussling in the dark with Death for a human being, and often overwhelmed at the sudden victory of his foe, by the conviction, that himself has opened to him the path. I refer now to the best of the medical guild, the few men of thought, feeling, and integrity. Such will feel, how sadly true is the self-reproach of Faust, who, on being hailed with honor and thanks by the peasants for having, a young assistant to his medical father, saved so many of them from the plague, exclaims that their praise sounds like scorn, and relates to his companion the blind, desperate nature of their treatment, concluding as follows:—

> And thus with most infernal pills,
> Among these valleys and these hills,
>   Far worse than did the Pest we blazed.
> Thousands did I the poison give;
> They withered off, and I must live
>   To hear th' audacious murderers praised.*

The common crowd of legalized botchers walk through their daily mischievous routine, partly in ignorant thoughtlessness, partly in insensibility.

"The whole baseless calamitous system of drug-poisoning," says a German expounder of Priesnitz's practice, "which has already snatched away many millions, had its origin in the misconception of primary or acute diseases. Because people did not perceive that these abnormal feverish conditions are only efforts at healing which the organism makes, they mistook these fever-symptoms for the disease itself, and finding that they could be

---

* So haben wir mit höllischen Latwergen
In diesen Thälern, diesen Bergen,
Weit schlimmer als die Pest getobt.
Ich habe selbst den Gift an tausende gegeben;
Sie welkten hin, ich muss erleben,
Dass man die frechen Mörder lobt.

allayed by blood-letting and drugging, they prized this fatal discovery. Then sprang up from this poisonous seeding a whole host of terrible deadly maladies. But because the afflictions did not show themselves immediately, within a few weeks after the medicinal suppression of the acute disease, no one had a thought that the drugs and bleeding were the cause of them." The same author thus writes of inflammation in case of wounds !—" In order to heal a wound, the organism must form on the part where the wound is, new flesh, new vessels for the new capillaries, &c. To be able to form this flesh, it is necessary that the material for it,— the forming sap, which is the blood,—be led to the part in abnormal quantity. Thus, too, plants heal an injury by sending to the injured spot sap in unusual abundance. Through this abnormal blood-life, increased warmth is produced in the part to be healed, which warmth, however, only then gets to real inflammation when the instinct of the wounded person for cold water inwardly and outwardly is not satisfied. Allopathy, in its stolidity, looks upon this streaming of the blood to the wounded part, and the exaltation of life therein to the point of heat, as disease, as something which must be removed, and lets blood. Hereupon, notwithstanding, the organism continues to send blood to the injured part, where it is needed, and the Doctor continues to let blood, sometimes until the extremities become bloodless and cold, and the patient often dies of weakness,—as is also the case with internal, so called, inflammations."

These views of fever and inflammation have been deduced from the facts observed and brought to light by Priesnitz. If any like them were ever before entertained, it was but in a partial, feeble way. They have never formed part of the medical creed; they have not been made the foundation of a school. As great as between the momentary illumination of lightning and the light of the day-long sun, is the difference between having a thought pass through the mind, and having it planted there till it grow to a fruitful conviction. Hereby is the Healing Art become, for the first time, what all Art ought to be, the handmaid of Nature, and thus, at last, what it never before was, a genuine healing art, and a blessing to humanity.

This broad, absolute condemnation of the drug and lancet practice, is at any rate not new. Hear some of the most famous physicians speak of their Art.

Van Helmont says:—" A murder-loving devil has taken possession of the medical chairs; for none but a devil could recommend to physicians blood-letting as a necessary means."

Boerhave :—" When one compares the good performed on the earth by half a dozen true sons of Æsculapius since the rise of the Art, with the evil done among men by the countless number of Doctors of this trade, one will doubtless think, that it were much better if there never had been a physician in the world."

Reil :—" It is perfectly clear that we do not know the nature of fever, and that the treatment thereof is nothing more than naked empiricism.—The variety of opinions is a proof that the nature of the subject is not yet clear; for when the truth is once found, certainty takes the place of hypothesis in every sound mind."

Rush :—" We have not only multiplied diseases, but have made them more fatal."

Majendie :—" In the actual condition of medical science, the physician mostly plays but the part of simple spectator of the sad episodes which his profession furnishes him."

Billing :—" I visited the different schools, and the students of each hinted, if they did not assert, that the other sects killed their patients."

Water too can kill, or it could not cure. Yet may it fearlessly be affirmed, that where one will be hurt or killed by the water-treatment, one hundred will be by drugs. Relatively, the water-cure is without danger; nay, it is so absolutely. Knowledge is needed to do anything, even to grow cabbages. An idiot may break his neck falling down steps safely used by thousands daily. But conceive knowledge with poisons for its instrument, and the same knowledge with one pure agent, and able with that one to bring out any and all the effects aimed at by the lancet and whole pharmacopœia. In the skilfullest hands, arsenic, prussic acid, copperas, oil of vitriol, mercury, iodine, strychnine, all medical poisons in constant use, suddenly cause death at times, to the confounding of the practitioner. Their remote effects in shortening and embittering life, are incalculable, unimaginable. In short, the water-cure, at once simple and philosophical, is dangerous only where there is clumsiness, rashness, or stupidity: drugs, virulent and treacherous, are full of immediate danger in the most prudent and sagacious hands, and are besides charged with evils distant and insidious.

By means of water, then, whose energizing and healing power has been to the full revealed by Priesnitz, chronic diseases, till now deemed hopeless, are eradicable, and acute ones cease to be alarming. By the thorough cure of acute attacks, chronic complaints,—mostly the consequence of suppressed or half-cured acute ones,—will be much fewer. Through the same influence, acute will become less frequent. Were this discovery to cause no other change of habits, the substitution of cold for warm baths and the general practice of cold bathing, will alone produce such bodily fortification as to ward off an immense amount of disease. But the change cannot stop there. Wedded as men are to routine, hugging custom as if life itself were intertwined with its plaits, still they do by degrees let in the light of new truths. When one of her great laws is discovered, Nature smiles joyfully and benignantly, as a mother on the unfolding of her infant's mind, and in man's heart is reflected the smile, the harbinger of new blessings. This discovery is already hailed by tens of thousands as pregnant with immeasurable good. It is so simple, so intelligible, so ac cessible, that it must spread its blessings in spite of prejudice, interest, and ignorance.

Health is nearly banished from Christendom. Even among those who lead an outdoor life of healthful labor, there is the debilitating counteraction of stimulants, in drink, in food, in tobacco. The wealthier classes are more the victims of drugs, the poor of alcohol. These two curses, poisoning the sources of life, have diminished the stature and strength of the race, far more even than vice and poverty, of which too alcohol is a prolific parent. That there is this diminution is proved, among other evidence, by the falling off in the standard of stature for soldiers in the principal countries of Europe, in England, in France, in Germany. Through these poisons, the natural instincts of appetite have been depraved. There is a general vitiation of the palate through the perverted nerves, brought about by the universal use of all kinds of foreign stimulants, medicinal, spirituous, and spicy. Water is deemed good to mix with spirits and wine, and milk with tea and coffee. Pure, they are insipid, and so deep has reached the corruption, that it is quite a common belief, that water is unwholesome! There is a general craving for stimulants. They are esteemed temperate who use them only at meals! Their hurtful effects upon the health, temper, strength and morals, cannot be estimated. Against all this, Nature protests by the sighs of weakness, the groans of disease, the pangs of conscience, and the agonies of premature death. Priesnitz would seem to be commissioned to re-utter the commands of Nature, to rouse mankind to a sense of its growing physical degeneracy, and to open the path towards health, refreshed life and enjoyment. Priesnitz has demonstrated, that for the preservation of health and restoration from disease there is an efficacy, a virtue in WATER, hitherto undreamt of; that all kinds of stimulants, under all circumstances whether in disease or in health, are always falsehoods, disguised like worse moral lies under cajoling flatteries; and this he enforces with the eloquence of cheerfullest, sweetest sensations, renovating, I might almost say, re-creating, the nervous system, and thus putting literally new life into the body.

GENEVA, September, 1841.

The last of July, after a six weeks' experiment of the water-cure, we left Boppart. These few weeks have made, I may say, an epoch in my life. It is not the bodily strength I gained,—and the time was much too short for a full restoration to health,—but the gain of new truths and convictions, which give me in a degree command over my bodily condition; the gain of insight and knowledge, whereby I can ward off attacks against which I, like others, before felt myself powerless. I have learnt to know the effects of stimulants, and am emancipated from their tyranny. As on the morning of our departure from Marienberg, we drove along the beautiful shores of the Rhine, I felt, that new and beneficent laws had been divulged to me, and that I was closer under the protection of Nature.

At Bingen, after exploring the Niederwald on donkeys, and visiting the Rheinstein,—a turretted old castle perched among rocks and woods high above the river, fitted up and inhabited by a Prince of Prussia,—we quitted the Rhine to take the road to Wiesbaden, where, as at other fashionable watering-places, Idleness holds an annual festival; for the proportion is small of those who are here solely for the business of cure. Thence a short railroad carried us to Frankfort, famous for its biennial fairs, where merchants thickly congregate; for the election and coronation in past centuries of the Emperors of Germany; and most famous of all as the birth-place of Goethe, who as boy, among the other sights and sounds that were teaching his young mind its powers, witnessed with greedy delight one of the imperial coronations, himself already appointed to a throne and a sway, firmer and wider than that of Emperors. Here were laid the foundations of a nature, the richest the earth has borne since Shakspeare.

Sir Egerton Brydges, that genial old man, says:—"A large part of the existence of a human being consists in thought and sentiment." Most true. Like air through the lungs, thought and emotion are curling unceasingly round the brain; they are the atmosphere of the soul, as impalpable, yet as real and vital, as that we breathe. Without this lively presence of feeling and thought, we cannot be as soul-endowed beings; it is the state of mental life. Our friends, our neighbors, our children, are far off from us, in comparison with this sleepless inward offspring of the mind. Is it well-limbed, healthy, clean, we live the erect, loving, steadfast life of a genuine man; is it deformed, crabbed; our life is narrow, suspicious, timid. What a task, then, how high, how deep, to feed, to purify, to enlarge, to enrich this spring of every human movement, endeavor, purpose, deed. Such is the Poet's function, the noblest, the most useful. Through his sensibility to the beautiful, he sees furthest into the nature of things, goes down to the root of the matter, discerns in each class of being the original type, wherein Beauty has its perfect dwelling. Embodying the visions thus had, in moulds which each creates for itself, he brings before his fellow-men mirrors, wherein they behold themselves, their thoughts and feelings, subtilized, exalted —magic mirrors, whose images, glowing with almost supernatural effulgence, are yet felt to be true. For poetry is a distillation of Beauty out of the feelings and doings of daily life, and a poem is but the finest, maturest fruit of impulses, which exist in, and openly or secretly control, the most prosaic worker in a trading community. Who so base or dull, but has had moments of spiritual abstraction, when his whole being was penetrated with unearthly light, whereby all things, as it were transfigured, looked calm and joyful? Breathes there a man, not blasted with idiocy in whom at times a gorgeous sunset would not awaken emotion, whose heart would not open to the mystic beauty of the midnight sky, who has not felt, though but for an instant, a quickening impulse towards perfection? Such moods the poet fosters, awakens, confirms. He teaches the mind to use its wings: he peoples it with richer possibilities. The Poet is the highest of educators. With the gushings of the young untainted heart, mingle his warm expansive thoughts, and as years ripen, we embrace more closely the truths he has melodiously unfolded, unconscious often whence they have come.

The fortune of worldly position and of length of years, favored the pre-eminent genius of Goethe, in performing the great task of the poet in a way unparalleled in these latter times. No man of the age has so widened the intellectual horizon of his country, so deepened and freshened the common sea of thought, so enriched the minds of his contemporaries with images of beauty and power. Among the heartless, senseless complaints against Goethe,—as such will be made against the greatest,—that of his want of patriotism is the most vapid. Let the man be pointed to who has done so much to enlighten, to elevate Germany. He has thus contributed more towards the liberty of his country than any score of "Liberals," even though they be genuine ones. There is a fitness in his being born at Frankfort, at once the capital of Germany and a free town. Saving Luther, there is none other who better deserves the title of Father of his country.

His fellow citizens are about to raise to him a colossal statue in Frankfort. In the neighboring town of Mayence, a noble one, designed by Thorwaldsen, has been lately erected to Gutemberg. Goethe and Gutemberg will be side by side. They belong together; the one, the German who invented types, the other, the German who has made the best use of them.

A day sufficed for Frankfort. The most beautiful thing they have to show, is Dannecker's statue of Ariadne. For our route towards Switzerland we chose what is called the mountain road, which traverses one of the most fertile plains of Europe, bounded on the East by a range of hills, sloping up into soft valleys and wooded heights, with here and there a ruined castle to connect the fresh-looking landscape with the olden time. Our first night was at Weinheim, an ancient town begirt with towers, and snugly seated, amidst orchards and vineyards, at the foot of the hills. Early before breakfast, I walked up to the old castle of *Windeck*. I met people going out to work; they looked mostly hunger-pinched and toil-bent. To how many is the earth a cold prison, instead of the fair warm garden Nature offers it. To none, even the most favored, is life what it might be. When will men's aims be truer, and their means juster, and existence cease to be a harrying scramble? The earth is yet shadowed by the scowl of man upon his fellow. Nature is most rich and bountiful, would we but live after her law. The resources are within and about us; and a Christian must believe that they will be awakened and improved, till man at last smiles upon man.

A night rain had sweetened the air and land for our morning drive to Heidelberg, which was the next stage. We spent an hour among the broad ruins of the famed castle, saw the streets lively with students, joyous intelligent looking youths, sought out two or three young Americans at their lodgings, and then went again rolling smoothly on our journey, to end the day at Carlsruhe (Charles' rest), the capital of the Grand Duchy of Baden. The next day we dined at Baden—Baden, the celebrated watering-place, lying beautifully in a stream-enlivened valley, between gentle hills, overrun for miles with shady walks and drives.

The *Cursaal*, containing the spacious public saloons and ball-rooms, and furnished like a palace, is the general resort in the evening. Here are the gambling-tables, three or four of them, all plying at the same time their silent gloomy trade. Round each large oval table, with its wheel of destiny in the centre, and its fine green cloth covered with figures and mystic divisions, was a crowd of spectators and players, standing or seated. To partake of the scene actively and from its midst, I joined one of them, throwing down occasionally among the twinkling gold pieces and fat piastres a pale florin, the lowest stake allowed. The players were of various conditions and ages and aspects; a few of them mere players, to whom it was an arithmetical trial, a sportful excitement, like one young Englishman who gaily scattered a handful of Napoleons at a throw, choosing, as though he could choose, the numbers to stake on, dallying carelessly with Fortune. But out of the fixed serious countenances of most, stared the Demon of gain. He must have laughed one of his bitterest laughs at his dupes. The scene would have adorned Spenser's cave of Mammon. In the glare of a large overhanging light, a circle of human beings intent upon gold, and all the features of Avarice concentrated in haggard unity on one little spot. A circle, but without bond of union; each pursuing his end in selfish isolation, unmindful of his neighbor, except when Envy stirred at his good fortune; absorbed, possessed by the one feeling; his whole nature quenched under its cold tyranny; his visage half petrified by the banishment of all other thought.—It had too its poetic side; the hope ever renewed; the mysterious source of the decree, coming out of unfathomable depths; its absoluteness, representing perfectly the inexorableness of Fate.

Before entering on our route through the Black Forest to Schaffhausen in Switzerland, we made a circuit of half a day by Strasburg, to see the Cathedral, one of the most beautiful of Gothic churches, the pinnacle of whose spire is the highest point ever reached in an edifice of human hands, being twenty-four feet higher than the great Pyramid of Egypt. These airy Gothic structures, rising lightly from the earth, as if they were a growth out of it, look, amidst the common houses about them, like products of another race. They have an air of inspiration. Their moulds were thoughts made musical by deep feeling.

They are the Poems of an age when Religion yearned for glorious embodiment. They declare the beauty and grandeur of the human mind, that it could conceive and give birth to a thing so majestic. Those high-springing vaults; those far-stretching aisles, solemnized by hues from deeply colored windows; those magnificent vistas, under roof; those outward walls, so gigantic, and yet so light with flying buttresses and the relief of delicate tracery; that feathery spire, which carries the eyes far away from the earth; to think, that the whole wondrous fabric, so huge and graceful, so solid and airy, so complex and harmonious, as it stands there before you, stood first, in its large beautiful completeness, in the brain of its architect, *Erwin von Steinbach.* Those great builders of the middle ages have not been duly known; their names are not familiar, as they should be, like those of the great painters.

Strasburg, and Alsace, of which it was formerly the capital, though long in the possession of France, are German still in language and customs. The original character of a people clings to it through all kinds of outward vicissitudes. This is strongly exemplified in the French themselves. The exact similarity between certain prominent features in the ancient Gauls and the modern French, shows with what fidelity mental qualities are transmitted through advancing stages of civilisation, and what permanent unfailing effects, soil, atmosphere and climate exert upon the character of a people. The Gauls were as noted for the fury of their first onset in their battles with Cæsar, as the French were at Agincourt and in the Spanish Peninsula, and seem to have been discomfited by the steadfastness of the Romans precisely in the way their descendants were by the cooler courage of the British. Winkelman, endeavoring to show the effects of air and nourishment on national character, states, that according to the Emperor Julian there were in his day more dancers in Paris than citizens, and I have somewhere seen this quotation from Cato;—*Duas res Gens Gallica industriosissime persequitur, rem militarem et argute loqui :*—Two things the Gallic people cultivate most diligently, military affairs and glibness of speech.

In a day and a half we reached Schaffhausen by Homberg and Donauschingen. At Schaffhausen we had to resign the comfort of post-horses. The inn-keepers of Switzerland, a numerous and wealthy class, have influence enough, it is said, to prevent the introduction of the posting-system, it being of course their interest to have travellers move slowly. On the way to Zurich, we stopped an hour a few miles below Schaffhausen, to see the Falls of the Rhine, the finest in Europe, and well deserving their fame. In the afternoon we had the first view of the snow-capt mountains. Far before us, fifty or sixty miles off, they lay along the horizon like a bank of silver. We approached Zurich, descending among gardens, and vineyards, and villas, with the lake and town in view. The evening hour of arrival is always a cheerful one to the traveller, and it is trebly so, when the smiling welcome of " mine host" is preceded by such a greeting as this from Nature. We had time before dark to enjoy the wide prospect from the top of the Hotel. The sublimities of Switzerland were still remote, but we were already encompassed by its beauties.

The next morning we started early, intending to sleep that night on the top of the Righi. Crossing before breakfast Moun: Albis, from whose southern side the mountains about the Lake of the four Cantons came grandly into view, we descended upor' Zug, passing through which and along the northern shore of it: lake, we reached Arth at one ; whence, at half-past two, we com menced the journey up the Righi on horseback with a guide. The ascent begins a mile east of Goldau, one of the villages destroyed by the fall of the Rossberg in 1806. Conceive of a slip of rock and earth two miles long, one-fifth of a mile wide, and one hundred feet thick, loosened from the summit of a mountain five thousand feet high, rushing down its side into the valley below. It overwhelmed three villages with five hundred of their inhabitants, and spread desolation over several miles of the valley. We passed through the terrific scene, a chaos of rock and rubbish, where Goldau had been. Huge blocks of stone, as large some of them as a small house, were forced up the Righi far above the site of Goldau. There are traditions of similar slides from this same mountain in past ages, and still higher up were scattered other blocks which the guide said had come on one of those occasions from the Rossberg, three or four miles distant. We were more than three hours ascending, and went up into a cloud, which enveloped the top of the mountain, so that we had no sunset. The cloud passed away in the night.

The next morning before dawn, with cloaks about us, we were out. From the top of this isolated peak, a mile above the lakes at its base, we saw light break slowly over the earth, as yet without form in the darkness. We had almost a glimpse of the creative mystery. We were up in the heavens, and beheld the Spirit of God move upon the face of the earth. We witnessed with magnificent accompaniment the execution of the mandate,—Let there be Light. The peaks in the sun's path rose first out of darkness to meet the coming dawn, their jagged outline fringed with grey, then with gold. Day had hardly broke about us, when off to the south fifty miles a rosy tint shone on the snowy heads of the Bernese Alps, the first to answer the salutation of the Sun. Soon, the summits of all the mountains rose up in the growing day, a world of peaks, the giant offspring of the Earth awakened by the Morning. Below was still twilight. Gradually light came down the mountains and rolled away the veil of night from the plain. The Sun grew strong enough to send his rays into the valleys, and opened the whole sublime spectacle,—a spectacle affluent in sublimities, that lifted the Thoughts out of their habits, and swelled them to untried dimensions. The eye embraced an horizon of three hundred miles circuit; the Mind could not embrace the wealth of grandeur and beauty disclosed. Towards the west, the view ranged over what from such a height seemed an immense plain,.bounded by the far dim Jura; an indistinct landscape, with woods, and rivers, and lakes; or, rather, a hundred landscapes melted into one, that took in several of the largest, most fertile cantons, covering thousands of square miles. Turning round, we stood amazed before the stupendous piles of mountain. From five to fifty miles away, in a vast semicircle, rose in wondrous throng their wild bulks—rugged granite or glittering snow, towering in silent grandeur, an upper kingdom, their heads in the sky. They looked alive as with a spectral life, brought from the mysterious womb of the Earth. You gaze, awed, baffled, in their majestic presence, overwhelmed by the very sublimity of size.

We had come up by the north path, we went down by the south. What a walk on a sunny morning! Down we went, nearer and nearer to the beautiful lake right under us, plunging deeper and deeper into the magical scenery of its shores. We reached Weggis in two hours and a half. The perpendicular height from the level of the lake to the pinnacle of the Righi is about a mile; in the descent I must have walked seven or eight. By steamboat we reached Lucerne at one. From Lucerne we looked back down the lake at the throng of mountains that rose out of its waters·and crowded the eastern horizon. A slight haze made the sun shine on them more warmly. The scene was like a vision, so strange was it and beautiful.

The same afternoon we left Lucerne and slept at Entlebuch, whence the next day we came to Berne, traversing the broad cantons of Lucerne and Berne, through a country abundant in crops and landscapes. ·Our attempt to see some of the splendors of the Bernese Oberland was frustrated by the weather; so that, after going from Thun to Brienz, through their two lakes, we turned back in the rain, having merely got a momentary glimpse at Interlaachen of the *Yungfrau*. We made a long day from

Berne to Lausanne, passing through Freyburg, the stronghold of Romanism in Switzerland, remarkable for the singularity and picturesqueness of its position, high up in one of the bends of the river Saane; for its suspension bridge—the longest in the world—one hundred and seventy feet above the river which it spans; for its Convents and Jesuits' College, and for the dirtiness of its streets. A transparent morning for the drive from Lausanne along the shore of Lake Leman to Geneva, gave us a clear view of Mont Blanc, more than sixty miles off. We reached Geneva on the 17th of August.

Calvin, Rousseau. An old town that hasn't its great men is tasteless to the traveller. These two give the flavor to Geneva. Of necessity far apart in time, for one would think the spirit of Calvin must have been well-nigh worn-out or dormant ere the little Republic could have engendered a Rousseau. I figure Calvin as gaunt, fleshless; a man of a gritty substance, on whom flesh couldn't grow. A nature tough as steel, unbending as granite—as was needed for his task. With what a bold biting lash he scourged the sensualities of his time! How he defied the principalities of the earth! How he scorned the tempests of papal, and regal, and popular, wrath! They did but invigorate his will, sublimate his genius, for the building up of a power that was to stretch over many nations and endure for ages. He would not have been Calvin had he not burned Servetus. This crime was the correlative of his virtue. It condensed with the heartiness and earnestness, the austerity and narrowness of Calvinism. His followers continued and continue to burn Servetuses after a different fashion. Honor to the patriarch of the Puritans.

Calvin, who was not born in Geneva, became there a ruler; Rousseau, who was, doesn't seem to have been held of much account by his townsmen, until lately, when they have erected to him a statue, more out of pride probably than love. Rousseau was made of anything but granite; an unstable tremulous nature, devoured by passions which yet hadn't life enough to energize him. His life-long sorrows were of the Werterian kind, but he had'nt the strength to shoot himself. He was a Werter *manqué*. Yet he too did a large share of good. In a time of coldness and misbelief, he helped to bring men to the knowledge of the truths and beauties of Nature, and of the resources of their hearts, through which knowledge alone can there be fruitful love of God. And this indeed, in different moods, is the office of all thinkers. Even Rousseau's sentimentality, insipid or sickening now, was savory and healing to his sophisticated generation. Had his writings had no other effect than to re-awaken in the hearts of so many mothers the duty of nursing their own infants, he would deserve well of the Christian world.

FLORENCE, October, 1841.

We remained at Geneva a fortnight, preparing for Italy. On the third of September we set out by the route of the Simplon, along the southern shore of the Lake and up the valley of the Rhone, sleeping the first night in Martigny, the second in Brigg, at the foot of the pass. The valley of the Rhone is generally level, barren, and subject to inundation. The long day's drive from Martigny to Brigg was of less interest than any we had had in Switzerland. The valley, almost unpeopled, without deep verdure or the softness of tillage, desolate without being wild, offers no pictures to the eye; and the mountains that enclose it, are bare and cold without elevation enough for grandeur. This is one of the worst regions for goitre and cretinism. Before noon we stopped to change horses in the public square of *Sion*, the capital of the canton of Valais. Happening to be a market day, there was a throng of people in the square. An assemblage of such unsightly human beings I never beheld. Nearly all looked as if they were more or less under the blight, whose extreme effect is the idiocy called cretinism. Mostly of a pallid Indian hue, with lank black hair, they had a strange weird look.

At Brigg, whilst we were getting ready to start in the morning the master of the hotel, whose son or son-in-law had the furnishing of horses, came to inform me that I should have to take six for the ascent. I represented to him that for a carriage like mine four would be as sufficient as six, and that it would be unreasonable, unjust, and contrary to his own printed regulations to impose the additional two upon me. The man insisting, I objected, then remonstrated, then protested. All to no purpose. I then sought out the burgomaster of the town, to whom with suitable emphasis I represented the case. He could not deny that the letter of the law was on my side. Whether or not he had the power to over-rule the post-master I don't know, but at all events my appeal to him had no practical result; the carriage came to the door with six horses. I had the poor satisfaction of letting the inn-keeper hear his conduct worded in strong terms, and of threatening him with public exposure in the guide-books as an extortioner, which threat acted most unpleasantly upon his feelings, and I hoped, kept him uncomfortable for some hours.

What a contrast between the irritations and indignations of the morning, and the calm awed feelings of the day! 'Twould be worth while for an army to be put into a towering passion at the base of the Simplon, just to have all anger quelled by the subduing sublimities of its sides and summit. As we went up the broad smooth road of Napoleon, the gigantic mountains opened wider and wider their grandeurs, heaving up their mighty shoulders out of the abysses, at first dark with firs, and later, as we neared the top of the pass, shining far, far above us in snow that the sun had been bleaching for thousands of years. We crossed the path of an avalanche, a hundred feet wide, that had come down in the spring, making as clean a swarth through the big trees as a mower's scythe does in a wheatfield. We passed under solid arches, built, or cut through the rock, to shield travellers against these opake whirlwinds, these congealed hurricanes, this bounding brood of the white giantess, begotten on her vast icy flanks by the near sun. On the summit of the pass, the snowy peaks still high above us, we came to the *Hospice*, and then descending quietly on the southern side a couple of miles, reached about sunset the village of Simplon. At the quiet inn we were greeted by two huge dogs of the St. Bernard breed, who, with waggings of tail and canine smiles, seemed doing the hospitalities of the mountain. Here we met two English travellers, and spent a cheerful evening as the close to such a day. After a sound sleep under thick blankets we set off early the next morning. What a starting point, and what a morning's drive! Ere noon we were to be in Italy, and the way to it was through the gorges of the Simplon.

With wheel locked, we went off at a brisk trot. The road on the Italian side is much more confined than on the northern. Yesterday, we had the broad splendors, the expanded grandeurs, of the scene ; to day its condensed intenser sublimities. We soon found ourselves in a tunnel cut through a rock ; then sweeping down deeper and deeper into what seemed an endless abyss; close on one side of us a black wall of rock, overhanging hundreds, thousands, of feet, and darkening the narrow path ; as close on the other a foaming torrent, leaping down as it were a wild creature rushing by us to head our track. Over dark chasms, under beetling precipices, across the deafening rush of waters, the smooth road carried us without a suggestion of danger, the wonders of the sublime pass all exhibited as freely as to the winged eagle's gaze ; as though Nature rejoiced in being thus mastered by Art. On we went, downward, downward. At last the descent slackens, the stream that had bounded and leapt beside us, runs among the huge rocky fragments, the gorge expands to a valley, the fresh foliage of chestnut trees shadows the road, the valley widens, the mountain is behind us, a broad even landscape before us, the air is soft, the sun shines hotly on fields where swarthy men are at work,—we are in Italy! It was a passage from sublimity to beauty. We were soon among vines and strong vegetation. This then is Italy. How rich and warm it looks! We entered Duomo d'Ossola, the first town: it looked solid and time-beaten. In a public square hard by where we stopped for a few minutes, was a plentiful show of vegetables and fruit, juicy peaches and heavy bunches of grapes. At a rapid pace we went forward towards Lake Maggiore. These are the " twice-glorified fields of Italy." This is beautiful, passionate Italy, the land of so much genius, and so much vice, and so much glory. This is the land, for centuries the centre of the world, that in boyhood and in manhood is so mixed in our thoughts, with its double column of shining names familiar to Christendom. It was late in the afternoon when at Fariolo we came upon the beautiful Lake. For ten or twelve miles the road ran on a terrace, whose wall was washed by its waters. About sunset we passed the Borromean Islands, the evening clear and bland. 'Twas after nightfall when we entered Arona.

We had to-day an incident, which gave assurance that we were arrived in Italy, as convincing as did the beauty and fruitfulness lavished upon this chosen land. Opposite in character to them, that have their source in bounty and love; this, in penury of spirit and hate. It came too from one of "God's Vicegerents on Earth," although its nature smacked of paternity in the Prince of Darkness. God floods his creation with liberty and light, the which his vicegerents, Kings and Popes, are ever busy to smother, lest men be maddened and blinded by the too free use of Heaven's best gifts. God's vicegerents! his counterworkers rather. They are oftenest the very antidotes of light. Their God is POWER, whom they worship with human sacrifices. Monarchies and Hierarchies are the tokens of man's weakness. The stronger they, the weaker he. As men strengthen, they dwindle. They are like props planted beside a young tree, that having insidiously taken root, divert into themselves nourishment due to it, so that the tree languishes and perishes, while they thrive and wax strong. They are the bridle put into the horse's mouth in the fable, for his help, as he foolishly thought, which became the instrument of his enslavement. They are the stewards of Custom, which is the tyranny of the lower human faculties over the higher. I once heard when a boy a stump-speaker at a "barbecue" declare, that a visit to Europe had made him a democrat. The process whereby this effect was wrought will be clear to most Americans who sojourn here for a time. As counterpoise to this, it will be but fair to mention that German Prince, who, becoming tainted with republicanism, was sent to the United States to be cured thereof,—and was cured. That man deserved a throne. But to the incident.

At the Piedmontese frontier, the custom-house officer, who as usual examined but one of our trunks, hit upon the one that contained books. "Ah! Books," said he; "I must make a list of them." Hereupon he ordered his assistant to take them all out, my representations that they were solely for my own use, and that I was merely passing through Piedmont, having no effect. On first alighting, I heard one say to the other, "Il Signore é militare;" a conclusion which was probably dispelled by the sight of the contents of the trunk, and not, I think, to my advantage. The making of the list was a long process, the officer having to write the titles that were not Italian letter by letter. The task seemed to him a hard and unaccustomed one. The subordinate displayed the title of each volume beside his principal, I superintending the orthography. The assistant handled the books carefully and even tenderly, as though in his eyes they were things precious. The poor man, I fancied, looked at me with an expression of deferential regard, as one who possessed and had free access to such a treasure. Among them was Silvio Pellico's story of his imprisonment, in Italian. He turned it in his hands, looked into it, gently shuffling over the leaves, and quietly glancing from the volume to me, not at all as if he would beg it, but as if he transferred towards me some of the feeling the book awakened in him. He probably had heard vaguely of Pellico's martyrdom. The list finished, the books were repacked, and the trunk was leaded, that is, tied round with stout twine, over whose knot was pressed, with long pincers, a small leaden seal. The trunk was replaced on the carriage, and a paper was given me certifying its contents and the operation it had undergone. This overhauling and list-taking was but the commencement of the vexation. The next day,—to make an end of the story,—on passing out of Piedmont, an officer was sent with us to see the sealed trunk delivered unbroken at the custom-house of Lombardy, some distance off. It was just as if I had had a criminal in company, and Piedmont warned Austria of his danger. Books, in truth, are criminals in both countries. On arriving at Milan I was obliged, before driving to the hotel, to go first to the custom-house, to leave in safe keeping the mysterious trunk, as big with mischief as the Grecian Horse to the Trojans, but luckily by the vigilance of Piedmont its diabolical purport was revealed to Austria. Quitting Milan I had to call for it, to leave it again at the Piedmontese custom-house on re-entering Piedmont on the road to Genoa; for I found that otherwise, owing to a press of business there, I should be delayed two or three hours. It came after me the next day to Genoa, where, not to have any more frontier troubles, I left it, to be sent to Florence, which it reached several days later, bringing with it a bill against me, for separate travelling charges, of ten dollars. This affair, trifling as it appears, marred the enjoyment of our first days in Italy. It makes a man, too, feel little, to find himself utterly defenceless against such pitiful abuses from low officials.

Through the bountiful plains of Lombardy, we had a short day's drive from Arona to Milan, passing near the first battle-field between Scipio and Hannibal. Entering Milan by the arch of the Simplon, we came first upon the broad Parade, or *Place d'Armes*, where the cannon are kept always loaded, Milan being the capital of the Austrian Lombardo-Venetian Provinces, and residence of the Imperial Viceroy. The two principal objects of Milan are, Leonardo da Vinci's great picture of the last supper, and the cathedral, a vast, beautiful, gothic structure of white marble, from whose roof ascends a forest of light pinnacles and marble needles, surmounted by statues. Around, upon and within the church are two or three thousand statues, numbers of them the effigies of benefactors. Conspicuous on a pinnacle was one of Napoleon. A gift of cash to the church will obtain for the donor the honor of a statue, its prominence and elevation being measured by the amount bestowed. What inventive genius these solemn gentlemen of the robe have always shown in unloosing the clasp of money-clutching man! What a scent they have for the trail of gold! A traveller relates, that passing through "the noble little state of Connecticut," and stopping to bait in one of its dreariest townships, he asked a tall raw-boned man, who was measuring him keenly with his eye, what the people did in so barren a country for a living: "When we can catch a stranger, we skin *him*, and when we cant, we skin one another." I defy the leanest native in the stoniest part of Connecticut, to devise the means more shrewdly for compassing a given dollar, than these ghostly bachelors. From the roof of the cathedral we looked down into the opulent city beneath, and far away over the rich plain of Lombardy. To the west, as distant as the pass of the Simplon, was visible the snowy head of Mount Rosa.

We left Milan after forty-eight hours, and were a day and a half on the road to Genoa, sleeping the first night in a clean good inn at Novi. Some miles out of Milan, not far from Pavia, we stopped to see the famous *Chartreuse*, with its beautiful church and dozen little chapels, each one enriched with precious marbles exquisitely wrought and inlaid, whereon millions have been spent in work and materials. Madame de Stael said, that Genoa has the air of having been built by a Congress of Kings. We walked through its streets of palaces, searching the palaces themselves for pictures, which is the chief and pleasantest occupation of the stranger passing through Italian cities. From the best points we had a survey of the town and harbor. The port is very active, and Genoa is growing in population, commerce and wealth. What a country this beautiful Italy would be, if it could drive out the foreigner, if it could shake off ecclesiastical domination, if it could bind itself up into a single nation, if—but there are too many ifs.

We were glad to find ourselves on the third day out of Genoa on the road along the shore of the Mediterranean. It takes some time to get accustomed to Italian cities and ways. One has too a feeling of loneliness, which custom never entirely overcomes, in a large crowded town, where you know not a soul, and have speech with none but hirelings; so that, after having "seen all the sights," you are cheered by departure, and smile upon the Cerberus at the gate, who stops your carriage to learn from your passport that you have the right to go. Starting from Genoa in the afternoon, we slept the first night at Chiavari, the second at Massa. The Mediterranean on the right, valleys and hills on the left; the road winding, mounting, descending with the movements of the shore, where land and sea are gently interlocked; compact towns nestled in the green bosom of valleys, the mountains behind, the sea before them; vines gracefully heavy with purple grapes, festooned from tree to tree;—these are the chief features of the day-long picture. From Massa, seated by the water, with a shield of marble mountains against the north, we started early on the sunny morning of the 16th of September, wishing to reach Florence before dark. We soon left the sea, and crossing the mountain range, went down on the other side into the territory of Lucca, among hills clothed with chestnut and olive, and fields the gardens of Plenty, the sun shining warmly, the earth breathing fragrantly through its leafy abundance. Valery, in his excellent guide-book, recommended to me by Wordsworth (Murray's wasn't yet published) says of Lucca ;— " Un certain perfectionnement social et philosophique parait avoir prévalu pendant long temps dans ce petit état, qui n 'eut jamais de Jésuites. L'Encyclopédie y fut re-imprimée en 28 vol. folio, 1758–71." Surely the Lucchese were wise to keep out the Jesuits ; for priestly venom, which so poisons in Italy the cup of life, festers nowhere to bitterer virulence than in that dehumanized corporation. But the letting in of such a flood of French philosophy, as is implied by a reprint of the renowned *Encyclopédie*, that was a questionable proceeding. Yet after all, Voltaire, Diderot and their associates sharpened and helped to disenthral the intellect of the Christian world ; they opened the eyes of men, though they could not tell them what it was best to look at. Valery, whose book is that of a man of letters, and is a mine of minute historical, biographical and miscellaneous information, lets go no opportunity of bringing France and Frenchmen before his readers. Always cheerful and polished, he is a thorough zealous Frenchman, who neither disturbs nor is himself disturbed by the stiffest nationalism of another.

While changing horses in Lucca, we were tempted by voluble *domestiques de place* with enumeration of the sights of the town ; but our eyes and hearts were set upon Florence. The postmaster questioned us eagerly, how many carriages were behind. Now is his autumnal harvest. The English, to whom all other travellers are so much indebted for the cleanliness and comfort of the inns on the Continent, are swarming southward. Soon after quitting Lucca we entered Tuscany,—proud Tuscany, in bygone times, the intellectual centre of Italy, the home of her language, the warm nest of genius, the cradle of her giants, of

Dante, of Michael Angelo, of Bocaccio, of Petrarca, of Leonardo da Vinci, of Machiavelli, of Galileo. By Pistora and Prato, we drove along the south-western base of the Appenines, and through fields closely tilled up to the trunks of the olive, the mulberry, and the vine, and among white villas glistening in the western sun, we approached the high walls of Florence.

Nature and Art contend the one with the other in beautifying Florence. Except westward, where the Arno flows towards the sea, all about her are gentle hills that have come down from mountains, visible here and there in the distance. The Appenines and the Arno have scooped out a site, which man has made much of. The moment you pass out of almost any one of the gates, smooth gentle paths tempt you up heights, as if eager to exhibit some of the fairest landscapes even of Italy. In twenty or thirty minutes, you turn round to a view embracing the dome-crowned town, with its spacious leafy gardens, and far-stretching valley, and the countless heights and mountains which, bestudded with white villas, churches, convents, and clothed with the vine and olive, lie all round "the most beautiful daughter of Rome." Towards sunset, seen through that purple haze, which gives it a voluptuous, sleepy aspect, the landscape, so beautiful from its forms and combinations, looks almost like an illusion, a magical diorama. Carefully guarded within the walls, are many of the loveliest offspring of the Arts, ever fresh with the grace of genius; without them, Nature unrolls her indestructible beauties, heightened by Art and the associations of creative thought. Within the same hour, you may stand before the Venus of Cleomenes and on the tower of Galileo, which overlooks Florence and the vale of the Arno; before the Madonna of Raphael, and on the "top of Fiesole."

Even where the accumulations of Time are the most choice, the curiosities outnumber by much the beauties; so that the sight-seer has some weary and almost profitless hours, and re joices occasionally like Sterne, when the keys could not be found of a church he went to see. It is true, sight-showing has become so lucrative, that he seldom has that pleasant disappointment. Neither, on the other hand, does one like to miss anything, nor to do by halves what one has come so far to do. There are things too that are not much in the seeing, but that it is well to carry away the memory of having seen. The rapid traveller through crowded Italy, must therefore work nimbly with body and mind, from morn till night, to accomplish his labor of love. As we have the winter before us in Florence, we proceed here in a more idle and gentlemanly way. We can lounge among the marvels of the Pitti and the Uffizii, and let the mood of the moment prompt us what to sit before, without self-reproach, postponing the rest till to-morrow, or next week, or next month; or we can even let a whole day go over, without setting eyes on a picture or a statue or a church. Some of our first and pleasantest hours were spent in the studios and company of our own sculptors. It is much for a stranger, to have here fellow-countrymen of character and intelligence, who rank with the best as artists.

The first fortnight after our arrival, the town was enlivened by the presence of a Scientific Congress, numbering nearly nine hundred members, mostly Italians, to whom the amiable Grand Duke did the honors of his capital in graceful and munificent style. Among his hospitalities, was a dinner given at the *Poggio Imperiale*, one of his villas a mile out of the Roman Gate. Nine hundred guests were received in the suite of elegant drawing-rooms on the first floor, and sat down in the second to tables supplied with as much taste as luxury. 'Twas a brilliant animated scene. After dinner, toasts were drank, and short sprightly speeches made amidst vivas and bravos. The guests were all carried to and from the villa in carriages furnished by the host. As we drove back in the evening, my three Italian chance-companions vied in commendation of the courtesy and liberality of the Grand Duke. At last, one of them, a tall, stout, comfortable shrewd-looking man of about fifty, a priest too, I think, informed us, that he had come against orders, for he lived in the dominions of the Pope (who, with the arch-priestly dread of light, prohibits his subjects from attending these Congresses), and that he was the only representative from the papal states. To this disclosure the other two said not a word, and I dare say, what in me rose as a suspicion, mounted in them to pretty nearly a brimming conviction, namely, that our portly papal fellow-passenger was there for the purpose of taking notes quite other than scientific.

The crowning scene to the proceedings of the Congress was its last meeting in full session, in the large hall of the old Palace. Seven or eight hundred Italians, educated men, numbers of them men of thought, a noble-looking assemblage of heads. The purpose of their meeting I overlooked in the bare fact of such a convocation in that hall, where in the olden times of popular sovereignty were heard the stirring accents of free deliberation. May it be an omen of better days, when an assemblage as large and enlightened shall meet on the same spot for even higher objects, and with the new vivifying feeling, that at last they have become once more thoroughly men!

FLORENCE, May, 1842.

One can lead here for a season an intellectual life without much mental effort, with enough of activity to keep it in a receptive state; and the mind will lay up stores of impressions, to ripen hereafter into thought. The Past opens to the stranger rich pastures, wherein if he can but feed with healthy instincts, he will assimilate into himself abundantly of the old. The creative spirits of bygone periods invite him to communion; all they ask of him, is sympathy with their labor. Even the Poets exact not for the enjoyment of them, that vigorous co-operation in the reader, which Wordsworth justly intimates is necessary from his. The best Italian poetry is more superficial than the best English. It is based upon, not also impregnated throughout with thought. It has more of music and sentiment, of form and grace. Only Dante obliges you to gather yourself up as for a fraternal wrestle. Alfieri at first somewhat, until you have found the key to his mind, which has not many wards.

A scale of the occupations, pastimes, idleness, of a semi-passive half year in Florence, would have at its basis the walks and drives in the *Cascine* and environs. But first, a word about the climate. It is much like ours of the middle states, except that our winter is colder and drier. An American is surprised at this similarity on arriving in Italy, having got his notions from English writers, who, coming from their cloudy northern island, are enchanted with the sunny temperance of an Italian winter, and oppressed by the heats of summer. The heat is not greater than it is in Maryland, and our winter is finer, certainly than that of Florence, being drier, and though colder, at the same time sunnier. As with us, the autumn, so gloomy in England, is cheerful, clear, and calm, holding on till Christmas. They have hardly more than two cold months. Already in March the spring is awake, and soon drives back Winter, first into the highest Appenines, where he clings for a brief space, and thence retreats up to the topmost Alps, not to reappear for nine or ten months. Nor is that beautiful child of the light and air, the Italian sunset, more beautiful than the American.

Walking or driving;—the opera, theatre, and company;—the galleries of painting and sculpture, and the studios of artists;—reading and study at home. Thus and in this gradation would I divide the hours of a man of leisure in Florence, especially if he be one whose nerves oblige him to lead a life of much more gentlemanly idleness, than with a perfectly eupeptic stomach he would choose. I put walking and driving first, as being, although the most innocent, the most absolute forms of idleness. The

Cascine, a public promenade, just out of the western gate of the town, stretching a couple of miles down the right bank of the Arno, cannot be surpassed in situation and resources by anything similar in Europe. In warm weather, you have close shade, and in cold, the sun all along the margin of the stream, with a hedge and groves of pine and ilex as a cover against the *tramontana* or north wind. Thither on Sundays and other holidays resort the people at large, and every day in fine weather, the free and the fashionable, including among the former, monks, white and brown, whom I see here almost daily in shoals, with a sigh at the waste of so much fine muscle.

On the Continent, not a town of twenty thousand inhabitants,— nay, of fifteen or ten, but has its theatre, for operas or comedies at stated seasons. Music and the theatre are not, as with us, an occasional accidental amusement, but an habitual resource: they have an honorable place in the annual domestic budget, even of families of small means. Music is part of the mental food of the Italians. It is to them a substitute for the stronger aliment of freer countries. May it not be, that the bounds set to mental development in other spheres, are in part the cause of the fuller cultivation of this? Nature always strives to compensate herself for losses and lesions. Life, if cramped on one side, will often swell proportionably in another. Music has been to Italy a solace and a vent in her long imprisonment. This is not, of course, an endeavor to account for the origin of musical genius in Italy: original aptitudes lie far deeper than human reason can ever sound: but, that the people has musical habits, is probably in a measure owing to such influences. I don't remember ever to have heard an Italian whistle. They are too musical, the emptiest of them, for that arid futility. They sing as they go for want of thought; and late at night 'tis most cheerful to hear, moving through the street, laden with airs from operas, mellow voices that die sweetly away in the stillness, to be followed by others, sometimes several in chorus. To me there is always something soothing and hopeful in this spontaneous buoyant melody, the final sounds of the Italian's day.

As nothing in Art is more marketable than musical talent, London and Paris take, and keep, to themselves the first adepts. To the gifted songsters of the South,—whose warmth seems essential to the perfecting of the human musical organ,—showers of gold make amends for showers of orange-blossoms; and the dazzling illumination of palaces and sumptuous theatres, for the brilliancy of their native sky. Italy scarcely hears, in the fulness of their powers, her Pastas, Malibrans, Grisis, Lablaches, Rubinis. Their gifts once discerned, they are wafted across the Alps, to share the caresses, the triumphs, the largesses of the great northern capitals. When their career is run, the most of them come back to their never-forgotten home. The dear, beautiful, sorrow-stricken mother, who gave them their cradles,—and who alone could give them,—gives them too a tomb. Florence therefore has no richly equipt opera. In Italy itself, Naples and Milan have choice before her.

The Opera is not a perfectly pure form of Art. It is a forced marriage between language and action on the one side, and music. The poetry of the language is smothered by the music, while on the other hand words often clog the wings of melody. Language and action are definite, music is vague. In their union, the indefiniteness of music is resisted, the distinctness of words is obliterated by a haze, albeit a golden haze. In the compromise, whereby the union is brought about, some violence is done to the nature of each. The effect of music is best when its source is invisible. This mode of presentation accords with its nature; for music is a voice from the depths of the infinite,—a disembodied spirit, delivering its message through the least substantial medium of access,—sound. The glaring showiness, the pomp and corporeal effort of the stage, are an obstruction to its airy aspirations.

While to the dramatic reality the music imparts a lightness and poetic transparence, by these coarse material forms some of its own life is absorbed. Of all Art the genuine effect is, to exalt the tone of the mind, to refine its temper. Even the knowledge communicated is but incidental, altogether subsidiary to a fruitfuller gain. Facts, history, Art uses merely as vehicles, to convey to the mind its offerings of beauty. The results of Art are not, like scientific acquirements, tangible, measureable; they are chiefly in the mood awakened. The deepest, grandest truths, which it is the function of Art to reveal and illustrate, are presented in an indirect way. A noble poem leaves the mind of the reader in an expanded state. He feels a higher, clearer consciousness of life, a broader hope, a refreshed content. Available facts have not been piled away in his memory; but his best susceptibilities have been stimulated; his nature has been attuned on a higher key than common; he has a quickened sensation of freedom, of nobility. He is lifted into a higher state of-being, and in that state is apter for the performance of all practical duties. Herein consists the noble usefulness of poetry, of Art. This mental exaltation, this disenthralment of the spirit from all gross bonds, good music especially never fails to produce. Its opening voice is a grateful summons to the spiritual part of our nature. The glare, bustle and complex movements of the stage, make a confusion of effects. The spectacle, busying the senses, unstrings the rapt intentness of the spirit. The joyful calm and solemnity of the religious mood, always created by the best music, is ruffled.

For a really good society, two things are requisite; a high state of culture, and the habitual re-union of the most cultivated through genial and intellectual sympathies. But as social distinctions, in part factitious, prevail even in republican countries, this fusion into unity under high influences, is nowhere more than partially practicable. Gross and accidental advantages are still prized,—

and that even by the intellectual,—above those that are inherent and refined. They who possess, watch them jealously. Instead of the *salve*, printed in large letters on Goethe's threshold, they would like to inscribe on theirs, " No admittance to strangers ;" that is, to those who hav'n't the same interests to guard. Against a partition of their power, they in various ways protest; and now with the more emphasis, from a perception of the growing disregard of them. The land of Promise, where men and things shall be valued at their just worth, is much too remote for its remoteness to be measured; and we can only discover that we are less far from it, by a comparison of where we are with where we have been,—a comparison which, if made broadly and with a free spirit, will, in other domains of life as well as in this, induce hopefulness and trust.

The second requisite, therefore, is found, from general causes, as little in Florence as elsewhere, and less than in the great capitals. -As to the first, Florence has its creditable circle of men of Letters, Science, and Art. But while with those to whom rank and affluence give opportunities of education, they are but slenderly connected, they are at the same time sundered from the masses; they and the multitude cannot duly co-operate; their light scarcely pierces the blighting shade cast upon the people by the tangled brambles of priestly abuse. A community under Roman ecclesiastical dominion, cannot attain to the highest state of culture possible in its age. By the growth and diffusion of knowledge, through the long peace and the intercommunication among nations, the bonds of episcopal tyranny have been somewhat loosened in the Italian states. The body of the scientific and literary men have of course always lived in secret protest against this curse. But though they hate the tyrants and contemn their impostures, they cannot escape from them. The mind is stinted and thwarted in its wants and aspirations. Thought itself, free in the dungeon and on the rack, languishes where it has not free utterance by speech and pen. That under this long double load of political and religious despotism, the Italians have still kept alive the sacred fire of knowledge; have, through the thickest atmosphere, shot up into the sky, high enough for all Europe to see them, lights, poetic and scientific, proves, what deep sources of life, what elasticity and tenacity of nature there are in this oppressed people. Let those who for their abject state would despise them, think of this, and they will perhaps wonder that the Italians are not even more prostrate.

The political despotism to which Tuscany was subjected by the first Medici, has been, since the extinction of that bad breed, a paternal one, under a branch of the house of Austria. Still, though mild and forbearing in the hands of the present worthy Grand Duke, and his father, so justly beloved by the Tuscans, it is a despotism (and nothing else would be permitted by the other states of Italy), and as such, crushes in the people some of the richest elements of life. Florence, therefore, cannot be in advance of its sisters in social organization and spirit. Like other cities of its compass, it has nothing better than what, by a combination of the figures Amplification and Hyperbole, is termed "Good Society," composed here, as elsewhere, by those who have inherited, or by wealth acquired, social rank; embracing in Florence, besides the native *noblesse* and diplomatic corps, a large body of "nobility and gentry,"—in the phrase of the English newspapers,—from other lands, who for a season take up their abode in the Tuscan capital. The occupation of this circle is idleness. Start not at the apparent solecism. It is but apparent; for, to people who are not urged to exertion either by body or spirit; whose infinite natures are in a measure circumscribed within the animal bounds of the ephemera of the fields, their whole life revolving in a quick diurnal orbit; whose minds, left void by exemption,—not, however, entirely wilful,—from active duties and labors, are obliged, in order to oppose the pressure of time, literally to make something out of nothing ; to people thus dislocated from the busy order of nature, it becomes an occupation, requiring method and forethought, to resist the weight of their waking hours, and maintain the daily fight with ennui. Their insipidity of life is seasoned by a piquant ingredient, supplied by clouds of little cupids,—imps that, with their inborn perverseness, choose here to hover over nuptial couches, assaulting the hymeneal citadel with such vigor, that all, says dame Gossip, have not strength to withstand them. Their chief public performances are, to support the opera, and adorn the *Cascine* with their equipages and toilettes.

The Galleries of Painting and Sculpture come next in the scale, on which I have subdivided the hours of a stranger's Florentine sojourn. They might, without inaccuracy, take their place under the head of company. Genuine works of Art speak to you more clearly than most tongue-wagging speakers. In them is a soul which puts itself at once in connexion with yours. When at Antwerp, I never walked on the ramparts without feeling what companionship there was in the spire of the Cathedral : the mind felt its presence constantly and cordially. A shot-tower, you will say, of equal height, that met the eyes whenever they were turned towards the town, would have been just as much company. With this difference : that the one would be the company of a ponderous bore, the other, that of a buoyant poet.

Whenever your mood is that way bent, you betake yourself to the Grand Duke's residence, the Pitti Palace. Passing through its wide portal, you ascend, under the guidance of civil guards, by broad flights of steps, to a suite of spacious apartments, where are lodged Raphael, and Titian, and Claude, and Rubens, and Leonardo da Vinci, and Guido. From room to room, through a long series, you converse with these great spirits for hours together if you choose. Every day in the year, except Sundays and holidays, these refulgent rooms are thus courteously thrown open.

The servant at the door, who takes charge of your cane or umbrella, is not permitted even to accept anything for the service. A noble hospitality is this, to which strangers are so accustomed that they do not always duly value it. The Gallery attached to the old Palace over the *Uffizii*, where is the Tribune with its priceless treasures, daily invites the stranger in the same liberal way.

Among the studios of living Artists, the most attractive naturally to an American, are those of his fellow countrymen. Nor do they need national partiality to make them attractive. The first American who gained a reputation in the severest of the Fine Arts was GREENOUGH. For some years he was the only sculptor we had, and worthily did he lead the van in a field where triumphs awaited us. I happened, five or six years ago, to travel from Boston southward with him and Powers, and heard Greenough then warmly second Powers' inclination, and urge him to hasten to Italy. Powers was soon followed by Clevinger, who, in turn, received from him encouraging words. The three are now working here harmoniously together.

Artists of merit have seldom much to show at their rooms; for their works are either made to order, and sent to their destinations as fast as finished, or they are sold almost as soon as seen. Sculptors have an advantage over painters, inasmuch as they retain the plaster casts after which each work is chiselled in marble. As Greenough does not always finish the clay model up to the full design in his mind, but leaves the final touches to the chisel itself, he is not forward to exhibit his casts taken from the clay, the prototypes of the forms that have been distributed to different quarters of the world. He has just now in his studio, recently finished in marble for a Hungarian nobleman, an exquisite figure of a child, seated on a bank gazing at a butterfly, that has just lighted on the back of its upraised hand. In the conception there is that union of simplicity and significance, so requisite to make a work of plastic Art, especially of sculpture, effective, and which denotes the genial Artist. The attitude of the figure has the pliable grace of unconscious childhood; the limbs are nicely wrought; and the intelligence, curiosity, delight, implied and expressed in its gaze at the beautiful little winged wonder before it, impart vividly to the work the moral element; wanting the which, a production, otherwise commendable, is not lifted up to one of the high platforms of Art. The mind of the spectator is drawn into that of the beautiful child, whose inmost faculties are visibly budding in the effort to take in the phenomenon before it. The perfect bodily stillness of the little flexible figure, under the control of its mental intentness, is denoted by the coming forth of a lizard from the side of the bank. This is one of those delicate touches whereby the artist knows how to beautify and heighten the chief effect.

Another work of high character, which Greenough is just about to finish in marble, is a head of Lucifer, of colossal size. The countenance has the beauty of an archangel, with the hard, uncertain look of an archangel fallen. Here is a noble mould not filled up with the expression commensurate to it. There is no exaggeration to impress the beholder at once with the malevolence of the original which the sculptor had in his imagination. The sinister nature lies concealed, as it were, in the features, and comes out gradually, after they have been some time contemplated. The beauty of the countenance is not yet blasted by the deformity of the mind.

Greenough's Washington had left Italy before my arrival in Florence. By those best qualified to judge, it was here esteemed a fine work. Let me say a few words about the nudity of this statue, for which it has been much censured in America.

Washington exemplifies the might of principle. He was a great man without ambition, and the absence of ambition was a chief source of his greatness. The grandeur of his character is infinitely amplified by its abstract quality; that is, by its clean-ness from all personality. Patriotism, resting on integrity of soul and broad massive intellect, is in him uniquely embodied. The purity and elevation of his nature were the basis of his success. Had his rare military and civil genius been united to the selfishness of a Cromwell, they would have lost much of their effectiveness upon a generation warring for the rights of man. No these, but the unexampled union of these with uprightness, with stainless disinterestedness, made him Washington. If the Artist clothes him with the toga of civil authority, he represents the great statesman; if with uniform and spurs, the great General. Representing him in either of these characters, he gives preference to the one over the other, and his image of Washington is incomplete, for he was both. But he was more than either or both; he was a truly great man, in whom statesmanship and generalship were subordinate to supreme nobleness of mind and moral power. The majesty of his nature, the immortality of his name, as of one combining the morally sublime with commanding practical genius, demand the purest form of artistic representation,—the nude. To invest the colossal marble image of so towering, so everlasting a man, with the insignia of temporary office, is to fail in presenting a complete image of him. Washington, to be best seen, ought to be beheld, not as he came from the hand of the tailor, but as he came from the hand of God. Thus, the image of him will be at once real and ideal.

That Greenough's fellow-countrymen, by whose order this statue was made, would have preferred it draped, ought to be of no weight, even if such a wish had accompanied the order. To the true Artist, the laws of Art are supreme against all wishes or commands. He is the servant of Art only. If, bending to the uninformed will of his employers, he executes commissions in a way that is counter to the requirements of Art, he sinks from the Artist into the artisan. Nor can he, by stooping to uncultivated tastes, popularize Art; he deadens it, and so makes it ineffective. But by presenting it to the general gaze in its severe simplicity, and thus, through grandeur and beauty of form, lifting the beholder up into the ideal region of Art,—by this means he can popularize it. He gradually awakens and creates a love for it, and thus he gains a wide substantial support to Art in the sympathy for it engendered, the which is the only true furtherance from without that the Artist can receive.

A statue which is a genuine work of Art, cannot be appreciated,—nay, cannot be seen, without thought. The imagination must be active in the beholder, must work with the perception. Otherwise, what he looks at, is to him only a superficial piece of handicraft. The form before him should breed in him conjecture of its inward nature and capacity, and by its beauty or stamp of intellect and soul, lead him up into the domain of human possibilities. The majestic head and figure of Washington will reveal and confirm the greatness of his character, for the body is the physiognomy of the mind. That broad mould of limbs, that stern calmness, that dignity of brow, will carry the mind beyond the scenes of the revolution, and swell the heart with thoughts and hopes of the nobleness and destiny of man. Let the beholder contemplate this great statue calmly and thoughtfully; let him, by dint of contemplation, raise himself up to the point of view of the artist, and it will have on him something of this high effect. He will forget that Washington ever wore a coat, and will turn away from this noble colossal form in a mood that will be wholesome to his mental state.

This attempt to justify Greenough's work by no means implies a condemnation of other conceptions for a statue of Washington. A colossal figure,—but partially draped,—seated, the posture of repose and authority,—Greenough's conception, seems to me the most elevated and appropriate. Artists have still scope for a figure, entirely draped in military or civil costume, on horseback or standing. Only, this representation of Washington will not be so high and complete as the other.

Powers left America with a goodly cargo of busts in plaister, carrying them to Italy, there to execute them in marble. With these he opened his studio in Florence. The first that were finished he sent to the public exhibition. All eyes were at once drawn to them. Here was something totally new. Here was a completeness of imitation, a fidelity to nature never before approached, never aimed at by modern sculptors. Even the most delicate blood-vessels, the finest wrinkles, were traceable in the clear marble. Nor did the effect of the whole seem to be thereby marred. People knew not whether their astonishment ought to pass into admiration or censure. The Italian sculptors gathered themselves up. This man's Art and theirs were irreconcileable. They felt,—we must crush him, or he will overmaster us. They crowded the next exhibition with their best busts. Powers too was there. In the Tuscan capital, a young American sculptor not merely contended publicly with a host of artists for superiority; he defied to mortal combat the Italian school in this department of Art as taught by Canova. It was a conflict not for victory solely, but for life. Where would be the triumph, was not long doubtful. Powers' busts grew more and more upon the public eye. The longer they were looked at, the stronger they grew. By the light they shed upon the art of sculpture, the deficiencies of their rivals became for the first time fully apparent. Connoisseurs discovered, that they had hitherto been content with what was flat and lifeless.

The principle of the academic style of bust-making, thus suddenly supplanted, was, to merge the minor details into the larger traits, and to attempt to elevate,—to idealize was the phrase,— the subject, by preserving only the general form and outline. The result was, that busts were mostly faithless and insipid, their insipidity being generally in proportion to their unfaithfulness.

Powers made evident, that the finest traits contribute to the individuality of character; that the slightest divergence from the particularities of form vitiates the expression; that the only good basis of a bust is the closest adherence to the material form, as well in detail as in gross. So much for the groundwork. Hand in hand with this physical fidelity, must go the vital fidelity; that is, a power to seize life as it plays on that beautiful marvel, the human countenance. From the depth of the soul comes the expression on the countenance; only from the depth of a soul flooded with sensibility, can come the power to reproduce this tremulous mystical surface. Nay, this susceptibility is needed for the achievement of the physical fidelity itself. Without it, the lines harden and stiffen under the most acute and precise perception. Finally, to this union of accuracy in copying the very mould and shape of the features, with sympathy for the various life that animates them, must be added the sense of the Beautiful. This is the decisive gift, that turns the other rich faculties into endowments for Art.

The Beautiful underlies the roughest as well as the fairest products of Nature. It is the seed of creation. In all living things this seed bears fruit. In the embryo of each there is a potentiality, so to speak, to be beautiful, not entirely fulfilled in the most perfect developments, not entirely defaced in the most deformed. This spirit of beauty, resplendent at times to the dullest senses, lambent or latent in all living forms, pervading creation, this spirit is the vitality of the Artist. In it he has his being. His inward life is a perpetual yearning for the Beautiful; his outward, an endeavor to grasp and embody its forms; his happiness is, to minister in its service; his ecstasy, the glimpses he is vouchsafed of its divine splendors.

As sympathy with the motions of life is needed, to copy physical forms, so this loving intimacy with the Beautiful is needed, to refine and to guide this sympathy. In short, a lively sense of the Beautiful is requisite, not merely to produce out of the mind an ideal head,—an act so seldom really performed,—but likewise, to reproduce a living head. He who would copy a countenance must know it. To know a human face,—what a multiplex profound knowledge! Not enough is it, to have a shrewd discriminating eye for forms; not enough, to peer beneath the surface through the shifting expression. To get knowledge of any individual thing, we must start with a general standard. You cannot judge of a man's height, unless you bring with you a generic idea of measures and a notion of manly stature. So of a man's mind,—though the process be so much deeper,—and so too of his head and face. A preconceived idea of the human countenance in its fullest capability of form and expression, an aboriginal standard must illuminate the vision that aims to take in a complete image of any face. What mind can compass this deep-lying idea, except one made piercing, transparent, "visionary," by an intense inborn love of beauty? Each face is, so to speak, an offshoot from a type; each is a partial incarnation of an ideal, all ideals springing of course out of the domain of Beauty. It is only by being able to go back to this ideal, which stands again closely linked with the one, final, primeval, perfect idea of the human countenance; it is only by thus mastering, I may say, the original possibility of each face, that you can fully discern its characteristics, its essential difference from other faces—learn why it is as it is and not otherwise. A vivid, electric sensibility to the Beautiful, in active co-operation with the other powers, is the penetrating, magnifying telescope wherewith alone the vision is carried into the primitive fields of being. Thus is every face, even the most mis-shapen, brought within the circle of the Beautiful; cannot be fully seen, cannot be thoroughly known, until it is brought within that circle. Under the homeliest, commonest countenance, there is an inner lamp of unrevealed beauty, casting up at times into the features gleams of its light. These translucent moments,—its truest and best states,—the Artist must seize, in order to effect a full likeness. This is the genuine idealisation. And these states he cannot even perceive without the subtle expansive sense of the Beautiful.

The unexampled excellence of Powers's busts was soon acknowledged. In this department of Art, the Italian sculptors yielded to him the first place. Thorwaldsen, on coming, astonished, out of Powers's studio, declared that he could not make such busts, that there were none superior to them, ancient or modern. The cry now rose, that Powers could make busts, he could copy nature, but nothing more. This false inference sprang not wholly from jealousy, but in part from the false school of Art long dominant in Italy, where students were taught to study the antique more than Nature; whereby the perceptions and mental powers became so weakened and sophisticated, that it was no longer felt, what a task, how high and intense it is, truly and vitally to copy Nature. Conceive what is a human countenance,—the most wonderful work of God that our eyes can come close to! What an harmonious blending of diverse forms, what a compact constellation of beaming features, what concentrated life, what power, what variety, what unfathomable significance, in that jewelled crown of the body, that transparent earthly temple of the soul! Adequately to represent this masterpiece of divine workmanship, what a deed! He who can reproduce it in its full life and truth and character, must be a great Artist; that is, a re-maker, in a degree, of God's works,—a poet, a creator. To copy Nature, forsooth; the words are very simple: the act is one of deep insight, of noble labor, anything but a superficial work. He who performs it well, co-works with Nature, his mind exalted the while by poetic fervor. Hence none but Artists of the first class have left good portraits.

The faculty for the Ideal is then indispensable to the execution of a good bust. It is the key-stone which binds the other endowments into the beautiful arch, whereby works of human hands grow stronger with time. The basis in plastic Art is always, unerring accuracy in rendering physical forms. Sense of beauty and correctness of drawing, are thus the two extremes of the Artist's means. Between them,—and needed to link them in effective union,—is fullness of sensibility, to sympathize with and seize the expression of, all the passions and emotions of the soul. These, with imitative talent and manual dexterity, embrace the powers needed as well in the portrait-artist as in him whose subjects are inventions. I speak of the plastic Artist without distinguishing the sculptor from the painter. The difference between them is in the inequality of their endowment with the faculties of form and color; the sculptor requiring a severer eye for form than the painter, and dispensing with an eye for color. The moment the Artist begins, by the working of his imagination, to compose a subject, then comes into active play the Reason; the faculty whereby, in every department of work, prosaic as well as poetic, the mind selects and adapts,—the faculty whereby the means within reach are picked and arranged for the completest attainment of the end in view. This, it seems to me, is the only power needed in larger measure for the artist who composes groups, than for him who would make the best portrait.

It is the completeness of his endowment with all the requisites for sculpture, that stamps Powers with greatness. In the circle of his genial gifts there is no chasm. They are compactly knit together. To his ends they all co-operate smoothly, through that marvellous instrument, the human hand. Such is the precision of his eye, that he who exacts of himself the most faithful conformity to Nature's measurements, never needs the help of compasses to attain it. Such his sense of the Beautiful, that he does justice to the most beautiful countenance, and has given a new grace even to draperies. Such his sympathy with life, that with equal ease he seizes the expressions of all kinds of physiognomies, so that you cannot say that he does men better than women, old better than young; and hereby, in conjunction with his mimetic talent, he imparts such an elastic look to his marble flesh, that the spiritual essence, wherewith all Nature's living forms are vivified, may be imagined to stream from his finger-ends while he works. Such his manual dexterity, that in twenty hours he can turn out one of these great busts in its unparalleled completeness. And as if nothing should be wanting which could serve in his calling, Nature has bestowed on him a talent, I may call it a genius, for Mechanics, which,—had it not been overborne by superior faculties, destined to lift him up into the highest field of human labor, —would have gained for him a name and living as an inventive and practical machinist. It is now the pliant servant of nobler qualities; helping him to modelling tools, to facilities and securities for the elevation or removal of clay models, and to other contrivances in the economy of his studio.

Powers had not been long established in Florence, ere he set about his first statue, the Eve. This work was planned before he came to Italy. Almost precisely as it stands now embodied in attitude and character, he described to me in America the image he had there evolved in his mind. The figure is above the average height, undraped and nearly erect. The only support it has from without is a broken stem by the side of the left leg, representing the tree whence the fruit has just been plucked. On this leg is thrown the weight, the other being slightly bent at the knee. The head, inclined to the right, follows the eyes, which are fixed upon the apple, held in the right hand, raised to the level of the breast. The left arm hangs by the side, the left hand holding a twig of the tree with two apples and leaves attached. The hair, parted in the middle and thrown behind the ears, falls in a compact mass on the back. Round the outer edge of the circular plot of grass and flowers, which is the sole basis of the statue coils the serpent, who rears his head within a few inches of the right leg, looking up towards the face of Eve.

Here, without a fold of drapery to weaken or conceal any of Nature's lineaments, is the mature figure of a woman; nearly erect, the posture most favorable to beauty and perfectness of proportion; the body unconsciously arrested in this upright attitude by the mind's intentness; while the deed over which she broods, without disturbing the complete bodily repose, gives occupation to each hand and arm, throwing thereby more life as well into them as into the whole figure. Thus intent and tranquil, she stands within the coil of the serpent, whose smooth but fiery folds and crest depict animal fierceness, and contrast deeply with the female humanity above him. Both for moral and physical effect the best moment is chosen, the awful pause between obedience and disobedience. Her fresh feet pressing the flowers of Eden, Eve, still in her innocent nakedness, is fascinated against her purer will,—the mother and type of mankind, within whose bosom is ever waging the conflict between good and evil. What fullness combined with what simplicity in this conception, which bespeaks the richest resources of imagination under guidance of the severest purity of taste.

How shall I describe the execution? Knowledge and skill far exceeding mine, would fall short of transmitting through words an image of this marvel of beauty. The most that the pen can do before a master-piece of the pencil or chisel, is, to give a vivid impression of the effect it makes on the beholder, and a faint one of the master-piece itself.

In executing his Eve, Powers has had twenty or thirty models. From one he took an ankle, from another a shoulder, a fragment from the flank of a third; and so on throughout, extracting his own preconceived image piece by piece out of Nature. From such a labor even a good Artist would recoil, baffled, disheartened. To none but a supreme genius does Nature accord such familiarity. With instantaneous discernment his eyes detect where she comes short, and where her subtle spirit of beauty has wrought itself out. He seizes each scrap of perfection, rejects all the rest, and so, out of a score of models, re-compounds one of Nature's own originals. Such is the movement on the surface, that the statue has the look of having been wrought from within outward. With such truth is rendered the flexible expression imparted to flesh and blood by the vital workings, that the great internal processes might be inferred from such an exterior. The organs of animal life are at play within that elastic trunk; there is smooth pulsation beneath that healthy rotundity of limb. The capacity and wonderful nature of the human form fill the mind as you gaze at this union of force, lightness, and buoyant grace. In spite of that smooth feminine roundness of mould, such visible power and springiness are in the frame and limbs, that, though now so still, the figure makes you think of Eve as bounding over shrub and rivulet, a dazzling picture of joyous beauty. Then, again, as the eye passes up to the countenance, with its dim expression of mingled thought and emotion, the current of feeling changes, and the human mind, with its wondrous endowments, absorbs for awhile the beholder. But mark; it is by the power of Beauty that he is wrought upon. Through this, humanity stands ennobled before him. By this, the human form and capability are dilated. This awakens delight, breeds suggestion. By means of this, the effect of the statue is full, various; its significance infinite. Take away its beauty, and all is a blank. The statue ceases to be.

The head of Eve is a new head. As it is beautiful, it is Grecian; but it recalls no Greek model. Nor Venus, nor Juno, nor Niobe, can claim that she helped to nurse it. Not back to any known form does it carry the mind; it summons it to compass a new one. It is a fresh emanation from the deep bosom of Art. In form and expression, in feature and contour, in the blending of beauties into a radiant unity, it is a new Ideal, as pure as it is inexhaustible. Lightly it springs into its place from the bosom and shoulders. These flow into the trunk and arms, and these again into the lower limbs, with such graceful strength, that the wholeness of the work is the idea that establishes itself among the first upon the mind of the beholder. To the hollow of a foot, to the nail of a finger, every part is finished with the most laborious minuteness. Yet, nowhere hardness. From her scattered stores of beauty Nature supplied the details; with an infallible eye, the Artist culled them, and transferred them with a hand whose firm precision was ever guided by grace. The Natural and the Ideal here blend into one act, their essences interfused for the unfolding of a full blossom of beauty.

What terms are left to speak of the Venus of the Tribune? None stronger are needed than such as are used in speaking of the Eve of Powers. Let who will cry presumption at him who places them side by side. Art always in the end vindicates her favorite children. The Eve need fear comparison with none of them.

The clay model of Eve being finished, Powers's mind is busy with another work, also a single female figure, which he will set about immediately. It will represent a modern Greek captive, exposed in the slave-market of Constantinople. Like Eve, the figure will be without drapery; like her, it will not fail to be a model of female beauty, though in frame, size, age, character and expression, altogether different.

CLEVINGER has been here but a short time, and is zealously at work upon the crowd of busts which he brought with him from America, and several that he has modelled in Florence. Among the former is a fine one of Allston; among the latter, one of Louis Bonaparte, ex-king of Holland, so admirably executed, that it awakens regret that there is none of equal fidelity extant of the Emperor Napoleon.

Two American painters are established here, who give promise of reaching a high excellence; Brown and Kellogg. Brown devotes himself chiefly to landscapes, for which he displays rare aptitude. He has just finished a view of Florence, admirable in all respects, but chiefly for the truth with which it gives the rich hue of the Italian evening sky. An evidence of his gifts for this department, is the style in which he copies Claude Lorraine, reproducing the character, tone, and magical coloring of that great Artist with a fidelity that might impose upon a practised connoisseur.

Kellogg, by the progress he has made since he came to Florence, has shown that his ability is equal to his zeal. With an empty purse, and a spirit devoted to Art, he landed in Italy eighteen months since. In that period his genius, through industry and judicious study, has developed itself in a way that gives assurance that he will reach a high rank.

I will conclude this Florentine chapter with a few chips of "fragments" picked up in that division, which the despotism of nerves over the intellectual as well as the physical man, obliged me to put last in my scale of occupations and pastimes.

Among my disappointments are Petrarca and Macchiavelli. I am disappointed in Petrarca that his sonnets are written more out of the head than the heart. They sparkle with poetic fancy, but do not throb with sensibility. In his pleasant little autobiographical memoir, Petrarca ascribes to his love for Laura all that he was and did. For twenty years, it was the breath of mental life to him. Happily he was not of an energetic, glowing nature (his portrait might be taken for that of a woman), or his love would have consumed instead of animating him, or, worse still, would have had perhaps a quick close in success. I am sorry to conclude, that he was very far from being the most miserable man of his generation.

Macchiavelli is not the searching thinker that one unacquainted with his works might infer him to be, from his so long sustained reputation. He is a vigorous, accomplished writer; a clear, nervous narrator. Subtlety in the discussion of points of political expediency, seems to me his highest power. Princes, nobles, and populace, are to him the ultimate elements of humanity. The deep relations of man to man, and of man to God, do not come vividly within his view. He has no thorough insight into the moral resources of man; he does not transpierce the surface of human selfishness. There is in him no ray of divine illumination, whereby he might discern the absolute. But it is unjust to reproach him with a want which he has in common with most of his brother historians.

A just reproach against him is, that in his History he flattered the Medici, and has handed down a misrepresentation of them. From his pages no one would learn that the first Medici were usurpers, successful demagogues. Sismondi and Alfieri counteract the false report of Macchiavelli, and disclose the long-concealed ugliness of these vulgar tyrants. Describing the state of Italy at the death of Lorenzo, and the loss of independence with that of liberty, Sismondi says:—" Florence, mastered for three generations by the family of Medici, depraved by their licentiousness, made venal by their wealth, had learnt from them to fear and to obey." The hollowness and worthlessness of Pope Leo X., his prodigality, dissoluteness, and incapacity, are exposed by Sismondi, who describes as follows Pope Clement VII., another Medici, and the one to whom Macchiavelli, in a fulsome address, dedicated his History of Florence:—" Under the pontificate of Leo X., his cousin, when times were prosperous, he acquired the reputation of ability; but when he came to confront distress not brought about by himself, then his unskilfulness in matters of finance and government, his sordid avarice, his pusillanimity and imprudence, his sudden resolutions and prolonged indecision, rendered him no less odious than ridiculous." Sismondi relates, that Lorenzo de

Medici, being on his death-bed, sent for Savonarola, the celebrated preacher of ecclesiastical reform and devotee to liberty, who had hitherto refused to see Lorenzo, or to show him any respect. Nevertheless, Lorenzo, moved by the fame of Savonarola's eloquence and sanctity, desired to receive absolution from him. Savonarola did not refuse to him consolations and exhortations, but declared, that absolve him from his sins he could not, unless he gave proof of penitence by repairing as much as in him lay his errors. That he must pardon his enemies, make restitution of his ill-gotten wealth, and restore to his country its liberty. Lorenzo, not consenting, was denied absolution, and died, says Sismondi, in the possession of despotic power, " mori in possesso della tirannide."

Lorenzo dei Medici,—whose portrait in the gallery here is that of an intellectual sensualist, whose largesses, pecuniary liberalities and sensual sumptuosities won for him the equivocal title of " il magnifico,"—Lorenzo and Leo X. have the fame of being the munificent patrons of Poets and Artists. All the fame they deserve on this score is, that they had taste to appreciate the men of merit who lived in their day. These men were the last offspring of the antecedent energetic times of liberty. By the receding waves of freedom they had been left upon the barren shore of despotism. What had Leo X. to do with the forming of the eminent writers and artists who adorned the age to which the servility of men has given his name ? Patrons of Poets and Artists ! A curse upon patronage. Let it be bestowed upon upholsterers and barbers. Poets and Artists don't want patronage : what they do want is sympathy. Patronage is narrow, is blind ; its eyes are egotistical ; it is prone to uphold mere talent, mediocrity. Sympathy is expansive, keen-sighted, and discerns and confirms genius.

Leonardo da Vinci, Dante, Boccaccio, Petrarca, men too great to be patronised, were the children of republican Florence. By

Democracy, turbulent Democracy, were they nursed into heroic stature. When the basis of her government was the sovereignty of the people, when nobles had to put away their nobility to be admitted to a share in the administration of affairs, then it was that the bosom of Florence was fertile and wide enough to give birth to the men who are the chief glory of modern Italy. Compare Florence as she then was, vigorous, manly, erect, productive, with her abject, effeminate, barren state under the Medici. Or contrast the genius generated by democratic Florence with that of aristocratic Venice.

Alfieri tells, that he betook himself to writing, because in his miserable age and land he had no scope for action; and that he remained single because he would not be a breeder of slaves. He utters the despair, to passionate tears, which he felt, when young and deeply moved by the traits of greatness related by Plutarch, to find himself in times and in a country where no great thing could be either said or acted. The feelings here implied are the breath of his dramas. In them, a clear nervous understanding gives rapid utterance to wrath, pride, and impetuous passion. Though great within his sphere, his nature was not ample and complex enough for the highest tragedy. In his composition there was too much of passion and too little of high emotion. Fully to feel and perceive the awful and pathetic in human conjunctions, a deep fund of sentiment is needed. A condensed tale of passion is not of itself a Tragedy. To dark feelings, resolves, deeds, emotion must give breadth, and depth, and relief. Passion furnishes crimes, but cannot furnish the kind and degree of horror which should accompany their commission. To give Tragedy the grand compass and sublime significance whereof it is susceptible, it is not enough, that through the storm is visible the majestic figure of Justice: the blackest clouds must be fringed with the light of Hope and Pity; while through them Religion gives vistas into the Infinite, Beauty keeping watch to repel what is partial or deformed. In Alfieri, these great gifts are not commensurate with his power of intellect and passion. Hence, like the French classic dramatists, he is obliged to bind his personages into too narrow a circle. They have not enough of moral liberty. They are not swayed merely, they are tyrannized over by the passions. Hence, they want elasticity and color. They are like hard engravings.

Alfieri does not cut deep into character: he gives a clean outline, but broad flat surfaces without finish of parts. It is this throbbing movement in details, which imparts buoyancy and expression. Wanting it, Alfieri is mostly hard. The effect of the whole is imposing, but does not invite or bear close inspection. Hence, though he is clear and rapid, and tells a story vividly, his tragedies are not life-like. In Alfieri there is vigorous rhetoric, sustained vivacity, fervent passion; but no depth of sentiment, no play of a fleet rejoicing imagination, nothing "visionary," and none of the "golden cadence of poetry." But his heart was full of nobleness. He was a proud, lofty man, severe, but truth-loving and scornful of littleness. He delighted to depict characters that are manly and energetic. He makes them wrathful against tyranny, hardy, urgent for freedom, reclaiming with burning words the lost rights of man, protesting fiercely against oppression. There is in Alfieri a stern virility that contrasts strongly with Italian effeminateness. An indignant frown sits ever on his brow, as if rebuking the passivity of his countrymen. His verse is swollen with wrath. It has the clanger of a trumpet that would shame the soft piping of flutes.

Above Alfieri, far above him and all other Italian greatness, solitary in the earliness of his rise, ere the modern mind had worked itself open, and still as solitary amidst the after splendors of Italy's fruitfulness, is Dante. Take away any other great Poet or Artist, and in the broad shining rampart wherewith genius has beautified and fortified Italy, there would be a mournful chasm. Take away Dante, and you level the Citadel itself, under whose shelter the whole compact cincture has grown into strength and beauty.

Three hundred years before Shakspeare, in 1265, was Dante born. His social position secured to him the best schooling. He was taught and eagerly learnt all the crude knowledge of his day. Through the precocious susceptibility of the poetic temperament, he was in love at the age of nine years. This love, as will be with such natures, was wrought into his heart, expanding his young being with beautiful visions and hopes, and making tuneful the poetry within him. It endured with his life, and spiritualized his latest inspirations. Soberly he afterwards married another, and was the father of a numerous family. In the stirring days of Guelfs and Ghibellines, he became a public leader, made a campaign, was for a while one of the chief magistrates of Florence, her ambassador abroad more than once, and at the age of thirty-six closed his public career in the common Florentine way at that period, namely, by exile. Refusing to be recalled on condition of unmanly concessions, he never again saw his home. For twenty years he was an impoverished, wandering exile, and in his fifty-sixth year breathed his last at Ravenna.

But Dante's life is his poem. Therein is the spirit of the mighty man incarnated. The life after earthly death is his theme. What a mould for the thoughts and sympathies of a poet, and what a poet, to fill all the chambers of such a mould! Man's whole nature claims interpretation; his powers, wants, vices, aspirations, basenesses, grandeurs. The imagination of semi-Christian Italy had strained itself to bring before the sensuous mind of the South an image of the future home of the soul. The supermundane thoughts, fears, hopes of his time, Dante condensed into one vast picture—a picture cut as upon adamant with diamond To enrich Hell, and Purgatory, and Paradise, he coined his own soul. His very body became transfigured, purged of its flesh, by the intensity of fiery thought. Gaunt, pale, stern, rapt, his "visionary" eyes glaring under his deep furrowed brow, as he walked the streets of Verona, he heard people whisper, " That is he who has been down into Hell." Down into the depths of his fervent nature he had been, and kept himself lean by brooding over his passions, emotions, hopes, and transmuting the essence of them into everlasting song.

Conceive the statuesque grand imagination of Michael Angelo united to the vivid homely particularity of Defoe, making pictures out of materials drawn from a heart whose rapturous sympathies ranged with Orphean power through the whole gamut of human feeling, from the blackest hate up to the brightest love, and you will understand what is meant by the term *Dantesque*. In the epitaph for himself, written by Dante and inscribed on his tomb at Ravenna, he says:—"I have sung, while traversing them, the abode of God, Phlegethon and the foul pits." Traversing must be taken literally. Dante almost believed that he had traversed them, and so does his reader too, such is the control the Poet gains over the reader through his burning intensity and graphic picturesqueness. Like the mark of the fierce jagged lightning upon the black night-cloud are some of his touches, as awful, as fearfully distinct, but not as momentary.

In the face of the contrary judgment of such critics as Shelley and Carlyle, I concur in the common opinion, which gives preference to the *Inferno* over the *Purgatorio* and *Paradiso*. Dante's rich nature included the highest and lowest in humanity. With the pure, the calm, the tender, the ethereal, his sympathy was as lively as with the turbulent, the passionate, the gross. But the hot contentions of the time, and especially their effect upon himself,—through them an outcast and proud mendicant,—forced the latter upon his heart as its unavoidable familiars. All about and within him were plots, ambitions, wraths, chagrins, jealousies, miseries. The times and his own distresses darkened his mood to the lurid hue of Hell. Moreover, the happiness of Heaven, the rewards of the spirit, its empyreal joys, can be but faintly pictured by visual corporeal images, the only ones the earthly poet possesses. The thwarted imagination loses itself in a vague, dazzling, golden mist. On the contrary, the trials and agonies of the spirit in Purgatory and Hell, are by such images suitably, forcibly, definitely set forth. The sufferings of the wicked while in the flesh are thereby typified. And this suggests to me, that one bent, as many are, upon detecting Allegory in Dante, might regard the whole poem as one grand Allegory, wherein, under the guise of a picture of the future world, the poet has represented the effect of the feelings in this; the pangs, for example, of the murderer and glutton in Hell, being but a portraiture, poetically colored, of the actual torments on earth of those who commit murder and gluttony. Finally, in this there is evidence,—and is it not conclusive?—of the superiority of the Book of Hell, that in that Book occur the two most celebrated passages in the poem, —passages, in which with unsurpassed felicity of diction and versification, the pathetic and terrible are rounded by the spirit of Poetry into pictures, where simplicity, expression, beauty, combine to produce effects unrivalled in this kind in the pages of Literature. I refer of course to the stories of Francesca and Ugolino.

Dante's work is untranslateable. Not merely because the style, form, and rhythm of every great Poem, being the incarnation of inspired thought, you cannot but lacerate the thought in disembodying it; but because, moreover, much of the elements of its body, the words namely in which the spirit made itself visible, have passed away. To get a faithful English transcript of the great Florentine, we should need a diction of the fourteenth century, moulded by a more fiery and potent genius than Chaucer. Not the thoughts solely, as in every true poem, are so often virgin thoughts; the words, too, many of them, are virgin words. Their freshness and unworn vigor are there alone in Dante's Italian.

Of the modern intellectual movement, Dante was the majestic Herald. In his poem, are the mysterious shadows, the glow, the fragrance, the young life-promising splendors of the dawn. The broad day has its strength and its blessings; but it can give only a faint image of the glories of its birth.

The bitter woes of Dante, hard and bitter to the shortening of his life, cannot but give a pang to the reader whom his genius has exalted and delighted. He was a life-long sufferer. Early disappointed in love; not blest, it would seem, in his marriage; foiled as a statesman; misjudged and relentlessly proscribed by the Florentines, upon whom from the pits of Hell his wrath wreaked itself in a damning line, calling them, " Gente avara, invida, e superba;" a homeless wanderer; a dependant at courts where, though honored, he could not be valued; obliged to consort there with buffoons and parasites, he whose great heart was full of honor, and nobleness, and tenderness; and at last, all his political plans and hopes baffled, closing his mournful days far, far away from home and kin, wasted, sorrow-stricken, broken-hearted. Most sharp, most cruel were his woes. Yet to them perhaps we owe his poem. Had he not been discomfited and exiled, who can say that the mood or the leisure would have been found for such poetry? His vicissitudes and woes were the soil to feed and ripen his conceptions. They steeped him in dark experiences, intensified his passions, enriching the imagination that was tasked to people Hell and Purgatory; while from his own pains he turned with keener joy and lightened pen to the beatitudes of Heaven. But for his sorrows, in his soul would not have been kindled so fierce a fire. Out of the seething gloom of his sublime heart shot forth forked lightnings which still glow, a perennial illumination, —to the eyes of men, a beauty, a marvel, a terror. Poor indeed he was in purse; but what wealth had he not in his bosom! True, he was a father parted from his children, a proud warm man, eating the bread of cold strangers; but had he not his genius and its bounding offspring for company, and would not a day of such heavenly labor as his outweigh a month, aye, a year of crushed pride? What though by the world he was misused, received from it little, his own even wrested from him; was he not the giver, the conscious giver, to the world of riches fineless? Not six men, since men were, have been blest with such a power of giving.

Pisa, February, 1843.

Here is a wide chasm of time. A goodly space of ground, too, has been gone over. Without much stretching, a volume might be put in between this date and the last. That trouble, however, shall be spared the writer and the reader. Let us see whether in a few pages we cannot whisk ourselves through Switzerland into Germany, and back to Italy.

Starting northward from Florence, in the afternoon of June 7th, 1842, in less than an hour we were among the Appenines, over whose barren, billowy surface we rolled on a good road to within a few miles of Bologna, where we arrived the next day at three.

The Italian intellect is quick at expedients. With freedom the Italians would be eminently practical. Free people are always practical; hence, the superiority of the English and Americans in the useful and commodious. From necessity and self-defence, the acute Italians are adepts in the art of deception. Hypocrisy they are taught by their masters, temporal and spiritual; a substitution of the semblance for the substance being the foundation of civil and religious rule in Italy.

The fictions of the Catholic Church are mostly unsuitable to the Arts. Martyrs and emaciated anchorites cannot be subjected to the laws of beauty. The Greek divinities were incarnations of powers, qualities, truths, which, though not the deepest, were shaped by beauty. The Romish saints, with their miracles and macerations, want capability of beauty together with dignity and respectability, and are thence doubly unfit for the handling of Art. The highest genius cannot make them thoroughly effective. In the gallery of Bologna one is often repelled even from the best execution by the offensiveness of the subject. The geniality of Art is shown as much in the selection of subjects as in the treatment. One tires of heavy virgins that would be thought to float, and old men on their knees to them, trying to look *extasiés;* and more still, of the distortions of mental and bodily agony.

Leaving Bologna at noon, by Modena and Reggio, we arrived at Parma after dusk, through a country, level, fertile and well tilled. Along the road vines hung in graceful festoons from tree to tree, and peasants were gathering mulberry leaves for silkworms.

After running to the Gallery, just to have a momentary look at the two famous Correggios, we started from Parma at nine in the morning, and coming on rapidly through Piacenza and Lodi, entered Milan just before dark.

By the grandeur of the Cathedral we were even more moved than when we first beheld it. Then we explored its populous roof; now we descended into its vaults, peopled too with statues and busts, some of silver to the value of more than a million of francs. About the tomb of St. Charles Borromeo there is gold and silver to the amount of four million francs. Guard it well, Priests. 'Twill be a treasure on that day, which *will* come, when this people's deep, smothered cry shall end at last in a triumphant shout. From the Cathedral we betook ourselves to the barn-like place, which contains Leonardo da Vinci's fresco of the Last Supper. Here is the inspiration of genius. To produce that head of Jesus, what a conception must have been long nursed in the great painter's brain, and with what intense force of will must he have embodied it, to stamp upon human features such pre-eminence, such benignity, such majesty! With this, the vigor and variety in the superb heads of the apostles, the grace and spirit of the grouping, bring the scene before you with such speaking presence, that one sees how pictures can strengthen and keep alive religious belief. By its vivid reality, its beauty and character, this sublime picture proclaims the truth of what it sets forth, and takes the mind captive with its power and its fascination.

As we approached Como, we enjoyed much the contact again with mountains. After an early breakfast, June 12th, we were on board the steamboat at seven, to explore the beautiful lake. At nine, about midway, we landed, in order to see and have the views from the Villas Serbelloni, Melzi, and Somariva.

The villa Somariva has some fine sculpture by Thorwaldsen and Canova, and a number of Italian and French pictures. The French Ideal is a medium of the human form taken from measurement of the antique. The genuine Ideal is attainable only through an earnest loving study of nature, directed by a sure eye and a warm sense of the beautiful. Modern French art has an eccentric look; whereas, Art should always be concentric, seeking, that is, the centre of all forms and expressions, the concentration into an individual of the best qualities of many. Hence, high Art looks always tranquil and modest. French Art is apt to have an excited, conceited air.

Stopping as we did where the Lake branches, we had followed the advice of a Milanese gentleman, who accosted us in the boat. Had we gone on, we should not have made by a good deal so much of our morning; for the upper end of the lake has less interest and beauty than the middle. On re-embarking, as the boat returned, between one and two, we renewed conversation with the friendly giver of such good counsel. He had spent his Sunday in a passive enjoyment of the rich soft beauties of the Lake. This was the easy and highest form of worship for a nature like his. He was a man past forty, of rather more than middle stature, with a well made, somewhat stout frame, inclined to fullness. His complexion was of that rich creamy tint, seen oftener in Italy than elsewhere, with blue-black hair and smooth whiskers; a handsome man, with regular, bold features, that didn't look bold, from the gentleness of his expression; for his graceful mouth and large white teeth were formed for smiling, and his black eyes were not those glowing Italian orbs, in whose depths so much of good or evil lies sleeping,—you know not which,—they were shallow, handsome, happy eyes. He ordered coffee, and pressed me to take a cup. After this, he offered me a cigar from his case, and upon my declining that too, he seemed to conclude that I lived a very poor life. For himself, he let not an hour in the day go by, he said, without regaling his body with some or other fragrant stimulant. He urged us, should we revisit Milan, to stop at the hotel where he lodged, whose *cuisine* and wines he praised with thankful animation. Yet, he was not one of those who spend their mornings in expectation of their dinner. He was too subtle an epicurean for such a dead diurnal vacuity. Though his dinner was the chief circumstance of his being, still, after his mode, he valued time, and knew how to bridge over the wide gulfs between meals upon pillars constructed of minor enjoyments, including among them easy acts of kindness and courtesy.

We got back to Como at four, and started immediately for Lugano, our resting-place that night. The Lake of Lugano pleased us even more than that of Como. There is greater variety in the forms of the mountains. These fairy Lakes, uniting Italy to Switzerland, combine the beauties of both.

As you advance from Lugano, the mountains close in upon you, the scenery growing bolder and grander. Through an opening not far from Lugano, we had a clear distant view down into Lake Maggiore, and then we came upon the picturesque old town of Belinzona, flanked with turrets, the turrets flanked with mountains. Towards evening we approached the southern sublimity of this pass, a rent in the mountain nearly a mile long, where the river Ticino,—which till now had this deep gorge all to himself,—has been forced by the engineer to make room for a road, the angry, headlong torrent being thrice crossed and recrossed in the course of the mile. As we emerged from this magnificent passage, the mountains stretched up into Swiss stature, their sides clothed with firs as with a plumage. 'Twas dark when we drove into Airolo, at the foot of the St. Gothard, where good beds awaited us.

First through green fields and firs, then rugged wastes, and finally, torrents, snow, and bare rock, up, up, up we went for three or four hours, the steep road making its way zigzag on terraces. The summit of the pass, a scene of cold dreary sterility, is a great geographical centre; for within a circuit of ten miles are the sources of four of the chief rivers of Europe, the Rhine, the Rhone, the Reuss, and the Ticino.

Now we set off in a race with the Reuss, who bounds five thousand feet down the mountain in a series of cataracts, to rush into the Lake of the Four Cantons at Fluellen. We crossed the Devil's Bridge, the northern sublimity of the St. Gothard pass; and the *Pfaffensprung,* so called from the tradition of a monk having leapt from rock to rock, across the torrent, with a maiden in his arms. That's a fine tradition. One cannot but have a kind of respect for the bold amorous monk. He deserved the maiden—better than any other monk. The beautiful maiden,—for beautiful she could not but be, to inspire a feat so daring,—must have been still and passive in the arms of her monastic Hercules; for had she made herself heavy by scratching and kicking, whilst in mid air over that fearful chasm, I fancy the tradition would have been more tragical. Never was maiden more honorably won—by a monk. We passed through Altdorf, Tell's Altdorf, and taking the steamboat at Fluellen, traversed under a serene sky the Lake of the Four Cantons, with its sublime scenery, landing in Lucerne after sun-down. Thus, from dawn to twilight we had crossed one of the grand Alpine passes, and the whole length of the most magnificent Lake in Europe. This was a rich day.

The next morning, before starting for Thun, we took time to walk a few steps beyond one of the gates to see the colossal lion, cut in the side of a rock, as designed by Thorwaldsen, in commemoration of the faithful Swiss, who fell defending the royal family of France in the Tuileries in 1792. By the Emmendale we reached Thun the following day. Here, in this beautiful portal to the sublime scenery of the Bernese Alps, we sat ourselves down in quiet lodgings, by the water's edge, near where the river issues from the lake.

In the grandeurs, sublimities, movements of Nature in Switzerland, the creative energy reveals itself in doings and voices that astound the imagination. Nature seems here more than elsewhere vivified by the breath of God. Those gigantic piles of riven rock, fixed in sublime ruggedness, proclaim with unwonted emphasis, the awful hand that arrested their upheaving. Those terrific fields of eternal ice, the nourishing mothers of great rivers, tempt the imagination towards the mysterious source of Nature's processes. The common forms and elements of our globe are here exaggerated. Hills and valleys become mountains and gorges; winter dwells on the peaks throughout summer; streams are obliged to be torrents. Walking in a meadow, you come suddenly on a streamlet, that looks in the grass like a transparent serpent at full speed, it runs with such startling velocity, as though it had a momentous mysterious mission. The Rivers rush out of the Lakes, as if they had twice the work to do of other rivers.

At the end of a month, we quitted Thun, about the middle of July, to return, for the rest of the summer, to the water-cure establishment at Boppart. 'Twould have been wiser had we gone to Graefenberg. Priesnitz understands his own discovery better than any one else, and inspires his own patients with a deeper confidence. At Graeffenberg, moreover, there is mountain air and the coldest water. Through the secluded Münster valley we reached Basle, whence by railroad, post, and steamboat we rapidly descended the Rhine to Boppart. The Rhine suffers at first by being seen when one's vision has just been enlarged and sublimated by Switzerland.

The left, the wooded, shore of the Rhine was golden with autumnal foliage, the right pale with fading vineyards, when in the middle of October we again turned our faces southward. 'Twas eleven o'clock, a chilly moonlight night, when, at the gate of Frankfort, the officer questioned us, "Are you the Duke?"—"No, I am an American."—"Oh, then," to the postillion, "drive on."

Our former admiration of Dannecker's statue of Ariadne was somewhat qualified, for since we first saw it, our eyes had been strengthened in Italy. The composition is admirable, the attitude graceful; but the limbs want rounding and expressive finish, and the head is stiff, as mimicry of the antique always is.

It being too late to re-enter Italy by the Splügen pass, we bent our course more eastward towards Munich and the Tyrol, through the fine old German towns of Würzburg and Augsburg. We might have been present at the festival held to celebrate the completion of the *Walhalla*, a magnificent temple on the shore of the Danube, erected by the King of Bavaria, in honor of German worth and genius, to be adorned with the statues and busts of Germany's great men, from Arminius to Schiller. When I learnt afterwards that from this temple Luther is to be excluded, I was glad that we had not gone out of our way to see it. Figure to yourself the Apollo of the Vatican with the head purposely taken off, or the Cathedral of Strasburg with the spire demolished, and you will have some notion of the grossness of this outrage. A German Pantheon without Luther! The grandest national temple that Architecture could devise, and sculpture adorn with the effigies of German greatness, yet left bare of that of Luther, could never be but a fragment. The impertinence of this petty, transitory King, to try to put an affront on the mighty, undying Sovereign, Luther!

In Munich there is a noble collection of pictures; but the city, with its fresh new palaces, and churches, and theatres, has a made up look. It seems the work of Dilettantism: it is not a warm growth out of the wants and aspirations of the time. It is as if it had been said: Architecture and Painting are fine things; therefore we will have them. The King of Bavaria, the builder and collector of all this, has been a great "Patron" of the Arts. Latterly his patronage is said to have taken another direction, and he has become a patron of Religion. The one is as proper a subject for patronage as the other.

We entered the Tyrol on the 22d of October, after a light fall of snow, which weighed just enough on the fir trees to add a grace to their shapes, and on their dark green foliage sparkled in the sun, like a transparent silver canopy. Tyrolese scenery we saw in its most picturesque aspect. Our road went through Innspruck, the Capital of the Tyrol, lying in a capacious valley encompassed by mountains; thence over the Bremer through Botzen, historical Trent, and Roveredo. Coming down from the chilly mountains, the sun of Italy was luxurious. What a fascination there is in this warm beautiful land!

We stopped half a day at Verona. Dante and Shakspeare have both been here; Dante in person, as guest of the Scaligers, Shakspeare in Juliet, that resplendent diamond exhibited by the lightning of a tropical night-storm. Just out of the town they show a huge, rough, open stone coffer, as Juliet's tomb; and in one of the principal streets, our cicerone pointed to a house which he said was that of the Capulets. Preferring to believe, we made no further inquiries. So, we have seen Juliet's tomb, and the house of the Capulets. We saw too the palace of the Scaligers, wherein, at the table of *Can-grande,* Dante hurled at his host that celebrated sarcasm. One can readily figure the sublime, thoughtful, sorrowful man, sitting silent as was his wont, scornful of the levities and follies of speech around him, and not keeping his scorn out of his great countenance, when, after some coarse sally from a favorite buffoon, the prince, turning to the poet, said, " I wonder that this man, who is a fool, can make himself so agreeable to us all, while you, who are called wise, have not been able to do so." —" You would not wonder," answered Dante, " if you knew that friendship comes of similarity of habits and sympathy of souls."

At Verona we turned from our southward course, and went off due east to Venice, without halting in Vicensa and Padua, that lay in our path. We rowed in Gondolas, saw Titian's picture of the Assumption, walked over the Rialto, inspected the Arsenal, stood near the Bridge of Sighs, took chocolate in the place of St. Mark, and rowed back in the Lagune to Mestre, whence by Padua and Rovigo we came to Ferrara. From the people a traveller has to do with on the highways of Europe, he gets much of the caricature of what in the world is called politeness, namely, a smooth lie varnished.

A scarcity of post-horses detained us a day in Ferrara, and the bridge over the Po having been swept away by late floods, we had to make a circuit to reach Bologna. The Manuscripts of Tasso and Ariosto in the Library, Ariosto's house and Tasso's prison, beguiled the time in the desolate old town of Ferrara.

Off the beaten highways, from which the floods forced us, the people looked fresh and innocent. Wherever strangers throng, there knavery thrives. Hence, on the great routes of Europe, the traveller is constantly vexed and soured by impositions, from the most brazen to the most subtle. From the obsequious innkeeper to the coarse postillion, he is the victim of the whole class with whom he has to deal. Yet he would be very unjust who should thence infer that cheating and lying are habitual with the people among whom by these classes he is so often plagued and wronged. The country between Ferrara and Bologna overflows with population. Under this warm sun, the fertile valley of the Po yields meat, drink and clothing all at once; silk, vine and grain growing in plenteous crops at the same time in one field.

At Florence we found Powers with his model of the Greek Slave nearly finished. What easy power there is in genius! Here is one of the most difficult tasks of sculpture,—a nude female figure,—conceived and executed with a perfectness that completely conceals all the labor of thought and hand bestowed upon it. Most worthy to be a daughter of the Eve, this figure is altogether of another type, slender and maidenly. Like Eve, it is a revelation of the symmetry, the inexhaustible grace, the infinite power and beauty of the human form. What an attitude, —how naturally brought about,—what a wonderful management of the resources of such limbs for expression! It is a figure

"To radiate beauty everlastingly."

From it one learns what a marvellous work is the human body. One feels himself elevated and purified, while contemplating a creation so touching and beautiful. Of this statue a distinguished American clergyman, whom we had the pleasure to meet in Italy, said, that were a hundred libertines to collect round it, attracted by its nudity, they would stand abashed and rebuked in its presence.

This is the fourth ideal female head that Powers has produced, and yet there is not between any two of them the slightest resemblance. Each one is a fresh independent creation. Not to imitate himself evinces in a sculptor even a still greater depth of resource than not to imitate the antique. It is proof of a mastery over the human countenance. Its elements and constituents Powers carries in his brain. This is the genuine creative energy.

Greenough was absent in America, and his studio was closed. Clevinger was at work at the model of his Indian, his first ideal effort.*

Pisa, famous for its leaning tower and its University, which has able professors, is, for one who wants quiet, a pleasant place to spend three months of winter. The Arno, flowing through it from east to west, for nearly a mile in a gentle curve, cuts the town into two parts, united by three bridges. Our front windows look out upon the river and its western bridge, and from one in the rear there is a view of the long jagged outline of the distant Appenines running towards Genoa, the highest peaks covered with snow. Our walks along the Lung-Arno carry us daily by the palace of Byron, the memory of whom does not seem to be much cherished by the Italians here.

On the 22d of February we found ourselves in lively, dirty, commercial Leghorn, which vulgar cacophonous dissyllable is intended to be a rendering into English of the melodious Italian name of this town, which is Livorno. That the Mediterranean well deserves its reputation of being a very ugly sea in winter we had sickening proof. In a stout French steamboat we were two nights and a day, instead of one night, in getting from Leghorn to Civita Vecchia.

FRIDAY, February 24th, 1843.

We cast anchor in the small harbor of Civita Vecchia at seven,

* The last time I saw Clevinger, he was standing before this work, with his frank, manly countenance animated by the pleasure and intentness of the labor. In the budding of his fame, he was cut off, a loss to his family, his friends, his country

landed at eight, and at ten set off for Rome. For several miles the road ran along the sea shore, through a desolate but not barren country, with scarce a sign of population. A few massive fragments of a bridge from the hands of the Romans, gave a sudden interest to the deserted region, and kept our minds awake until three o'clock, when, still eleven miles distant from Rome, we came in sight of St. Peter's, which drew us towards it with such force, that we wondered at the languor of the postillion, who drove his dull hacks as if at the end of our journey there were nothing but a supper and a snug hostelrie. We soon lost sight of St. Peter's. The fields,—and this is not strictly part of the *Campagna*,—still looked dreary and abandoned. Up to the very walls of the ancient mistress of the world, and the present spiritual mistress of many millions more than the Cæsars ever swayed, the land seems as if it had long lain under a malediction. At last, towards sundown, after an ascent, whence we overlooked the "Eternal City," the Cupola of St. Peter's filled our eyes of a sudden, and seemingly within a stone's throw of us. Descending again, we entered Rome by a gate near the Church, and, escorted by a horseman, whose casque led one to imagine him a mimic knight of Pharsalia, we drove close by the gigantic colonnade that encloses the court of St. Peter's, crossed the Tiber by the Bridge of Adrian, and after several turns through narrow streets, drove up to the temple of Marcus Aurelius Antoninus, with its front of fluted marble columns, under which we passed into the interior and there halted. 'Twas the Custom House, whence a dollar having quickly obtained for us release from the delay and vexation of search, we drove at dusk through the Corso to the *Hotel de l'Europe* in the *Piazza di Spagna*. Here we spent the evening in planning, and in trying to think ourselves into a full consciousness that we were in Rome.

SATURDAY, Feb. 25th.

Before breakfast I took my first walk in Rome up the broad

stairway from the *Piazza di Spagna* to the Pincian Hill; but the atmosphere was hazy. Later, I walked down the Corso, whose Palaces look wealth and luxury. A Palace without political power, what is it but a gilded Prison, where refined sensuality strives to beguile the intellect in its servitude! A scarlet gilt coach rolled by, with gorgeous trappings and three footmen in flaunting liveries crowded together on the foot-board behind; an exhibition, which shows manhood most disgustingly bemasked, and is an unchristian ostentation of the mastery of man over man. 'Twas the coach of a Cardinal! of one who assumes to be the pre-elect interpreter of the invisible God! of one whom millions believe to be among the most divinely-enlightened expositors of the self-denying Jesus' words! Truly, God rights the wrong in our little world by general laws and stoops not to an individual; else, it were neither unreasonable nor profane to expect that the sleek horses of this silken-robed priest might refuse to carry him to the altar, raised to him, who declared it to be hard for a rich man to enter into the kingdom of heaven. Possibly he is self-deluded; for so great is the power of man upon man, that the world-wide and time-heaped belief in his sanctity may have persuaded even himself, that between his life and his doctrine there is no wide-gaping inconsistency. Some too, being stronger in religious sentiment than in intellect, are blinded, under the bandage o'' custom, to the monstrous imposture. But many a one, having capacity for and opportunities of culture, must be the conscious worshipper of ambition and the knowing defiler of the Holy, and his life therefore—what I leave each reader to name for himself.

This is a gala-day in Rome, being one of the last of the Carnival. At two we drove to the Corso, where we fell into a double file of carriages going in opposite directions. The Corso is the principal street of modern Rome, about a mile long, proud with palaces, columns, and open squares. Out of most of the numerous windows streamed long crimson silk hangings. At short intervals were dragoons as a mounted police. The street was thronged with people, many in masks and fantastic costumes; the windows were crowded with gaily dressed spectators. But the chief source of animation to the gay scene, is the practice of throwing bonbons and boquets from carriage to carriage, or in or out of the windows, or from or at the pedestrians, a general interchange in short of missile greetings. Most of the bonbons are of clay, or paste and flowers, and hence can be dealt out profusely without much cost. You assail whom you please, and wire masks are worn by those who are careful of their eyes. 'Tis an occasion when the adult lay aside their maturity and put on childhood again, and, as among children, there is the fullest freedom and equality. We knew not a soul in the throng, and dealt our handfuls of powdered pills into carriages and windows, and received them in turn, with as much glee as if we had been harlequins in a pantomime. We came in towards six.

Sunday, Feb. 26th.

We drove first to the Forum. Here then had been the centre of the Roman world! There before you is a door of the ancient Capitol! A few straggling columns and arches stand up still manfully against time. You think 'tis something to find yourself face to face with what has heard the voice of Cicero and the Gracchi, to shake hands, as it were, across a gulf of twenty centuries, with the cotemporaries of the Scipios; when you learn that all that you behold are relics of the Imperial epoch. They showed us too the walls and two columns of a temple of Romulus with a door of well-wrought bronze. Although one likes to believe on such occasions, we had to turn incredulous from these, and settled our minds again into positive faith before the arch of Titus, which stands at the end of the Forum opposite the Capitol, and is enriched with sculpture illustrating the destruction of Jerusalem, in commemoration of which it was erected to the

Emperor Titus. Passing under this, which Jews to this day will not do, we drove down the *Via Sacra* to the Colosseum, near which is the arch of Constantine. Conceive of an elliptical Theatre with stone seats all round rising row back of row, to hold one hundred thousand spectators, who came in and out without delay or confusion through seventy inlets. Here in this vast arena may be said to have been represented the conflict between paganism and Christianity. Here were slaughtered tens of thousands of Christians, thrown to wild beasts as the most grateful spectacle to the Roman populace. The arena itself is now a Christian temple, sanctified by the blood of the faith-sustained victims.

From the Colosseum we went to the Church of St. John of the Lateran, where, if what they tell you were true, are preserved the heads of St. Peter and St. Paul. We were shown too what the exhibiting priest said is the table on which Jesus took the last supper with the apostles. This with other relics is declared to have been brought from Jerusalem by Helen, the mother of Constantine. This is the oldest church in Europe, and is called the mother of all others.

In the afternoon we drove to St. Peter's. I had not imagined the entrance to be so colossal. Before passing the immense portal, I was filled with wonder, which was not diminished by the view within. It is a symbol of the power and hopes of man. What a majestic work of human hands! All its magnificent details are swallowed in its immensity. The one all-absorbing idea is vastness.

ONDAY, Feb. 27th.

Our first visit to-day was to Crawford's studio. His Orpheus is here reputed a statue of high merit. The conception is at once simple and rich. The attitude is well adapted to display life and grace, the long line from the hindmost foot to the end of the curved arm, being one of the finest sweeps the human body can present. The act of protecting the eyes with the hand, imparts life as well by the shadow it casts on the countenance as by its characteristic propriety. The large fabulous-looking heads of the music-subdued Cerberus sleep well, and the group takes at once such hold of the imagination, that their expression seems that of involuntary sleep. 'Tis in itself a great merit in a work of art to make the mind of the beholder assist its effect. The selection of the subject and the execution are equally happy, and denote the genial Artist. We went next to Thorwaldsen's studio. Here I was somewhat disappointed.*

At the Barberini Palace we saw the Beatrice Cenci of Guido. People go to see it on account of her most awful story; and the story is not fully told to one who has not seen the picture. Guido was wrought up to his highest power of execution. The face is of the most beautiful, and through this beauty streams the bewildered soul, telling the terrific tale. It looks like a picture after which the artist had taken a long rest. It is wonderful. We next went hastily through the Doria Gallery, one of the richest private collections in the world.

Tuesday, Feb. 28th.

After breakfast I walked to the Minerva church to see the funeral ceremony for a Cardinal. In the square before the church was the Pope's carriage with six horses, and a score of the scarlet carriages of the Cardinals. The interior of the church was hung with black and gold. The body of the deceased Cardinal lay in state, in the centre of the nave, on a broad bulky couch raised about ten feet. Around it at some distance were burning purple candles. The music of the service was solemn and well executed, in part by *castrati*. The Pope descended from his throne, and, supported on either side by a Cardinal, and at

---

* It will be seen that this first impression was afterwards removed.

tended by other ecclesiastical dignitaries, went to the front of the couch and pronounced absolution upon the deceased. He then walked twice round the body, throwing up incense towards it out of a golden censer. His pontifical robe was crimson and gold. He evidently performed the service with emotion. The whole spectacle was imposing and luxurious. The gorgeous couch and habiliments of the deceased, the rich and various robes, the purple candles, the sumptuous solemn hangings, the incense and the mellow music, compounded a refined feast for the senses. Such ceremonies can speak but feebly to the soul. In the crowd that filled the large church, there was observable some curiosity, and a quiet air of enjoyment, but very little devotion. After the service, as the Pope's carriage on leaving the square passed close by me, an elderly man at my side dropped suddenly on his knees, shouting "Santo Padre, la benedizione," which the Pope gave as his horses went off in a trot, and of which I too, from my position, had a share.

In the afternoon we hired seats in the Corso, to see the last day of the Carnival. The Italians, disciplined by Church and State, know how to run wild on such an occasion without grossness or disorder. People all shouting and fooling, and no coarse extravagances or interruptions of good humor. At sunset the street was cleared in the centre, and half a dozen horses started at one end, without riders, to race to the other. After this, the evening ended with the entertainment of the *mocolo*, which is a thin wax lighted taper, wherewith one half the crowd provide themselves, while the others, with handkerchiefs and similar weapons, strike at them to put them out. This makes an illumination of the whole street, and keeps up a constant noisy combat. Thousands of people in masks and fantastic costumes.

Wednesday, March 1st, 1843

If priests were raised nearer to God by distinguishing them

selves from their fellow-men through the means of gorgeous garniture and pompous ceremony, the exhibition we this morning witnessed at the Sistine Chapel would have been solemn and inspiring. Up flight after flight of the broad gently ascending stairway of St. Peter's, we reached the celebrated Chapel. Seated on the pontifical throne, on one side of the altar at the further extremity of the Chapel, under Michael Angelo's Last Judgment, was the Pope. On his head was a lofty mitre of silver tissue, and his stole was of crimson and gold. To his right, on an elevated broad ottoman that ran along the wall of the Chapel and crossed it about the middle, were ranged more than twenty Cardinals in robes of light purple silk and gold. Around the Pope was a crowd of ministering Prelates, and at the foot of each Cardinal sat, in a picturesque dress, an attendant, apparently a priest, who aided him to change his robe, an operation that was performed more than once during the long service. The folio missal, out of which the Pope read, was held before him; when he approached the altar from his throne his robe was held up; and in the same way one of the attendant prelates removed and replaced several times his mitre. Part of the service consisted in kissing his foot, a ceremony which was performed by about a hundred bishops and prelates in various ecclesiastical costumes. This being the first day of Lent, Ash-Wednesday, the benediction of the ashes is given always by the Pope, and on the heads of those who have the privilege of kissing his toe (Cardinals don't go lower than the knee) he lays a pinch of the consecrated ashes.

When I look back to the whole spectacle, though only after the lapse of a few hours, I seem to have been present at some barbaric pageant. The character of the exhibition overbears my knowledge of its purport, and I could doubt that I have witnessed a Christian ritual.

Afterwards in passing over Monte Cavallo, we came suddenly upon the colossal statues by Phidias and Praxiteles 'Twas a rich surprise. Like St. Peter's and the Colosseum they sur passed my expectation. Their heroic forms stood out against the sky like majestic apparitions come to testify to the glories of old Greece.

In the afternoon we went to Gibson's studio, where we were pleased both with the artist and his works.

THURSDAY, March 2d.

First to the Capitol, built, under the direction of Michael Angelo, on the foundation of the ancient. Innumerable fragments and statues. In the Colossal River-God in the Court, the grace and slumbering power of the large recumbent figure are remarkable. According to our custom at the first visit, we went hastily through the gallery, only pausing before the dying Gladiator. Here, as in all master-pieces of Art, is the intense infusion of the will of the Artist into his work. This is the inscrutable power of genius.

Thence to the Church of Santa Maria Majore, the nave of which is supported by thirty-six beautiful columns, taken from a temple of Juno. Modern Rome is doubly enriched out of the spoils of ancient.

In the afternoon we drove to the Vatican. What a wilderness of marble! You walk, I was about to say, for miles through avenues of sculpture. Of the Apollo, Laocoon, and Antinous, I can say nothing to-day, except that great statues lose much in casts. What an edifice! Drove to the Villa Borghese.

FRIDAY, March 3d.

Our first stage to-day in our daily travel over Rome was at the baths of Caracalla, one of the most emphatic testimonials of Roman magnificence. The ruins, consisting now of little else than the outer and dividing walls, cover several acres. Sixteen hundred persons could bathe at a time. Besides the baths, there were halls for games and for sculpture, and here have been dug up several masterpieces. Here and there a piece of the lofty roof is preserved, and we ascended to the top of one of the halls, whence there is a good view of a large section of the region of ruins. Except in the Fora and Arches, one sees nowhere columns among the ruins. These, as well as nearly all marble in whatever shape, being too precious to be left to adorn the massive remnants of Pagan Rome, have been taken to beautify the Churches and Palaces of her Christian heir.

From the baths of Caracalla we went along the Appian way, passing the tomb of the Scipios, and under the arch of Drusus, to the tomb of Cecilia Metella, a large massive round tower, the largest monument ever raised to a woman. Thence to the Columbarium or tomb of the household of the Cæsars. The name is derived from the resemblance of the structure to a pigeon-house, as well in its general form as in that of the little semi-circular receptacles for the ashes.

In the afternoon we visited among other churches that of *Santa Maria Degli Angeli*, formerly the Baths of Diocletian, which was adapted to the shape and purpose of a church by Michael Angelo. A grand one it is with its immense pillars of Egyptian granite.

As according to Roman Catholic usage, several masses are performed in one morning to as many different congregations, a given number of inhabitants would require as Catholics a much smaller number of churches than it would being Protestant. But were the whole people of Rome to assemble at worship, at the same hour, in as many churches as would be needed for easy accommodation, even then, nine tenths of them would be empty. For three or four centuries the population has been at no time more numerous than it is now, and seldom so numerous; and owing to civil and foreign wars previous to the fifteenth century, and to the seventy years' absence of the Papal Court, it has probably not been greater than at present since the downfall of the Empire. So that there always have been ten times as many churches as are needed. Rome has a population of about one hundred and sixty thousand souls, and counts over three hundred churches. With thirty, all her people would have ample room for worship. Had half of the thought, labor, and money, wasted in building, adorning and preserving the others, been bestowed upon schools and seminaries, there would have been not less religion, and far more mental culture and morality; and Rome might now be really the intellectual and spiritual capital of the world, instead of being the centre of a decrepid form of Christianity, to which she clings chiefly by the material ties that bind men to an ecclesiastical system which embosoms high places of worldly eminence.

Nothing is shallower than carpingly to point out how communities or individuals might be better than they are. The above estimate is not made in a spirit of barren detraction; it shows into what extravagant abuses of God's best gifts man is prone to run. There is at any rate comfort in the evidence here presented,—if such were wanting,—of great spiritual vitality in human nature. Part of the gross misdirection thereof may be ascribed to the mental darkness during many of the first ages of Christian Europe, and part to the selfishness necessarily inherent in a body constituted like the Roman Catholic priesthood. The darkness has been greatly diminished, and individual independence has been sufficiently developed not to abide much longer corporate usurpations, civil or ecclesiastical. There may be hope, that through this natural fund of spirituality, under healthier development and clearer guidance, humanity will go on righting itself more and more, and that under its influence even Rome shall be rejuvenated, and cease to be the hoary juggler, that out of the spiritual wants of man wheedles raiment of gold for her own body and mansions of marble.

Drove out to Mount Sacer, and afterwards to the Pincian.

Saturday, March 4th.

Rain every day. Among the curiosities we this morning inspected in the library of the Vatican, were a collection of cameos and other small antiques dug up in Rome; several of the bronze plates whereon were inscribed the decrees of the Senate, but of the fallen Senate under the Emperors; specimens of Giotto and Cimabue; manuscript of Cicero's Treatise on the Republic, made in the fifth century, and written over by St. Augustine, with a treatise on the Psalms; manuscript of Petrarch; illuminated edition of the Divina Comedia; papyrus. To us as well as to the Pope it is a convenience that St. Peter's and the Vatican are cheek by cheek. On coming out of the library we entered the great church to enjoy its beautiful vastness.

In the afternoon we went to see Michael Angelo's colossal statue of Moses in the church of St. Peter in chains, a beautiful church (the interior I mean) with twenty fluted Parian columns. Here are preserved, 'tis said, the chains of St. Peter. The Moses is a great masterpiece. It justifies the sublime lines of the sonnet it inspired to Zappi:

> Questi é Mosé quando scendea del monte,
> E gran parte del Nume avea nel Volto.*

Power and thought are stamped on the brow; the nose breathes the breath of a concentrated giant; an intellectual smile sits on the large oriental mouth, which looks apt to utter words of comfort or command; the long, thick, folded beard bespeaks vigor, and gives grandeur to the countenance; and the eyes, of which, contrary to the usage of high sculpture, the pupils are marked,

> * This is Moses when he came down from the mountain,
> And had in his countenance a great part of the Deity.

absolutely sparkle. The figure is seated, with however one foot drawn back, as if ready to rise, an attitude correspondent to the life and fire of the countenance. From this grand work one learns what a mighty soul was in Michael Angelo.

In the sacristy is a beautiful head by Guido, representing Hope, as rapt and still as an angel listening to the music of Heaven. In this church was held under the Emperor Constantine, as says an inscription in it, a council, which condemned Arian and other schismatics, and burnt their books. We next visited St. Martin on the Hill, also constructed with columns from an ancient temple. Through the church we descended into a vault below where had been Imperial baths, and afterwards a church of the early Christians before Constantine. Adjoining this venerable spot was an opening that led into the catacombs, where the persecuted Christians used to conceal themselves. On slabs in the upper church were inscribed the names of many martyrs w ose tombs had been found below; among them those of several Popes. Thence towards sunset, we went to the church of the Jesuits, laden, like so many others, with pictures and marbles and sparkling altars, and sepulchral monuments. The grand altar just finished cost upwards of one hundred thousand dollars. On one side of the church a thin sallow Jesuit in a dark robe and cap was preaching to about a hundred persons, chiefly of th. poorer class. I regretted that I had not come in time to hear m re of his sermon, for a purer pronunciation and sweeter voice I never listened to. His elocution too was good and his gesticulation graceful, and his matter and manner were naif and unjesuitlike. He told his auditors that what the holy Virgin required of them, especially now during Lent, was to examine their souls, and if they found them spotted with sins to free themselves therefrom by a full confession, and if not, to betake themselves more and more to the zealous cultivation of the virtues. There was a sincerity, simplicity and sweetness in the feeling and utterance of this young man, that were most fascinating. When he had finished, he glided away into the recesses of the dim church like an apparition.

Sunday, March 5th.

To-day we remitted our labors. Late in the morning I walked up the stairway of the Trinity of the Mount to the garden of the Villa Medici; and afterwards to Monte Cavallo to behold again the two colossal Greek Statues. They must be seen early or late, for at other hours the sky dazzles the sight as you attempt to look up at them.

In the afternoon we drove to St. Peter's. Its immensity enlarges at each repeated beholding. 'Tis so light,—the interior I mean, —so illuminated, that it looks as though it had been poised from above, and not built upward from an earthly foundation. In one section of it is a series of confessionals, dedicated to the various languages of Europe. In each sat a priest ready to listen to and shrive in the tongue inscribed over his portal. Vespers at four. The voices were fine, but the music, not being sacred, was not effective in a church. One hears at times in music cadences of such expression, that they seem about to utter a revelation; and then they fade of a sudden into common melody, as though the earthly medium were incompetent to transmit the heavenly voice.

We drove afterward to the Pincian Hill in a cold north wind.

Monday, March 6th.

Walked before breakfast to Monte Cavallo. Our first stage after breakfast was to the house of Nero, over which were built, in part, the Baths of Titus. This is one of the best preserved bits of old Rome. The walls of brick are from three to five feet thick, the rooms nearly forty high. On some of the ceilings and walls are distinct specimens of Arabesque. Thence to look at the holy staircase of the Lateran, said to be of the house of Pontius Pilate. The feelings that would arise on standing before such an object is checked by doubt that *will* come up as to its authenticity. No one is permitted to mount the stairs except on his knees; and being of stone, they are kept covered with wood to preserve them from being worn out. In the Church of Santa Croce in Gerusalemme, founded by St. Helen, the mother of Constantine, is preserved, 'tis said, the cross of one of the thieves crucified with Jesus.

In the Gallery of the Colonna Palace we saw this morning several fine portraits and a beautiful St. Agnes, by Guido, with that heavenward look he delighted to paint, and painted so well. In the magnificent Hall of the Palace we were shown the portrait of the Colonna who commanded at Lepanto. In the afternoon we went for the second time to the Vatican. How the most beautiful things teach you to admire them! Genius, which is by its essence original, embodies its idea, the totality whereof even the most genial sympathy cannot at first take in. By repetition the whole spirit of the creation is imbibed, and only then does the mind receive the full image of what it beholds, learning thus, by a necessary process, from beauty itself to appreciate its quality. Thus the Apollo will go on growing into our vision until we can, if not entirely, yet deeply enjoy its inexhaustible beauty. On coming out of the Vatican we walked again into St. Peter's. Are its proportions perfect and its colors all in unison, or is it its vastness that tones down all the constituents to harmony? It fills me always with delight and wonder.

Towards sunset we drove to the church of St. Peter, in Montorio, whence, from the terrace, is a sweeping view of Rome. We looked down over the "Eternal City." Directly in front, and east of us about a mile, was the majestic Colosseum. Between us and the Tiber was the Camp of Porsenna. To the left, beyond the Tiber, was once the Campus Martius, now the most thickly peopled quarter of modern Rome. An epitome of a large portion of the world's history lay at our feet. There stood the

Capitol of the Republic, and beyond, the ruins of the Palace of the Cæsars, and all about us were the Palaces and Churches of their papal heir. Back of the Church is the Fontana Paolina, built of stone from the Forum of Nerva, by Pope Paul V., a Borghese. The water gushes out through five apertures in volume enough for a Swiss cascade.

TUESDAY, March 7th.

We drove out this morning to the Villa Pamphili, the grounds of which, having a circumference of four miles, are the most extensive of the Roman villas. Here are stately umbrella-shaped pines. Fields of grass, thickly studded with flowers, verified what had hitherto been to me a poetic fiction. From the top of the house is a wide noble prospect. Returning, we drove through part of the Jews' quarter to the Square of Navona, the largest in Rome, in ancient times a race-course, now a vegetable market. In the afternoon we went to the Pantheon, the best preserved remnant of ancient Rome, built by Agrippa, the son-in-law of Augustus, as the great Hall of the public baths by him established, afterwards converted into a temple to Jupiter, then to all the Gods, whence its name, and as early as the seventh century consecrated a Christian Church, under the name of St. Mary of the Martyrs, by Pope Boniface IV., who buried under the chief altar twenty-eight wagon loads of relics of the martyrs. The light (and rain) comes in through a wide circle left open at the top of the dome. The pavement is of porphyry. Here Raphael is buried. We drove afterwards to the villa Borghese, crowded with ancient marble, among which is a long series of busts of Roman Emperors in " antique red." The heads are nearly all of one type, and denote the energetic, practical character of the Romans. The statue of Pauline, one of the treasures of the villa, is the most beautiful work I have seen of Canova. Returning, we saw near the gate some rich Italian faces. Italy reminds one at times of a beautiful Guido Magdalen, her tearful countenance upturned towards heaven, so lovely in her affliction, such subdued passion in her luxurious features, such hope in her lucent eyes.

WEDNESDAY, March 8th.

We spent most of the morning in the studios of sculptors, and the afternoon in churches. What a multiplication of the human form in marble! The Churches are peopled with statues brown with age, and in the studios they dazzle you with youthful whiteness.

To describe in verse the surface of a man's mind is not to write poetry; nor is the imitation of the human body the exercise of a fine Art. The Sculptor's function is to concentrate in one body the beauty and character of many. When he does this he creates, and until he creates, he is not up to his vocation. Nature is not always beautiful, but at the bottom of all her phenomena is the spirit of beauty. Her essence is beauty, and this essence the worker with the chisel must extract and then embody, else is he a barren Artist.

We saw this morning Guido's Aurora. Here is a subject most apt for pictorial representation. The idea has sufficient intensity to irradiate the whole body. In few large compositions is there soul enough in the thought to animate the members; or if there be fire, there is lack of beauty. Here the idea, the parent of the whole work, is both strong and beautiful, and the execution being correspondent, the effect is complete. Afterwards, in the Minerva Church, we saw a statue of Christ, by Michael Angelo. It wants character and beauty. The subject is not suited to Michael Angelo's genius.

THURSDAY, March 9th.

We visited this morning the studio of Wolf, a German sculptor of reputation. A sweet dancing girl and a graceful Diana attracted us most. The foreign Artists in Italy seem well nigh

to take the lead of the native, owing, probably, to the enjoyment
of greater liberty, the Italians being more under the chilling sway
of academical rules, and the influence of the by no means pure
example of Canova. We walked afterwards in the garden of the
Villa Medici, the prison of Galileo during his trial, now the French
Academy ; and into its hall of plaster casts, where is a collection
of the best antiques. This is going into the highest company.
These are genuine aristocrats, choice specimens of manhood and
womanhood. With many of them, time and ignorance have
dealt roughly. Some are without arms, others without legs,
and some without heads, but still they live. In their mythology,
what a Poem the ancient Greeks gave birth to and bequeathed
to the world. We next went to one of the Churches, to hear a
sermon from an English Catholic Prelate. During Lent, there
is daily preaching in many of the Churches. Chairs were set for
two hundred persons, but there were present not more than fifty.
The preacher was evidently a man of intellect, but dry and argu-
mentative. The drift of his discourse was to show that priests
are essential to salvation.

Men, with all their selfishness, and perhaps through a modifica-
tion thereof, have ever been prone to give up their affairs in trust
to others, the trustees dividing themselves into the three hitherto
inevitable classes, the legal, the medical, and the theological.
Some even avail themselves to the full of all these helps and substitutes, abandoning the conduct of their worldly possessions to
their man of business, their bodies passively to their physician,
and their souls as passively to their pastor. These languid nega-
tives are of course few. By degrees the axiom is getting to be
valued, that to thrive, whether secularly or spiritually, a man
must look to his own interests. People are beginning to discern,
that health is not a blessing in the gift of Doctors, that Religion
is independent of hierarchies, and that the first preachers of
Christianity were quite a different kind of men from most of the

atest. Some men are pre-eminently endowed to develope and feed the spiritual element of our nature, and most reverently do I regard and cordially hearken to such wherever I meet with them. As in the preacher before me, I perceived no marks of such inspiration, and as there was neither eloquence nor art to give his discourse the attraction of an intellectual entertainment, we soon left the church, a movement which can be effected here without notice. He handled his argument not without skill, and doubtless the sermon was edifying to most of his auditors, their minds having been drilled by him and his colleagues into the habit of acquiescence.

The ordinary service was going on at the same time independently in a side chapel, where a very aged ecclesiastic, in a white satin embroidered robe, was saying mass, which to us, in the outskirts of the English Company, was quite audible. He was entirely alone, having no assistant at the altar and not a single worshipper; until just before he concluded, a bright-faced boy, ten or twelve years of age, came in with a long staff, to put out the tall candle. Ere the venerable father had ceased praying, the little fellow had the extinguisher up, thrusting it now and then half over the flame with playful impatience. The instant the old man had finished, out went the candle, and the boy, taking the large missal in his arms, walked off, looking over towards us for notice, and restraining with difficulty his steps to the pace of the aged priest, who tottered after him.

On leaving the church, we went for the first time to the Borghese Gallery, freely open to strangers, and to artists, of whom, in the different rooms, there were several taking copies. Strangers in Rome owe much to the unexampled liberality of the Italian nobles, in opening to them the treasures of their palaces and villas.

In the afternoon to the Vatican, where again we had a cloudy sky, and were therefore again disappointed before the great frescoes of Raphael, which, from the darkness of the rooms wherein they are painted, hav'n't light enough even on the sunniest days. On coming out we took our accustomed walk up under the dome of St. Peter's.

FRIDAY, March 10th.

We visited this morning the Corsini Gallery, in which is the bound Prometheus of Salvator Rosa, with his fiery stamp upon it. The horror which a lesser genius could excite, cannot be subdued by any mastery of art. The keeper of the rooms, with the hostile feeling reciprocated among the inhabitants of the different sections of Italy, remarked, that none but a Neapolitan would choose so bloody a subject. Another remarkable picture in this collection, is a head of Christ bound with thorns, by Guercino. The agony, the fortitude, the purity are all there, and in the upcast translucent eyes is an infinite depth of feeling, as of mingled expostulation and resignation, that recalls vividly the touching words, "My God, my God, why hast thou forsaken me?" 'Tis one of the masterpieces of Rome.

At twelve we found ourselves in St. Peter's, to witness the ceremony which takes place every Friday during Lent. The Pope, attended by his household and a numerous body of Cardinals and other prelates, says prayers successively at several different altars. The Swiss Guard, in the old-time costume with pikes, formed a hollow oblong, within which the Pope and the whole cortége of priests knelt. For the Pope and Cardinals a cushion was provided; the others knelt on the marble pavement. The Pope prayed inaudibly, and seemed to do so with heart. The strange uniform of the Guards, the numerous robed priests kneeling behind their chief, the gorgeous towering vaults above them, and the sacred silence, made a beautiful scene.

In the afternoon we drove to the Villa Mills, built above the ruins of the House of Augustus, on Mount Palatine. Through a door in the garden, round which clustered lemons, roses, and oranges, we descended to several of the rooms of Augustus, the floor whereof is about thirty feet below the present surface. From various points in the garden we had views of the majestic remnants of imperial Rome,—the Colosseum, the baths of Caracalla, the temple of Peace, part of the Forum, the temple of Vesta, the Pyramid of Caius Cestius, the tomb of Cecilia Metella, interspersed with convents and churches and scattered buildings. Over the wall on the southern side of the Villa grounds, you look directly down upon some remains of the Circus Maximus, which occupied the valley between the Palatine and Aventine Hills, and where took place the rape of the Sabines. It will take a long while for Niebuhr to efface belief in the reality of those early Roman doings. At last we ascended to a terrace built over a spot where had once been a temple of Juno, whence was a prospect of modern Rome with its throng of cupolas. We next mounted the Capitol Hill, to go into the Church Aracœli.

SATURDAY, March 11th.

We visited this morning the Convent of the *Sacré Cœur* on the *Trinitá del Monte*. This is a sisterhood of French ladies, some of them noble, devoted to the education of the upper classes. The establishment looked the model of neatness. The pupils, who had a uniform dress, rose and curtsied to us as we entered the rooms. They looked healthy and happy. The sisters had the manner and tone of well-bred ladies, chastened by seclusion from the rivalries of the world. It is one of the results of Catholic organization and discipline, that in an institution like this, a field of utility is opened to those whom disappointment, or distaste for excitement, or a natural proneness to piety, disposes to withdraw from the world. Through the principle of association, the various resources of many are centred upon a high object, and much activity, that would otherwise have lain dormant or have been wasted, is turned to excellent account. From one of the lofty dormitories, with its numerous clean white beds, we looked out into a broad garden belonging to the convent, and beyond this to the Ludovisi grounds and Villa.

Afterwards, at the room of Flatz, a Tyrolese painter, we were charmed with the artist and his works. His subjects are all religious, and are executed with uncommon grace and feeling. A pupil of his, too, Fink, is a young man of promise.

There are people with minds so exclusively religious, that Religion does not,—as is its office,—sustain, temper, exalt their being; it fills, it is their being. When the character is upright and simple, such persons become earnest and calm; when otherwise, they are officious and sentimental. If their intellect is sensuous, they delight in the imagery and manipulating ceremonies of the Catholic worship, and then, having of course, by their original structure, no intellectual breadth or power, they will be liable, under the assaults of a picture-loving mind and absorbing devotional feeling, to become Romanists even in Rome itself!

SUNDAY, March 12th.

This afternoon we returned to the chapel of the *Sacré Cœur*, to hear the music at the evening benediction. 'Twas a hymn from the sisterhood, accompanied by the organ. The service commenced silently at the altar, round which curled profuse incense, that glowed before the lighted candles like silver dust. The few persons present were kneeling, when the stillness was broken by a gentle gush of sound from the invisible choir up behind us. It came like a heavenly salutation. The soft tones seemed messengers out of the Infinite, that led the spirit up to whence they had come. At the end of each verse, a brief response issued from deep male voices at the opposite end of the church, near the altar, sounding like an earthly answer to the heavenly call. Then again were the ears possessed by the feminine harmony, that poured itself down upon the dim chapel like an unasked blessing.

MONDAY, March 13th.

This morning, at the Spada Palace, we saw the statue of Pompey, which "all the while ran blood" when Cæsar fell under the blows of the conspirators in the Capitol. 'Tis a colossal figure, bout ten feet in height, of fine character, dignified, vigorous, and ife-like. We drove afterwards out to the English burying-ground, where lie the ashes of Shelley, " enriching even Rome," as his wife had a right to say. I revere the character, and admire the genius of Shelley, yet I was not moved by the presence of his tomb. Emotion cannot be summoned at will. I have at times, in a holy spot, found myself in a state of utter insensibility, and, instead of turning my eyes inward under its spirit-moving influence, have caught my lips playing with the reminiscence of a jest, as irrepressible as it was impertinent in such a place. For all that, the visit was not barren; the feeling would come afterwards.

In the afternoon, we visited the rooms of Overbeck, the distinguished German painter, a great master in drawing and composition. Like Flatz, his subjects are all scriptural.

Very few artists being able to achieve the highest triumph in execution, which is the transparence and vivid beauty of healthiest life, addict themselves naturally, in a critical age, to an emulous cultivation of those qualities which through study are more attainable, and then attach to them a kind of importance which they do not deserve. This seems to be the case just now with composition, an element which may shine in a picture unworthy of permanent regard, and which stands related to the genial quality in Art as the narrative does to the poetical in a printed volume. Under genuine inspiration, the parts of a work will always, when Art is out of its first rudiments, put themselves together competently to the development of the idea, although the artist may not excel in composition; but from the most skilful combination of the constituent parts, will never be generated that unfading charm of life and beauty, which genius alone can impart, and the production whereof even genius cannot explain. In short, composition is the intellectual department of painting, and will be ineffective until vivified by the fire of feeling.

We walked afterwards through the gallery of the Capitol, and then to the Tarpeian rock.

TUESDAY, March 14th.

We commenced the day, which was bright at last, with a walk on the Pincian. Visited in the morning a second time the rooms of the German painter Flatz, and his pupil. We drove afterwards through the sunny air past the Forum and Colosseum out to the grand church of St. John of the Lateran, where, in the court, is the finest obelisk in Rome, brought, like the others, from Egypt, the land of obelisks. It is a single shaft of red granite, more than a hundred feet high.

In the afternoon, we walked again on the Pincian, amidst a throng of people from all parts of the world, in carriages, on horseback, and on foot. How seldom you meet a fine old countenance; one that has been enriched by years, that has the autumnal mellowness of joyous and benignant sensations. Oftener you see on old shoulders a face corrugated and passion-ploughed, that may be likened to a river-bed, which, deserted by the turbid spring flood, shows a hard, parched surface, bestrewn with driftwood and unsightly fragments, that tell how high the muddy torrent has revelled. At six, we went to see the Colosseum by moonlight. The wondrous old pile grows more eloquent still at night; its vastness expands, its majesty grows more majestic; the dimness of the hour seems congenial to its antiquity. The patches of moonlight glistening among its arches, look like half revelations of a thousand mysteries that lie coiled up in its bosom. It has the air of a mystic temple sprung out of the gloom, for a Sybil to brood in and prophesy.

WEDNESDAY, March 15th.

This morning, we drove out of the *Porta del Popolo*, the northern gate, a mile and a half just over the bridge of Mole, and returning along the right bank of the Tiber, with the Villa Madama and *Monte Mario* on the right, we re-entered Rome near St. Peter's. Thence, passing through the busiest part of the modern city, we drove between the Palatine and Aventine hills, round the Colosseum, by the three columns that are left of the Forum of Nerva, into the gay Corso, passing thus, suddenly, as we do almost every day, from amidst the gigantic brown fragments that silently tell of the might of ancient Rome, into the bustle and ostentation of a modern capital. I spent an hour afterwards in Thorwaldsen's studio, with a still growing enjoyment. Great Poems are incarnations of a nation's mind, whence in weaker times it may draw nourishment to help to renew its vigor. The creations of Shakspeare and Milton rear themselves the steadfast mountains of the mental world of England, up to which the people can at all times ascend to inhale a bracing air. So, too, after-sculptors will be able to refresh themselves at the clear fountain of Thorwaldsen's purity and simplicity.

THURSDAY, March 16th.

We drove out to the new St. Paul's that they are building on the site of the old one, more than a mile out of the St. Paul Gate. This Church is one of the largest, and the Pope is rebuilding and adorning it in a style of unmatched magnificence. Nations and systems cannot, any more than individuals, pause in their career. Each must fulfil its destiny. From the bosom of Eternity they are launched forth, to perform a given circuit, and long after they have culminated, they continue, though under relaxed momentum, to give out sparks of the original fire, and decline consistently to their end. The Papal State is loaded with a growing debt; Rome has churches enough for ten times its actual population; advancing civilisation rejects more and more the sensuous as an auxiliary to the spiritual. Yet, at an enormous cost, this church is re-erected, dazzling with pillars and marble and gold capacious to hold tens of thousands, though distant from the city in the blighted Campagna; a token not only that the spirit of Romanism is unchanged, but that it has yet the will and vigor, in the face of material difficulties, and in defiance of civilisation, to manifest itself in mediæval pomp and unchristian magnificence.

On getting back within the walls of the city, we turned into the *Via Appia*, and stopped at the tomb of the Scipios, down into which I groped with a lighted candle twenty or thirty feet below the present surface, in a labyrinth of low vaults, where I saw several vertical slabs with inscriptions. After dinner, we drove to the Villa Mattei, whence there is a fine view southward, of the aqueducts and mountains. Late in the afternoon I ascended to the top of the tower of the Capitol. The sky was cloudless, and the unparalleled scene seemed to float in the purple light. Mountain, plain, and city, the eye took in at a sweep. From fifteen to forty miles in more than a semicircle ranged the Appenines, the nearest clusters being the Alban and the Sabine Hills. Contracting the view within these, the eye embraced the dim Campagna, in the midst of which, right under me, lay the noisy city beside its silent mother. Looking down from such an elevation, the seven hills, unless you know well their position, are not traceable; and most of the ruins, not having, as when seen from the plain, the relief of the sky, grow indistinct; only the Colosseum towers broadly before you, a giant among dwarfs, challenging your wonder always at the colossal grandeur of Imperial Rome. In the west, St. Peter's broke the line of the horizon. From countless towers, spires, cupolas, columns, obelisks, long shadows fell upon the sea of tiled roof. The turbid Tiber showed itself here and there, winding as of old through the throng. I gazed until, the sun being set, the mountains began to fade, the ruins to be swallowed up in the brown earth, and the whole fascinating scene wore that lifeless look which follows immediately the sinking of the sun below the horizon, the earth seeming suddenly to fall asleep.

FRIDAY, March 17th.

Through the high walls that enclose the gardens and Villas in Italy, we drove out to the Villa Albani, reputed the richest about Rome in antique sculpture. There is a statue of Tiberius, which makes him shine among several of his imperial colleagues in grace and manly proportions, a distinction which he probably owes to the superiority of his Artist; a fragment from the bas-reliefs of the Parthenon at Athens, and other esteemed antiques in half size and miniature, amidst a legion of busts, among them one of Themistocles, of much character. Unhappily, on these occasions you cannot give yourself up to the pleasure of believing that you gaze on the features of one of the great ancients; for even the identity of the bust is seldom unquestionable, and of course still less so is the likeness. It were a goodly sight to behold an undoubted portrait of Plato, or Socrates, or Brutus. The villa is in a florid style of architecture, and the grounds are laid out in straight walks between walls of evergreen. The day was balmy, and the parterre walls were alive with lizards darting about in the sunshine. We next drove out of the St. John Gate to get a near view of the aqueducts, which have been well likened to Giants striding across the Campagna. On re-entering the Gate, the front of St. John of the Lateran presented itself very grandly. It is purer than the façade of St. Peter's, in which the perpendicular continuity is broken, a fault almost universal in the fronts of Italian churches. The statues, too, on the St. John, from being colossal and somewhat crowded, have a better effect than statues in that position generally have.

In the afternoon we drove and walked in the grounds of the

Villa Borghese. The entire circuit is at least two miles, and the grounds are varied both by art and nature. Strangers can hardly be sufficiently grateful to the family that opens to them such a resource. I should have stated, when speaking of the statuary in the villa, that the original and celebrated Borghese collection of antiques was sold to the Paris Museum, in the reign of Napoleon, for thirteen millions of francs. The present collection has been made since that period.

SATURDAY, March 18th.

This morning we began with the Sciarra Gallery, one of the most choice in the world. In a single room, not more than twenty-five feet square, were thirty or forty pictures, estimated to be worth three hundred thousand dollars, comprising masterpieces by Titian, Raphael, Guido, Leonardo da Vinci, and others. For the celebrated *Modesty and Charity* of Leonardo, the size of which is hardly four feet by three, the good-humored old keeper told us an English nobleman offered fifty thousand dollars. These marvels of the pencil teach with glowing emphasis, that the essence of the Art is beauty. If this be a truism, the crowds of prosaic works one daily passes justify its reiteration. Thence we went to Mount Palatine, to explore the ruins of part of the Palace of the Cæsars, adjoining the house of Augustus which we had already seen. Each of his successors for several generations seems to have enlarged the imperial residence, until, under Nero, it spread over the whole of the Palatine and Cælian hills and part of the Esquiline. What we saw to-day covers several acres. The habitable part, of which there are only left fragments of thick brick walls, was built on high arches. The view from the top embraces the greater part of the ancient and modern cities, extending over the Campagna to the mountains. 'Tis now a vegetable-garden, and where Emperors have dined, grows a luxuriant crop of artichokes. A bright-looking woman, who was peeling onions, and who plucked for us a boquet of hyacinths, told us that she paid for it seventy dollars annual rent. From the Palace we drove to the tomb of Augustus, where among other bones we saw the half of a skull, which the keeper protested was ancient Roman, and was ready to protest to be that of Augustus.

In the afternoon we went to the rooms of Maes, a Belgian Artist of talent, and then drove out to the church on Monte Mario, whence the view is very fine. A lad, who had care of the church, told us, that in the Convent adjoining lived two Dominican friars, there not being means to support more. Each of them receives five dollars a month, besides twenty cents a day for saying mass, making about eleven dollars a month to each for clothing and food. A man here can keep his body well covered with flesh for ten cents a day. His meat will be chiefly maccaroni and his drink water, a good fare for longevity. Be it as it may, there is no class of people in Italy with fuller skins than the friars.

In the evening we saw, at about seven o'clock, the long bright tail of a comet.

Sunday, March 19th.

This morning I heard a sermon at the Church of the Jesuits. The subject was the perfections of Joseph as husband and father, who, the preacher often repeated, had all the realities of the matrimonial union without its chief function, and performed all the functions of a father without having the reality. He enforced, happily and with pure feeling, from the example of Joseph, the sanctity of the marriage tie, and the supreme obligation of duty. It was a practical, animated, sound discourse, which commanded earnest attention from his audience, that consisted of the middle and lower classes, and was very numerous, filling nearly the whole area of the large church.

In the afternoon, we went to hear a celebrated French Jesuit preach, at the church called St. Louis of the French. In a discourse of more than an hour, to which a large, educated auditory listened with unwearied attention, the preacher summed up with skill and eloquence the chief arguments of the Roman Catholic Church against Protestantism. In an emphatic and adroit manner he presented the best that can be said in favor of the unity and infallibility of the Roman Church. He laid down, that Religion could be preserved but by one of three means; either, first, by God making a separate revelation thereof to each individual man; or secondly, by his having embodied it in a book, which each was to interpret for himself; or thirdly, by instituting a Church to whose guardianship he committed it. After endeavoring to show, that the third was the only means consistent with the simplicity of the divine government, he went on to set forth, that Christ established one Church, that that Church was by its nature, origin, and design, infallible; and in a brilliant sophistical passage he attempted to demonstrate the inherent necessity of intolerance towards doctrine, concluding with the position, that without such a church there would be no faith, no religion.

What a pitiful piece of work were man, if to his fellow-man he owed the very enjoyment of his highest faculty. How ignoble and parasitical must that Jesuit deem his brother men! But it is just and inevitable, that they who by men have been unduly exalted, should look down upon those who have bowed the neck under thei yoke. Without any direct knowledge of the fact, it might be inferred, that no class of men have a lower opinion of mankind than the Romish priesthood. No religion without the Church! Why, the Roman and all other churches that have ever existed or will ever exist, are effects of religion, not its cause,— the creatures of man, not his masters—and, as such, obsequious ever to his movements; sucking blood when he has been cruel, relentless when he has been intolerant, humane when he has become humanized; presumptuous towards his inactivity, humble towards his independence; aristocratic in one country, democratic in another—here upholding slavery, there denouncing it; always a representative of the temporary condition of society. Why were the Catholic priests more openly rapacious and lustful before the Reformation than since? Why is the priest in Spain different from the priest in Sweden, or the Catholic priest of the United States more true to his chief vow than his fellow in Italy? There is but one unity, and that is the universal innateness in man of the religious sentiment. The form wherein it clothes, the creed wherein it embodies itself, depend upon civilisation, temperament, climate, policy, and to these the priest inevitably fashions himself. But as effects reflect often back upon their causes, creeds and hierarchies re-act, with more or less power, upon Religion itself; and it is a symptom of a baleful influence, and of an unmanly passiveness in man, when so degrading a doctrine gets to be part of his creed, as that he owes his religion to his priest.

To learn what priestcraft is, we need not however go so far as Catholic Italy, although there its deformity is the most revolting in Christendom. Some very unequivocal exhibitions of it may be seen among the Protestant *isms* of our country, notwithstanding that the mass of our population is in mental freedom and strength raised above that of Europe, and that comparatively, through the severance of Church and State, we enjoy religious liberty. Priesthood, performing a necessary part in human societies, is, like the other institutions for the furtherance of man's estate, subject under all forms and circumstances to corruptions. The benefits resulting from a priesthood, like the benefits resulting from a magistracy, are purely those of organization. In the earlier stages of culture, or when humanity is partially developed, priests form a distinct authorized power, which, being men, it is of course their tendency to abuse. As society through individual culture develops itself, this organization becomes more and more merged in the general social one. Priests are first dropped by the state and then by individuals, and the religious element, re-incorporated, as it were, into the whole nature, receives its cultivation along with the other nobler sentiments of man. Rituals and Hierarchies are but the forms through which for a time it suits Religion to express and cherish herself; they are transient, only Religion is perennial. Forms, in their healthiest state, waste somewhat of the substance they are designed to set forth. At their birth, they are tainted with insincerity; when mature, they grow hypocritical; and in their old age, they get to be barefaced falsehoods, and then they die. In religion, as in politics, and in all things, man becomes weak in proportion as he surrenders himself to the power or guidance of others. This surrender is totally different from helpful co-operation, as well as from reciprocal subordination according to inborn superiorities.

Monday, March 20th.

At Thorwaldsen's studio, I stood again long before the St. John preaching in the wilderness. This is a group of twelve parts, ranged in a line declining on either side from the central figure, to suit its destination, which is the tympanum of a church in Copenhagen. St. John, in his left hand a cross, which serves him too as a staff, and his right raised towards Heaven, stands in the centre, with a countenance mild and earnest, his look and attitude well expressing the solemnity of the tidings he proclaims.

The first figure on his right is a man, apparently about thirty, with the left foot on a high stone, and one elbow on his knee, his chin resting in his hand. His fixed look is not turned up as if to catch the falling words of the speaker, but is outward as though his mind were busy with something that had gone before.—Next to him is a group of two figures, the first a turbaned man of middle age, with hands crossed at his waist, in the simplest erect attitude of deep attention, his closely draped light body in the most perfect repose, while his bearded countenance is intent upon that of St. John with the animated expression of one accustomed to thought, and whose mind is now deeply wrought upon by the words he hears. Behind him, and gently resting on his shoulder, is a beardless youth, like the elder one before him, who may be his father, attentive but passive.—The third figure is a mother, half kneeling, behind her a boy seven or eight years of age, with chin on his hands that are crossed on her right shoulder.—The fourth, an old man seated, with long beard and turban, a tranquil venerable figure.—The fifth, and last to the right of St. John, is a youth recumbent, supporting his upturned head with his left arm.

The first figure on the left of St. John is a boy about fifteen, looking up into his face with half open mouth and a beaming expression, as if the words he was listening to had unlocked his soul.—Next to him is a middle-aged priest, with both hands before his breast resting on a staff. His countenance is strong and rugged, and his brows are knit as if his mind were in a state of resistance to what he heard.—The third figure is a hunter. He looks melted by the preacher, and has an aspect of devout acquiescence. By a band he holds a fine dog, upon which is fixed the attention of,—the fourth group, two bright children, a boy and girl of nine and eight, their faces alive with childish pleasure.—Behind them, the fifth figure, is a female seated, their mother apparently, who is restraining before her a third younger child.—The sixth and last figure is a shepherd, recumbent, with open mouth and joyful look.

This subject is peculiarly fitted to sculpture, from the union of perfect bodily repose with mental animation. The conception, which is the happiest possible for such a group; the ease, life, correctness and grace of the figures; the contrasts in their postures, ages, conditions, sex, expression; the calm power evident in the fertility and purity of the invention; the excellence of the execution; the distribution of the parts, and the vivid character of each figure, make this work one of the noblest of modern sculpture.

In the afternoon we went through the Gallery of the Vatican. From an unnecessary and ungracious arrangement, in order to see the pictures, you are obliged to walk nearly the whole length of the range of galleries in the two stories, a distance of more than a mile, so that you are fatigued when you come in front of the pictures, where, moreover, there are no seats.—We went afterwards to the church of St. Onofrio, not far from St. Peter's. Here I saw a representation in wax of the head of Tasso, from a mask taken after death. Were there any doubt as to the genuineness of this head, the cranium were almost sufficient to dispel it, being just such a one as is fitted to the shoulders of an excitable poet. The monks keep it in their library. Another treasure they possess is a Madonna and child in fresco, by Leonardo da Vinci, which, notwithstanding the injury of time, breathes forth the inspiration imparted to it by that wonderful genius. Neither this, nor the mask of Tasso, both being in the convent to which the church is attached, can be seen by women, except through special permission from the Pope. Below in the church is Tasso's Tomb.

TUESDAY, March 21st.

At the rooms of Vellati, an Italian painter of landscapes and hunting pieces, we saw this morning the Magdalen of Correggio recently brought to light, Vellati having discovered it under another picture which had been painted over it, and which he bought for fifteen dollars. With great labor, by means of the point of a needle, the upper painting was removed without injuring the gem beneath it. Its size is about fifteen inches by twelve, and the price asked for it is five thousand pounds sterling; but its value cannot be counted in money. It is the duplicate of the celebrated picture at Dresden. In the same rooms was a fine landscape by Rembrandt.

In the *Piazza del Popolo* is a meagre exhibition of pictures, the best painters always drawing amateurs to their private rooms. We went afterwards to the Farnesian gardens, which are entered from the Forum, to see remains of the palaces of Nero and Caligula and of the House of Augustus. We groped down into the baths of Livia. We walked through the Forum to the Colosseum, and afterwards in the Borghese Gardens.

WEDNESDAY, March 22d.

This morning we saw the Cenci again. What a gift of genius, to reproduce such a face in all its tremulous life! With a deep, awful, innocent look, it seems to peer into your soul and pray you for sympathy. Doubt has been thrown upon its genuineness. If it be a creation and not a portrait, it is the more wonderful. Its character is so perfectly in unison with the mysterious heart-rending story of Beatrice Cenci, that, had it been discovered long years after her tragic end and without any clue to its origin, it might and probably would have been appropriated to her. We drove afterwards to the church of *St. Peter in chains*, to see for the second time the Moses of Michael Angelo. I observed to-day, that with the instinct of genius (in the heads of the antique the ear is further forward) he has placed the ear far back, which heightens the intellectual character of the head. In gazing at this powerful statue again, I felt that in Art 'tis only beauty that ensures constancy. The Moses is grand and imposing, but one does not look forward to a third visit with that anticipation of growing enjoyment, with which one goes back to the Apollo or the Laocoon. Liberate the Laocoon from the constraints of force and pain, and it would stand before you a body pre-eminent for beauty and justness of proportion. On the other hand, suppose the body a common one, and the work sinks to a revolting mimicry of corporeal suffering.

One who resides long in Rome is liable to be sucked back into the past. Behind him is an ocean of movement and thought, out of which rise countless fragments and monuments, that daily tempt him to exploration. A man might here lean his whole being against antiquity and find it a life-long support. The present becomes but a starting point whence he would set out on voyages into the past.—Walked out at the Porta Pia.

Thursday, March 23d.

This morning we went to the Villa Negroni, the neglected grounds of which are in great part occupied by a vegetable garden. The sun was just enough veiled by thin clouds to make walking agreeable, and although the Villa is far within the walls, we strolled for half an hour over twenty or thirty acres of artichokes, onions and peas, enjoying a wide sweep of the mountains. —We then went to see Cardinal Fesch's gallery, containing altogether twenty thousand pictures. Exempt from the officious promptings of a Cicerone, we lounged from room to room, choosing for ourselves, and appealing to the voluminous catalogue to back our vision or resolve doubts. After one has obtained, by familiarity with galleries, some knowledge of the best masters, it is delightful to be let loose in this way upon a new collection. This one is celebrated for Flemish and Dutch pictures.

Great part of the afternoon we passed among the statues of the Vatican. The Perseus looks as if Canova had studied the antique more than nature. The one sole mistress in Art being Nature, all that the artist can gain from the works of others is the best mode of seizing the spirit of the one common model, of compassing her beauties, so that he shall be able to reproduce what shall be at once ideal and natural. Not to imitate their forms, but to extract from them how their authors imitated the best of nature so truly, should be the aim of the young sculptor in scanning the Apollo or Laocoon. If he can make the wondrous work before him reveal the process of the worker, then he can profit by the example. If he cannot, then he has not the innate gifts of a high artist. But this process of the great masters he will not only fail to detect, by copying the forms that have come from human hands, but by such servility (for it is servility, be the model Phidias himself) he weakens his original powers, and gradually disables himself from standing up face to face before his living mistress. To the young sculptor, the antique should be an armory where he can fortify his native powers for the loving conflict he has to wage with vigorous beaming nature. In the Perseus, 'tis apparent the free play of the artist's mind was under check. You behold the result of fine powers in partial servitude. Nevertheless, both it and the boxers beside it are noble works. I went next to the Capitol, whence, after gazing at the Gladiator, and examining the busts of Brutus and Cæsar, I walked down into the Forum about the base of the Capitol, among piles of broken columns.

FRIDAY, March 24th.

This morning I paced St. Peter's to get for myself its dimensions. Walking without effort, I counted two hundred and sixty steps as the length of the great nave, thirty-seven as its width, and one hundred and eighty as that of the transept. I counted wenty-six altars. Its statues, mostly of gigantic size, and its mosaic pictures, I did not undertake to count. It is reputed to have cost about fifty millions of dollars.

Do not Painting and Sculpture require for their excellence a predominance of the sensuous over the meditative? The Catholic religion, the parent, or, at least, the foster-mother of modern painting, appeals largely to the senses; and the Grecian mythology, the nurse of ancient sculpture, still more so. The present tendency is towards the spiritual and rational, and the foremost people of Europe, the English, possessing the richest written poetry in the world, is poor in the plastic Arts. The great features of the German, English and American mind, are deep religious and moral emotions, the fruits of whose alliance with reason are far-reaching ideas and wide-embracing principles, which sway the thoughts and acts of men, but which can be but faintly represented in bodily images.

This sounds well enough, but great modern names refute it. Your fair-looking edifice of logic proves but a house of paper before the breath of great facts.

SATURDAY, March 25th.

We went to look at the continuation of Cardinal Fesch's collection of pictures in a neighboring Palace, but all the best are in the first which we saw a few days since. The keeper unlocked a large room in which pictures were piled away in solid masses one against the other. I noted No. 16,059 on one of them. Fourteen hundred dollars a year rent is paid for the rooms the whole collection occupies.—We then went to the Minerva Church to witness a religious ceremony, in which the Pope is carried on the shoulders of his attendants. We got into the church in time to have a good view of him seated in a rich throne-like chair, which rose just above the dense crowd, borne rocking along, as on a disturbed sea of human heads. Carried on either side of him were two large fans of peacock's feathers, which might be called the sails of the golden vessel. We afterwards walked in the Gregorian Gardens, a public walk near the Colosseum, between the Cælian and Palatine Hills.—In the afternoon we drove out to see the Torlonia Villa.

Canova's statuary wants what may be called the under movement, which Thorwaldsen's has, and which is by no means given by pronouncing the muscles, but by a union of sympathy for vital

8*

forms with clean firm manipulation. In Powers this union is more intimate than in any modern sculptor.

SUNDAY, March 26th.

We walked this morning on the Pincian Hill, and in the afternoon drove three miles out of the Porta Pia to a Roman ruin, whence there is a fine view of the mountains and over the Campagna all round. Behind us was Rome, and stretching out from it over the plain towards the mountains were the aqueducts.

In Italy, the past is a load chained to the feet of the present. The people drags after it, like a corpse, the thought, feeling, act of by-gone generations. Tradition comes down like the current through a narrow strait, behind which is an ocean. Here, more than in most parts of old Europe, the health-giving transformations go on languidly; the old is not consumed to give place to the hourly created new. The dead and effete is in the way of the quick and refreshing. Hence, languor and irregularity in the currents of life, causing in the body-politic, obstructions and stoppages, and all sorts of social, religious, and political dyspepsias, congestions, rheumatisms, constipations.

MONDAY, March 27th.

Returned with renewed enjoyment to Thorwaldsen's studio. Naturalness and ease are his characteristics. He has not a very high ideal of beauty, and seems to avoid the nude, which is the severest test of the artist.—Thence we went to the Church of St. Lorenzo, in Lucina, where a fine voice was singing. To strive, by such factitious ceremonies as those of the Romish worship, to symbolize the divine, is a degradation of the holy that is in us. It is summoning the solemn spirits of the soul to take part in a fantastic pageant of the senses.—We walked afterwards in the Gregorian Gardens, and on the ruins of the Palace of the Cæsars. Thence to look once more at the marvels of the Sciarra Gallery

—In the afternoon, on coming out of Crawford's studio, we drove over the river to St. Peter's.

TUESDAY, March 28th.

We set out at nine for Frascati. Three miles from the St. John's Gate we passed under an aqueduct, still used, and near the erect ruins of another. The Campagna, without trees or enclosures, and almost without houses, is much less level than it looks from the heights in Rome. We passed several shepherds with their flocks, and parties of peasants ploughing, with large, long-horned, long-legged, meek, white oxen. The plough had one upright handle, and by this the men supported their weight on it, for the purpose of turning up a deeper furrow of the dark soil. As we drew near to Frascati, the Alban mountains, which from Rome present themselves in a compact cluster, broke up into separate peaks, the hill sides covered with olive trees, which looked darker and more leafy than I ever saw them, and Villas with their wooded grounds shining out distinctly. From Frascati, which is not half way up the range of mountains, you have a clear view of Rome, twelve miles distant, and of the Mediterranean. Immediately after arriving, we set out for Tusculum, which lies almost two miles higher up, near the summit of one of the peaks. Before we got half way rain began to fall, and the sky was entirely overcast when we reached the ruins, consisting of an amphitheatre and part of the walls of the ancient city of Tusculum. Descending, we were glad to take shelter in Cicero's house, which is on the other side of the ridge. What is left of it, is six or eight deep arched rooms in a row, without direct communication with one another, and all pointing south on a passage way or portico. My imagination refused to bring Cicero before me otherwise than as looking out from his arches impatiently on a rainy day. In a hard shower we descended to the tavern, and after dinner drove rapidly back to Rome.

WEDNESDAY, March 29th.

What is called the bust of young Augustus, in the Vatican, is much like Napoleon when he was General. We walked round the Rotunda, where are the Perseus of Canova, the Antinous, the Laocoon, and the Apollo. What a company! and what a privilege it is to behold them. We drove afterwards to the Colosseum and for the first time ascended among the arches. Its vastness and massive grandeur never cease to astonish me.

In the afternoon, when we had looked at the pictures in the Academy of St. Luc, we drove to the Pincian Hill at five. The whole Heaven was strewn with fragments of a thunderstorm. Through them the hue of the sky was unusually brilliant, and along the clear western horizon of a pearly green. Standing at the northern extremity of the Hill, we had, to the south, the maze of pinnacles, cupolas, towers, columns, obelisks, that strike up out of the wide expanse of mellow building; to the right, the sun and St. Peter's; and, to the left, a rural view into the grounds of the Borghese Villa, where, over a clump of lofty pines, lay the darkest remnants of the storm, seemingly resting on their broad flat summits. The gorgeous scene grew richer each moment that we gazed, till the whole city and its fleecy canopy glowed in purple. We walked slowly towards the great stairway, and paused on its top as the sun was sinking below the horizon. 'Twas an Italian sunset after a storm, with Rome for the foreground.

As, after returning to our lodging, I sat in the bland twilight, full of the feeling produced by such a spectacle, in such a spot and atmosphere, from the ante-room came the sound of a harp from fingers that were moved by the soul for music, which is almost as common here as speech. After playing two sweet airs, it ceased: it had come unbidden and unannounced, and so it went. This was wanted to complete the day, although before it began I did not feel the want of anything. There are rare moments of Heaven on Earth, which, but for our perversity, might be frequent hours, and sanctify and lighten each day, so full is Nature of gifts and blessings, were the heart but kept open to them. But we close our hearts with pride and ambition, and all kinds of greeds and selfishness, and try to be content with postponing Heaven to beyond the grave.

THURSDAY, March 30th.

We visited, this morning, the Hospital of St. Michael, an immense establishment for the support and instruction of orphans, and an asylum for aged poor. It is divided into four compartments; for aged men, of whom there are now one hundred and twenty-five; for aged women, one hundred and twenty-five; for boys, two hundred and twenty; and for girls, two hundred and seventy-five; making altogether seven hundred and forty-five, as the present number of its inmates. We saw a woman one hundred and three years old, with health and faculties good. The boys are taught trades and the liberal arts, and are entitled to the half of the product of their work, which is laid up for them, and serves as a capital to start with when they leave the institution at the age of twenty; besides which, each one receives on quitting thirty dollars for the same purpose. The girls weave and work with the needle, and, if they marry, receive one hundred dollars dower, and two hundred if they go into a convent. They, as well as the boys, are taught reading, writing, arithmetic, and vocal music. The superintendant, who was throughout exceedingly obliging and affable, let us hear several pieces of music, admirably executed by a number of the boys.

The income of this Institution, from foundations made chiefly by former Popes, is twenty-eight thousand dollars, to which is added upwards of five thousand paid by some of those admitted into its walls, or by their patrons. The arrangements and administration seem to be judicious. Order, industry, and contentment, were visible in all the compartments. It is a noble institution, which does honor to Rome.

In the afternoon, we visited the Villa Ludovisi, in olden time the garden of Sallust. Among several fine antique statues, that have been dug up in the grounds, is a magnificent colossal head of Juno. I afterwards walked home from the Colosseum, in the warm spring air, taking a look on the way at the Moses of Michael Angelo.

Friday, March 31st.

Through narrow lanes, enclosed by high garden walls, we walked this morning on Mount Aventine. In the afternoon, we drove out to the grotto and grove of Egeria. At the grotto, where is the fountain, they pretend to show the stump of a column of the original portico, and the trunk of a statue of Numa Pompilius, in whose day there were neither porticos nor statues. From this spot there is a fine view towards Frascati and the hills. On the way, we stopped at a church without the walls, where a friar showed a marble slab, indented with two foot-prints, which he said were made by Jesus Christ, when he quitted St. Peter, to whom he appeared to rebuke St. Peter for deserting his post at Rome. The impressions are rudely cut, and the toes of the feet are all nearly square, but they nevertheless probably keep the poor friar and some of his brethren in food and fuel the year round.

The ancient sculptors had an advantage over the modern, in the profusion of poetical subjects; for every deity of their prolific mythology is poetical, that is, unites in itself all the perfections of a class, and stands as the ideal representative or symbol of wants, desires, or ideas. The modern artist is tasked to find individuals that have a generic character or significance. The defect in sacred subjects is, that they must be draped, and thus do not admit of the highest achievement in sculpture, which is, to exhibit the human body in its fullest beauty of form and expression.

Saturday, April 1st.

In the morning we visited the rooms of Mr. Rosseter and Mr.

Terry, two young American painters of promise, and walked about the Colosseum. After taking a last look at the beautiful resplendent St. Michael of Guido in the Chapel of the Capuchins, we drove to see the drawing of the lottery, which takes place every Saturday at noon in the square of Monte Citorio. From a balcony, where priests presided, the numbers were drawn to the sound of music, the square well covered with people, mostly of the working classes. In the afternoon, after taking another look at Vallati's Correggio, we walked on the Pincian Hill.

Sunday, April 2d.

It is four o'clock in the afternoon. Seated against the huge base of a pilaster, beneath the dome of St. Peter's, I have taken out my pencil to note down what is passing around me. In front, near by, directly under the cupola, in the centre of the church, is the great Altar, beneath which in the vaults is the tomb of St. Peter. The steps that lead down to it are enclosed by a marble balustrade, round which burn unceasingly a row of brazen lamps. At this altar service is performed only by the Pope himself or a Cardinal. Round these lights is a favorite spot for worshippers; there is now kneeling a circle of various classes. People are walking, lounging or chatting, or gazing at monuments and pictures. Across the great nave nearly opposite to me, is a little crowd about St. Peter's statue, kissing one after the other his bronze toe. Yonder is a knot of soldiers. A group of three, the middle one a priest, is passing me in lively chat. A few yards to my left another priest is on his knees; his lips move rapidly, nor are his eyes idle, nor his nose, which he occupies with snuff. Here come a couple of unkempt artisans, laughing. Yonder a white poodle is rolling himself on the marble floor, and a black cur is trotting up to interrogate him. From under one of the great arches is issuing a procession of boys, young acolytes. They crowd up to St. Peter's statue, kiss the toe, pass on, kneel for a few moments before the illuminated sanctuary, and then disappear in the distance. Not far off stand three priests in animated talk. Across the transept, shines down obliquely through a lofty arch, an immense band of illuminated dust, denoting the height of a western window. I raise my eyes towards the dome; the gigantic mosaic figures on its rich concave are dwarfed like fir trees on a mountain. Half way down the great nave, people are standing or kneeling a little closer, for service is going on in one of the side altars, and vespers are about to be sung in a chapel opposite. Many hundreds of visitors and worshippers mingled together are in the church, but merely dot thinly the area whereon tens of thousands might stand at ease.

MONDAY, April 3d.

Mounted in the morning to the roof and to the top of the dome of St. Peter's. What a pulpit whence to preach a sermon on the lusts of power and gold!

In the afternoon we took farewell in the Vatican of the Apollo and his inspired companions. In the evening we went to hear an improvisatrice, Madame Taddei. When it is considered that this class of performers study for years their business, and that the Italian language runs so readily into verse, the performance loses its wonder. Moreover, the imagination has such scope, that they can and do spin off a subject very loosely.

WEDNESDAY, April 5th, 1843.

We left Rome at ten in the forenoon. The day was fine and our faces were turned homeward, whence, across the sea, blew a fresh breeze as we approached Civita Vecchia.

THE END.

www.ingramcontent.com/pod-product-compliance
Lightning Source LLC
Chambersburg PA
CBHW031847220426
43663CB00006B/530